[london]
houses

[london]
houses

a handbook for visitors
vicky wilson

batsford

British Library cataloguing in publication
A CIP record for this book is available from the British Library

Published by B T Batsford, A member of **Chrysalis** Books plc
64 Brewery Road, London N7 9NT
www.batsford.com

First published 2002
Text copyright © Vicky Wilson 2002
Illustrations copyright © Emma Brownjohn 2002
Design Claudia Schenk

ISBN 0 7134 8785 2

Printed in Great Britain by
Creative Print & Design (Wales), Ebbw Vale

For a copy of the Batsford catalogue or information
on special quantity orders of Batsford books please
contact us on 020 7697 3000 or sales@chrysalisbooks.co.uk

[contents]

Introduction **6**

Central London **11**

Battersea/Chelsea/Fulham/Kensington **77**

Wimbledon **113**

Hampstead **119**

Hackney/Islington **163**

Richmond/Twickenham **177**

West London **205**

Charlton/Eltham/Greenwich **257**

East London **279**

North-east London **297**

North-west London **313**

Carshalton/Cheam/Croydon **321**

Index **339**

INTRODUCTION

Shutting the door on the world outside and embarking on a journey through an historic house releases the magic of time travel. It's an opportunity to recreate imaginatively a specific era peopled by characters whose lives can only be guessed at, or to rerun incidents from a well-known biography in their actual setting. Sometimes teasing out the layers of successive architectural interventions takes on the compulsion of a detective novel; sometimes characters or architectural motifs pop up unexpectedly to create another link in the maze of historical interconnections. Emerging into the noise of the 21st-century traffic outside, or the drone of planes backing up for Heathrow, only emphasises the vividness and immediacy of the experience.

London houses offer not only an introduction to some of the city's finest buildings and to the lives of some of its more famous inhabitants, but also a broad insight into the capital's architectural and social history. The oldest house presented here is Headstone Manor in Harrow, originally probably a timber-framed aisled hall flanked by two cross-wings built c. 1310 and acquired 30 years later by the Archbishop of Canterbury for use as a staging post; the most recent is 9/10 Stock Orchard Street in Islington, an ecologically-minded home and office designed by and for Sarah Wigglesworth and Jeremy Till between 1996 and 2000. In social terms, the spectrum runs from the destitute who filled the purpose-built workhouse now known as Vestry House in Walthamstow, through servants and the bourgeoisie to the aristocracy and royalty.

The houses fall into two distinct, if occasionally overlapping categories: those that have been conserved because of famous former inhabitants and those that are of interest because of their architecture. In the first group are the homes of such people as Thomas Carlyle, Charles Dickens, Sigmund Freud, George Frideric Handel, William Hogarth,

Samuel Johnson and John Keats; in the second the aristocratic mansions clustered mainly to the west of London and such masterpieces as Queen's House in Greenwich and Spencer House in St James's Park. Overlaps include Horace Walpole's Strawberry Hill, Sir John Soane's houses in Lincoln's Inn Fields and Ealing, Frederic Leighton's house in Kensington and William Morris' Red House in Bexleyheath, as well as the three royal residences of Buckingham Palace, Hampton Court and Kensington Palace, if royalty interest you.

As the previous paragraph makes obvious, it's a history biased towards the rich and/or famous, most of whom were men. The dwellings of the poor or working class have not until recently been regarded as worthy of interest, and while some stately homes make efforts to recreate the spaces downstairs and research their occupants, most concentrate on the elegant upstairs rooms elaborately decorated for the leisured nobility. As for women, I have focused on their stories as much as possible, for two reasons. First, while information on, say, Thomas Carlyle is readily available to anyone who wants it, his wife Jane is a much less known (though arguably no less interesting) figure. (For a fuller picture of the couple's home life, Thea Holme's *The Carlyles at Home* is highly recommended.) And second, as sociological surveys sadly show us still to be the case today, the home was more often than not the woman's domain and many bear the imprint of her ideas.

Few of the houses featured here are actually lived in, though Fred Hauptfuhrer at Asgill House, the Forbes family at Old Battersea House, Doris Hollamby at Red House and Jeremy Till and Sarah Wigglesworth (along with Queen Elizabeth II) are to be commended for allowing the public into their homes. As for the rest, I have found the people working in these houses often exercise a near-proprietorial interest and are almost uniformly excited by the history and stories that surround them, supplying a fund of unsolicited anecdotes and information. Many buildings are open only as the result of public campaigns and many are staffed by volunteers. Their dedication should be commended, as should the efforts of several local authorities to protect their architectural heritage.

I have aimed in this book to give the information I would have liked to have had myself when I visited these houses. Sometimes this involves a summary of the architectural history, sometimes a description of the social context, sometimes a snapshot of the lives, loves and work of former inhabitants, sometimes all three. I have tended to restrict biographical detail to the years an individual spent in a particular house rather than attempting an overview. Information from guidebooks – the best of which are recommended in the text – has been supplemented by biographies, histories, architectural monographs and so on. Jenny Uglow's *Hogarth A Life and a World* offers a vivid recreation of a London inhabited by many of this book's key figures; Pevsner's London guides were a constant source of reference for architectural minutiae.

Any book about London has to come up with its own definition of the boundaries of the city. Here I have used the London that appears within the London *A–Z*. The book deals only with houses that are open to the public, and of these only houses that are open more than once a year. To have included all those buildings that welcome visitors only during Open House Weekend would have turned the volume into a listing rather than a useful guide. Another criterion is that the owners have to make available some information about their building's history. Thus the many public buildings that were once houses and now function as libraries, community centres, schools and the like are featured only if the visitor is given a minimum of information about their original architectural state and past occupancy. Some of the buildings here are constantly in use and visitors are asked to respect the privacy of those working or living within them and their concerns about security and confidentiality. Details of wheelchair access are included only (as often) where this is problematic.

Sadly the book is weighted towards the past, with very little from the 20th century except Eltham Palace, 2 Willow Road and 9/10 Stock Orchard Street, though the imminent rescue of Isokon's Lawn Road flats in Hampstead should add another venue worthy of inclusion. Among the buildings closed for refurbishment at the time of writing are

Kew Palace, due to reopen in 2004, Danson House in Bexley (a building by Robert Taylor, the architect of Asgill House) and 19 Princelet Street in Spitalfields. A project to restore Benjamin Franklin's house in Craven Street, WC2, is currently underway.

I started to write this book because I liked visiting houses – resplendent stately homes, homes of interesting individuals, recreations of life in other times. If I were to try to rationalise it, I'd say houses are fascinating for at least four reasons. First, because they appeal to our curiosity (or nosiness) by offering a sanctioned opportunity to stare openly at what is or was essentially private space. Second, because of the insight this gives us into the lives of former inhabitants – not only the rich and famous but also their friends, spouses, lovers and servants. Third, as shrines to people we admire, the place where those feet actually rested under the table, where those books were written, where those conversations took place. And fourth, as pieces of architecture – whether great palaces or simply the anonymous housing stock of their day. A look at current television schedules – with programmes on people who've built their own homes, given a historical house a remake or want to trace their home's history – indicates that the nation is drawing close to sharing my obsession.

Acknowledgements

I would like to thank Dermot Wilson for introducing me to the joys of many of the houses here and for his ever-challenging opinions. And Tom Neville for his never-flagging encouragement and perceptive comments on the text.

[central london]

Apsley House   **12**

Buckingham Palace   **18**

Dickens House Museum   **27**

Dr Johnson's House   **32**

18 Folgate Street   **39**

Handel House Museum   **45**

House of St Barnabas-in-Soho   **52**

The Sherlock Holmes Museum   **54**

Sir John Soane's Museum   **58**

Spencer House   **66**

John Wesley's House   **71**

APSLEY HOUSE

Originally known as No. 1 London because it was the first house after the toll gates at the top of Knightsbridge, Apsley House is a relatively modest Robert Adam silk purse turned into a pretentious sow's ear by Benjamin Wyatt for Arthur Wellesley, Duke of Wellington (1769–1852), following the latter's return to civilian life after his routing of Napoleon at the Battle of Waterloo in 1815. Built between 1771 and 1778 for the 2nd Earl of Bathurst (previously Baron Apsley), the house was bought by Wellington's elder brother in 1807 for £16,000, altered by James Wyatt and then sold to Wellington ten years later for £42,000 – an increase that makes the scale of more recent property-price inflation look modest. Wyatt's son Benjamin, formerly Wellington's secretary, then set about transforming Adam's five-bay house by adding a grand dining room to the rear (the north-east corner) in 1819 and in 1827 creating a two-bay extension running the full depth of the house to the west with a picture gallery on the first floor. Adam's red brick was encased in Bath stone and a massive portico tacked on to the centre of the new front elevation. By 1831 the alterations had eaten up £64,000 of the £400,000 Wellington had been granted by parliament for his defeat of the French and he was heard to complain.

Wyatt's two-bay addition has uncomfortably skewed the plan. You enter through the centre of the portico into the side rather than the centre of the outer hall, ruining any grand scheme for the room. The painting of the 1836 Waterloo banquet, an annual event held in the Waterloo gallery upstairs, depicts some 85 survivors of the battle, seated alongside the great and not-so-good who governed the country during Wellington's subsequent career as a Tory statesman. John Simpson's darkly romantic portrait of the duke shows a handsome man with pursed lips, a thin face and watchful eyes – charms apparently lost on his aristocratic

[central london]

Irish parents, who sent him into the army at the age of 17 in the belief that their 'ugly boy Arthur' (their fifth son) was 'fit food for powder'.

The plate and china room to the left (on the ground floor of Wyatt's 1827 addition) was created by Wellington's son to replace some small bedrooms. The dazzling array of gold leaf and silverware ranges from the vulgar to the surprisingly delicate, as in the muted blue and sepia Egyptian service Napoleon gave to Josephine on their divorce, but which she refused without even unpacking it. The collection as a whole represents a fat-cat golden handshake that bears witness to Europe's gratitude to the duke for securing Napoleon's defeat. There are also presents from the surviving officers of some of the divisions under Wellington's command during his early career in India (1797–1805), where he gained valuable experience as a commander and statesman.

The inner hall – the entrance hall of Adam's building – houses the ticket office. Along with a picture of the duke on one of his last public engagements – stooped but with the excellent bone structure of his face still discernible – there's a life-size portrait of the 7th Duke who bequeathed the house to the nation in 1947 in lieu of death duties. At the foot of Adam's graceful semicircular stairwell is a 3.5-metre nude statue of Napoleon posing as a Greek god. Commissioned from Canova by its subject (who didn't like the result), it was bought by the British government in 1816 and presented to Wellington, who no doubt got much pleasure from having his former enemy symbolically so thoroughly within his power. The Lawrence portrait of the duke, by contrast, depicts him as a dark hero – a model for Heathcliff – against a romantic landscape.

The Piccadilly drawing room retains Adam's frieze, doors and ceiling but has Wyatt's yellow colour scheme and unpleasant carpet. All that glitters probably is gold. Many of the pictures were appropriated by Napoleon's brother Joseph Bonaparte from the Spanish royal family. They were recovered from his coach following the defeat at the battle of Vitoria (June 1813) that marked the expulsion of the French from Spain. A mixed bunch – in some cases it seems hardly surprising the Spanish refused Wellington's offer to return them. *The Rape of Proserpina* and the jolly *Chelsea Pensioners Reading the Waterloo Despatch* – both acquired by the duke – sit ill with the calm Dutch scenes of the majority. The portico drawing room must originally have been light and pleasant, with views over Hyde Park to the west. We are told it functioned as an informal dining room and that the family sat out on the portico (whose placement fails to correspond to the internal plan, so its massive columns also obscure the view from one of the windows of the Piccadilly drawing room) for such occasions as Elizabeth II's coronation.

Wyatt's 28-metre-long, Louis XIV-style Waterloo gallery with its red plush walls, copious gilding, well-placed mirrors, top-lighting and increased ceiling height is certainly a dramatic space. Apparently the duke rebelled against his expensive architect by turning down a quote for £2000 for carved wood decorations in favour of £400 spent on gilded plaster putty (some of which was designed by his 'confidante' Harriet Arbuthnot). The paintings are hung in accordance with the duke's original scheme, which seems to be by subject (horses, saints, holy family, etc.) rather than style. His favourite was Correggio's *The Agony in the Garden* (north wall); I preferred the Velazquezs on the east wall.

The striped drawing room – a bedroom in Adam's original scheme – is done out to resemble a military tent and appropriately hung with portraits of Wellington's comrades-in-arms. Wyatt's dining room is dark and overbearing, lined with portraits of European royalty presented to the duke by their subjects.

During his 35 years at Apsley House Wellington pursued a career as a politician and statesman, with mixed success. His lack of sympathy with the liberal foreign policies of George Canning led him to resign his cabinet post in 1827 when Canning became prime minister, but following Canning's death shortly afterwards Wellington himself took on the role. His term in office was brief: his backing for the Catholic Emancipation bill lost him much support while his dogged resistance to parliamentary reform led to the fall of his ministry. (His distrust of 'commoners' was so profound he opposed the coming of the railways on the grounds they would encourage the lower classes to move around.) His nickname, 'the

Iron Duke', comes from the bars he put up at Apsley House's windows to protect them from rioters outraged at his refusal to extend the franchise. Wellington's home secretary was Robert Peel and it was the duke who drew up the template for the police force Peel famously introduced. He later served as foreign secretary (1834–35) and then as minister without portfolio (1841–46) when Peel was prime minister. He died at his favourite residence, Walmer Castle, one of the perks of his position as warden of the Cinque Ports.

Wellington proposed to Kitty Pakenham, great-great-aunt of the late Lord Longford, when he was just 24, but was rejected by her brother. They eventually married on Wellington's return from India in 1806, by which time he was heard to remark: 'She has grown ugly, by Jove.' Two sons were born in 1807 and 1808. Most biographers seem to agree that the marriage was a terrible mistake; Arbuthnot in a diary entry of 1822 claimed that Wellington told her that '[Kitty] did not understand him... and that he found he might as well talk to a child' while five years after her death in 1831 Wellington allegedly described Kitty to Lady Salisbury as one of the most foolish women who ever existed.

But there is no trace of the personal in this stuffy museum, administered by the V&A and reeking of institutionalism, until you get to the basement, where Wellington's death mask, dressing case and travelling canteen of cutlery at last make him seem human. The duke's family retains a basement flat (occupied at the time of writing by the 84-year-old 8th Duke) and an apartment upstairs (occupied by his heir), and disputes over parking spaces and the V&A's money-making functions have required mediation. Perhaps it's time to break a few more windows?

ADDRESS Hyde Park Corner, London W1J 7NT (020 7499 5676) **OPEN** Tuesday to Sunday, 11.00–17.00

ADMISSION £4.50/£3/over-60s and under-18s free **ACCESS** limited **UNDERGROUND** Hyde Park Corner

BUCKINGHAM PALACE

Like Asgill House, Red House and 9/10 Stock Orchard Street, Buckingham Palace is still very much lived in. So only the state apartments in the west range – where one of the richest women in the world, Queen Elizabeth II, and her gaffe-prone husband Philip entertain dignitaries – are open to the public. The palace also houses part of the royal collection, an art treasury on a vast scale amassed largely with tax-payers' money granted to various sovereigns. Are we being asked to pay the high entrance fee – rationalised by the fact that the palace is run purely on the profits from ticket and merchandising sales without government subsidy – simply to see what is rightfully ours?

The contradictions in the royal family's position as immensely wealthy individuals paid by the state to play a public role were inherent in Buckingham Palace from the start. The original Buckingham House was built by Lord Goring in 1633 and rebuilt by John Sheffield, Duke of Buckingham, in 1703–05. It was acquired by George III (1738–1820) shortly after his accession in 1760 through a dodgy compulsory-purchase deal made possible because half the property was on royal land. Over the next 14 years William Chambers was hired to remodel it as a family home for the king and his new wife Charlotte, with the ceremonial centre of the court remaining at nearby St James's.

The future George IV (1762–1830) set up his dysfunctional household in Carlton House on Pall Mall in 1783. (Two years later, in a saga that makes more recent royal shenanigans seem innocuous indeed, he secretly married the Catholic Mrs Fitzherbert, subsequently tenant of Marble Hill House, see page 192, with whom he continued an on-off relationship until 1803. The marriage was declared illegal in 1795 so he could wed his cousin Princess Caroline of Brunswick, whom he banished to Blackheath following the birth of their only daughter Charlotte the following

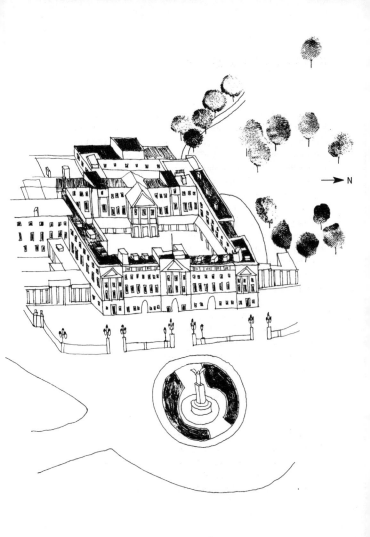

N

year.) After his accession in 1820 (following ten years as regent), George had Carlton House demolished and sold the site to pay part of the cost of converting Buckingham House into a full-scale residential and cere-monial palace. He chose as his architect the ageing John Nash (1752-1835) with whom he had worked on the development of Regent's Park and the remodelling of Brighton Pavilion. In the interests of economy Nash was forced to retain the core of the old house, which dictated the plan, the ceiling height of the ground floor and the proportions of many of the rooms. Ironically, this celebration of national greatness in the wake of the victories of the Napoleonic wars was far from English in inspiration, Nash drawing many of his architectural references and George IV most of his furnishings from France.

Nash doubled the size of the main block of the old house (now at the centre of the west range) by adding a suite of rooms to its garden side. He then demolished the side wings and replaced them with much grander structures to form a U-shaped plan. The fourth side of the courtyard was enclosed simply by railings with the monument now at Marble Arch in the centre. On his accession in 1830 George's brother William IV dismissed Nash – who had spent £640,000, almost three times the sum allocated by parliament, and still hadn't finished the work – and hired the much less inspired William Blore.

In 1837 William was succeeded by his niece Victoria (1819–1901) who became the first sovereign actually to live in the palace, by now almost 80 years in the making. Its shortcomings quickly became apparent after her marriage three years later to Prince Albert of Saxe-Coburg-Gotha and the birth of nine children within 15 years: first, there was no nursery, and second, no room large enough for a court ball. In 1847-50 Blore built an east wing enclosing the courtyard to provide apartments for distin-guished visitors on the first floor and nurseries on the second, financed in part from the sale of Brighton Pavilion. In 1853–55 new galleries, a dining room and a ballroom were added to the south-west corner by Nash's pupil James Pennethorne. Victoria's pleasure in her new home was relatively shortlived: following Albert's death in 1861 she retired to Windsor Castle for 40 years of widowhood and the palace was shut up until the next century when her philandering son Edward VII (see Southside House, page 116) tackled the interior redecoration and his son George V had the perishable Caen stone façade of the east wing refaced in Portland stone by Aston Webb to give it the insipid beaux-arts profile we know today.

The outline of Buckingham's relatively modest nine-bay house is still apparent in the quadrangle, giving a pleasant sense of domestic scale after the exhibitionism of Webb's 25-bay street elevation. The glory of Nash's golden Bath-stone façades with their finely carved Corinthian capitals and frieze and the elegant double portico is highlighted by contrast with the crude painted stucco of Blore's east wing. The queen's private apartments are in the north range; all in all the palace contains 52 royal and guest bedrooms, 188 staff bedrooms, 92 offices and 78 bathrooms in addition to the state apartments. It keeps 450 people off the dole.

Paying visitors enter through a door at the side of the central grand hall, part of Buckingham's original house and a surprisingly squat room given drama by Nash's lowering of the floor of the central area. George IV had spent much of his adulthood amassing furniture, porcelain and works of art – a particularly fruitful source being French palaces whose contents were sold off to raise funds following the revolution – and the state rooms were partly designed around his splendid collection, much of which is still in situ.

The entrance to Nash's grand staircase, however, is flanked by two sexy female nudes – Richard James Wyatt's *The Huntress*, 1850, and Jan Geefs' *Love and Malice*, 1859 – which were birthday presents from Victoria to Albert. The staircase itself is surprisingly small in scale: the effect of £3900 worth of sinuous gilded bronze balustrade and the finely engraved glazed cupola is jewel-like rather than imposing. The tiny guard room beyond, peopled by statues of Victoria and Albert in Greek fancy dress, their heavy features (and especially his dashing moustache) at odds with their costumes, is again distinguished by the intricacy of the craftsmanship – money spent on the painstaking labour of design and execution rather than on grand swagger. Around the lantern, from which

hangs one of the palace's several breathtaking glass chandeliers acquired by George IV for Carlton House, are studded etched-glass medallions – reminiscent of the ceiling mirrors used by John Soane (see page 62) – which break up the gilding to give a more ethereal effect.

The double-height green drawing room, above the grand hall, forms an anteroom to the throne room. Its most remarkable feature is the highly decorated ceiling, whose complex array of geometric forms, concave and convex coving and domes echoes the Mogul themes Nash elaborated in Brighton Pavilion. The sumptuous throne room has an equally superb ceiling below which – depicting scenes from the Wars of the Roses – runs England's answer to the Parthenon frieze purloined by Lord Elgin and sold to the nation just over a decade earlier. As in the green drawing room, Soanean mirrored doors – their outer edges decorated with hundreds of individually cast and positioned gilt-bronze fleurs de lys – increase the sense of space. The thrones themselves – emblazoned with ER and P rather like a Ford Capri windscreen – are set behind a spectacular proscenium in the form of two winged female figures holding suspended free-falling swags. The only picture is Angelica Kauffmann's portrait of Augusta, Duchess of Brunswick – sister of George III and mother of George IV's ill-treated wife Caroline and from 1807–13 a tenant of the Ranger's House (see page 275) – with her son Charles.

The picture gallery – an internal room between the enfilade from the grand staircase to the throne room and Nash's new additions to the garden front – runs the length of old Buckingham House. Nash's original ceiling design failed either to light the pictures or keep out water; it was modified by Blore and totally remodelled for George V in 1914 in its present plain-glazed barrel-vaulted form. The overall effect is a contrast to the opulence of the Nash rooms that precede it but the combination of modern ceiling and Grinling Gibbons-style carving is also something of a halfway house, a wasted opportunity to produce a more rigorously modern statement. Among the many paintings are Vermeer's *The Music Lesson*, bought by George III, and Rembrandt's *The Ship Builder and His Wife*, at £5250 George IV's most expensive acquisition.

The east gallery on the quadrangle side of Victoria's 1850s extension, its ceiling a delicately etched version of the long gallery's, is more unified and successful. Ill at ease among the stilted portraits of various official members of the royal family is John Hoppner's lively study of celebrated comic actress Mrs Jordan, for more than 20 years the loyal mistress of William IV – whose debts she would often pay off with her earnings – and the mother of ten of his children. Though it was painted before their liaison began in 1790, William didn't buy it until the 1830s, more than 15 years after he'd abandoned her to die in poverty in France and replaced her with Adelaide, a wife almost 30 years his junior from respectable German stock. The statue of the actress with two of their young children in the long gallery lobby – which William asked to have placed in Westminster Abbey – was commissioned following his accession in 1830. Another abandoned woman hanging here is George IV's wife Caroline, pictured in 1802 with her young daughter Charlotte (whom she saw for only a couple of hours a week) by Thomas Lawrence, with whom she is alleged to have had an affair. So disastrous was the marriage (George was drunk throughout the wedding ceremony and they lived together for only a year) that following his accession she was offered £50,000 to quit Blackheath and live abroad; when she refused she was barred from the coronation ceremony.

Queen Victoria's ballroom – 37.5 metres long, 18 metres wide and 14 metres high – is one of the largest rooms in London and undoubtedly impressive. A short video showing Elizabeth II gamely thumping a would-be knight on the shoulder and decorating the likes of Nelson Mandela and Elizabeth Taylor ends with the dispiriting spectacle of Prince Charles' fiftieth birthday celebrations ('for he's a jolly good fellow' sung to a Prince of Wales who, whatever his pretensions as a reformer, solemnly upholds the royal tradition of adultery). The tapestry-lined west gallery on the garden side leads to the state dining room, envisaged by Nash as a music room but completed by Blore for its present function. The relative coarseness of the detailing speaks of the financial constraints that followed Nash's dismissal; the dominating deep-red walls and carpet that deaden the pleasure of the garden views evoke an atmosphere reminiscent of the oppressive, inward-focused interiors of many a more modest Victorian dwelling.

The blue drawing room, music room and white drawing room – the enfilade Nash added to the garden side of Buckingham House – display a magnificence of proportion and decoration that could scarcely be bettered. The 21-metre-long blue drawing room (so-called because of the wallpaper installed by Queen Mary early in the last century) – divided into bays by pairs of gigantic Corinthian columns – has a ceiling whose billowing coves and bold console brackets show Nash at his most daring. The central music room with its dramatic bow – still decorated much as Nash intended – is perhaps the best in the house. Its air of light and space is enhanced by the shimmering vaulted and domed ceiling, gilded in a pattern of breathtaking intricacy echoed by the spectacular parquet floor. The ethereal chandeliers are probably the finest in the palace; as in the rest of the rooms on this floor, the five full-height windows in the bow are among the earliest surviving English uses of plate glass, a product developed in the 1820s. The white drawing room – which anywhere else would deserve a paragraph on its splendour but here fades into insignificance – retains its Nash ceiling but was redecorated in the late 19th century.

Blore's relatively modest ministers' staircase, at the foot of which is a Canova sculpture, as at Apsely House (see page 14), leads to the windowless marble hall, running below the picture gallery. The overelaborate gilded swags, added in 1902, that surround the family portraits arranged by Queen Victoria look like forgotten Christmas decorations. Visitors exit to the gardens through the elegant bow room below the music room.

ADDRESS Buckingham Gate, London SW1A 1AA (020 7839 1377; www.royal.gov.uk)
OPEN August and September: daily, 9.30–16.30 (by pre-booked timed ticket)
ADMISSION £10.50/over-60s £8/ under-17s £5/under-5s free/ family ticket £25.50
UNDERGROUND Victoria/ St James's Park

DICKENS HOUSE MUSEUM

When Charles Dickens (1812–70) leased 48 Doughty Street on 25 March 1837 for three years at £80 a year, the three-storey flat-fronted house, built c. 1807-09, stood in a smart private road closed off by gates manned by porters in livery. It was an impressive step up from the three back rooms he had rented at 13 Furnival's Inn, made possible by the enormous success of *Pickwick Papers*, which had been appearing in monthly parts for a year. On 2 April the writer celebrated the first anniversary of his marriage to Catherine Hogarth and on 8 April publishers Chapman and Hall organised a dinner to mark the serial's anniversary, giving Dickens a bonus cheque of £500. The Doughty Street household also included Dickens' 16-year-old brother Frederick and the couple's three-month-old son Charles.

The two years and eight months of the family's residency, before moving on to a larger, more upmarket property at 1 Devonshire Terrace, Regent's Park, were far from uneventful. Two more children were born – Mary on 6 March 1838 and Kate on 29 October 1839 – and in addition to completing *Pickwick Papers* Dickens wrote *Oliver Twist*, *Nicholas Nickelby*, *Sketches of Young Gentlemen*, the first chapters of *Barnaby Rudge*, the farce *The Lamplighter* and several pieces for *Bentley's Miscellany* (the journal he edited and in which *Oliver Twist* and *Nicholas Nickelby* were serialised) as well as rewriting for publication *Memoirs of Joseph Grimaldi*. The most momentous and emotionally scarring event, however, was the death of Catherine's 17-year-old sister Mary, who passed away in Dickens' arms in early May 1837 in one of the upstairs rooms after collapsing following a family visit to the theatre. The play the three had seen was the farce *Is She His Wife?* – an apt title since Dickens was to wear Mary's ring, which he slipped off the corpse's hand, for the rest of his life, planned to be buried next to her and idealised her in a way that can only have contributed to his disillusionment with his marriage to Catherine. Mary was the inspiration for Rose Maylie in *Oliver Twist*, whom Dickens was to allow to recover from her serious illness against his original intentions, and for Little Nell in *The Old Curiosity Shop*.

Run by the Dickens Fellowship, 'a society for Dickens' lovers', three of whose members raised a mortgage to save the house in 1923, the Dickens House Museum is endearingly tatty, its state of decoration conjuring a well-used home rather than a pristine heritage recreation, its scale evoking the informal hubbub of family life rather than the cultivated elegance of, say, John Soane's contemporary residence (see page 58). Only the drawing room, wash room and wine cellar are reconstructed; the other spaces house a selection of Dickens miscellany including two rooms of items from the collection of Comte Alain de Suzannet (1882–1950), a former vice-president of the fellowship. An extensive archive of letters, manuscripts, scholarly papers and some 8000 photographs is housed in the basement of No. 49, available free to researchers (call 020 7405 2127 to make an appointment).

The first impression on entering the house is the modesty of its scale – this was, after all, Dickens' home early in his career and tells nothing of the fame and fortune he was later to achieve. The walls of the hall and staircase are painted a bilious combination of lime green and orange matched from paint scrapings (admiration for Dickens the interior decorator may fall well short of respect for him as a novelist); the chequerboard floor is ingrained with the grime of what looks like a couple of centuries of footprints.

At the bottom of the stairs hangs the hall clock from Gad's Hill Place, the grand Georgian house near Rochester Dickens had dreamed of owning as a child and in which he lived for the last 12 years of his life. Below it is placed a letter to the clock-repairer that is more revealing of the author's personality than any number of teacups and quills: '…after enduring internal agonies of a most distressing nature, it has now ceased striking altogether. Though a happy release for the clock, this is not convenient to the household. If you can send down any confidential person with whom the clock can confer, I think it may have something in its works it would be glad to make a clean breast of.'

The dining room (ground floor, front) is a modest space given character by its curved rear wall and doors. The most striking feature here is the superb, overscaled mahogany sideboard Dickens bought late in 1839, presumably with the move to the larger Devonshire Terrace house in mind. Among the memorabilia is the quill pen Dickens used for writing his swan song *The Mystery of Edwin Drood*, a wooden lemon squeezer given him by his doctor and the reading glass he kept from 1834 until his death. The morning room (ground floor, rear) was used by the family as an informal sitting room, though no trace of that function remains. The displays, focused on Catherine, include her engagement ring and Charles' telling wedding present to her of a mother-of-pearl visiting-card case. Among the several letters in Dickens' surprisingly delicate writing is one describing the social triumph of the early stages of their 1842 trip to the United States – 'Imagine Kate and I – a kind of Queen and Albert... in newspapers and receiving all who come...' – along with a copy of a carefully worded letter of 1851 to Catherine, recovering from a 'nervous' illness in Malvern, preparing her for the news of their 18-month-old daughter Dora Annie's death. Dickens' apparent pride in his young wife in the former and concern for her feelings in the latter reveal nothing of the increasing frustration with the relationship that was to lead him cruelly to reject her in 1858.

On the first floor are the drawing room and Dickens' study. The former, at the front of the house, is crammed with furniture, evoking the claustrophobic conditions of Victorian family life, even among the aspiring middle classes. Some of the furniture is Dickens' own; other pieces are similar to items he is known to have possessed. The lilac decor is believed from paint scrapings and documentary evidence to approximate Dickens' colour scheme – another regrettable choice. The study at the rear is a repository of memorabilia rather than a reconstruction; for something of the atmosphere that might have been created look at the engraving *The Empty Chair*, based on a sketch of Dickens' Gad's Hill

Place study made by *Edwin Drood* illustrator Luke Fildes on the day of the writer's death. However, the simple writing table from the garden chalet at Gad's Hill Place at which Dickens wrote his last words and the ugly china monkey he kept on his desk are guaranteed to send tremors up the spines of the many devoted foreign pilgrims while the several fragments of manuscript including *Pickwick Papers* and *Oliver Twist* – pristine but for a few insertions and scorings out – bear witness to the remarkable fluidity with which he wrote.

The unatmospheric Mary Hogarth room (second floor, rear) has some relics of Dickens' personal saint including a copy of part xv of *Pickwick Papers* in which the author manages to make light of the tragedy to his readers, explaining that the interruption in the serial's publication is due to 'a severe domestic affliction of no ordinary kind', not, as rumours have it, to his having been 'killed outright… driven mad… imprisoned for debt… sent per steamer to the United States'. The rest of the displays are devoted to Dickens and the theatre including an engraving of a painting of the writer as the boastful but cowardly soldier Bobadil in Ben Jonson's *Every Man in His Humour* that captures his ease as an actor.

Dickens' bedroom and dressing room at the front of the house contain items from the Suzannet Collection. The bedroom continues the theme of lost love with a display of material related to Maria Beadnell, the banker's daughter the 18-year-old Dickens fell for but whose parents (in a less-than-shrewd financial judgement) discouraged from the match. The tiny dressing room, probably used as Frederick's bedroom, contains evidence of the enormously successful series of showman-like public readings which Dickens, billed as The Sparkler of Albion, engaged in during the last 12 years of his life, including a record by his doctor of the increase in his pulse rate after performances.

In the basement are the wash house and wine cellar. What used to be the kitchen, at the front of the house, is now a library of first editions where, in the museum's only concession to interactivity, you can copy Dickens' signature with a quill pen. In the still room you can watch a half-hour video about his life.

In Dickens' study hangs *Dickens's Dream*, the melancholy unfinished painting done five years after the author's death by R W Buss, one of *Pickwick Papers'* original illustrators. It shows the author, in colour, seated in his Gad's Hill Place study surrounded by fairy-scale pen-and-ink sketches of the characters of his imagination, one of whom is sitting on his knee as if begging him to confer her with immortality. The effect is something like that of the museum itself – a mass of borrowings from different sources through which we hope to come closer to genius, but which requires someone of Dickens' imagination to bring it to life.

ADDRESS 48 Doughty Street, London WC1N 2LX (020 7405 2127; www.dickensmuseum.com)
OPEN Monday to Saturday, 10.00–17.00

ADMISSION £4/£3/£2
ACCESS ground floor only
UNDERGROUND Russell Square

DR JOHNSON'S HOUSE

Dr Samuel Johnson (1709–84) rented this gem of a Queen Anne house, built c. 1700 for a city father by the name of Gough or Goff, from 1749 to 1759 for £30 a year. He chose it because of its proximity to the premises of William Strahan, the printer for the *Dictionary* he was to compile and deliver letter by letter. The house is reached through a network of alleys from Fleet Street, at the time part of the thoroughfare connecting Westminster to the City and a bustling conglomeration of shops, theatres, taverns, coffeehouses and chophouses with a somewhat seedy reputation. The double-fronted three-storey brick house, on a corner site, was occupied until 1911, when it was bought by Liberal MP Cecil Harmsworth and restored, many of its original features having been saved by years of neglect. The garret suffered severe damage during the Blitz of 1941–42.

Johnson's residency at Gough Square was a time of poverty and continuing financial crises – he was under arrest for debt in 1756 for the sum of £5 18s, which he was able to borrow from the more successful Samuel Richardson, author of *Pamela* and *Clarissa* – and it wasn't until 1762 that the award of a crown pension of £300 per annum brought financial security. The *Dictionary* (contracted in 1746 by a syndicate of booksellers for which he was to be paid £1575 for an anticipated three years' work) took eight years to complete, during most of which his supposed patron Lord Chesterfield (see Ranger's House, page 273) ignored him (patron in the *Dictionary* is famously defined as: '…Commonly a wretch who supports with insolence, and is paid with flattery'). In 1749 actor and theatre manager David Garrick, a former pupil and lifelong friend, staged Johnson's play *Irene*, which earned him £300, and the gloomy, profoundly personal poem *The Vanity of Human Wishes* was sold for 15 guineas. From 1750 to 1752 he wrote a twice-weekly journal *The Rambler*, often completed amid a roomful of people with the printer's boy waiting at the door, containing essays designed to 'inculcate wisdom or piety [while] refining our language to grammatical purity.' It was not a success. In 1758 he began a weekly series of essays published in a newspaper and known as *The Idler*, which were scarcely more popular.

Johnson's wife Elizabeth (Tetty), a widow 20 years his senior whom he married when he was just 25, died in March 1752. Though the marriage had not been without its problems – she was known for her extravagance and drunkenness and from the late 1740s had refused to have sex with him – he greatly respected her judgement, took pleasure in her skill at reading aloud, was never unfaithful and missed her sorely. A bear-like, shambling man unable to control his rolling head and the near-constant convulsions that shook his shoulders, his appearance became even more slovenly and unkempt and the house disordered and dirty following his wife's death. In 1759 his mother died (he covered the funeral expenses from the sale of the *Candide*-like story *The History of Rasselas, Prince of Abissinia*, which he wrote in a week) and he decided to move to cheaper lodgings in Staples Inn.

Johnson hated to be alone – according to his wife's friend Elizabeth Desmoulins: 'The great business of his life (he said) was to escape from himself; this disposition he considered to be the disease of his mind, which nothing cured but company.' An impoverished friend Anna Williams was staying with the Johnsons when Tetty died and he gave her a home. Two weeks later he took in the ten-year-old Francis Barber, a slave separated from his family and imported to England from Jamaica then given his 'freedom' on his master's death. Francis ran away from Johnson twice during this period – mainly because he didn't get on with Williams – but he eventually became Johnson's manservant and principal heir. Dramatist Arthur Murphy (whose portrait hangs in the dining room) described Johnson's homelife: 'He took no exercise, rose about two, and then received the visits of his friends. Authors, long since forgotten, waited on him as their oracle... His house was filled with a succession of visitors till four or five in the evening. During the whole time he presided at the tea-table.' He would then move on to a tavern, which he would usually be among the last to leave. After the move to Staples Inn he would invariably take tea with Williams – one of many female friends he sought out following Tetty's death – on his way home, sometimes arriving as late as five in the morning.

Visitors to Dr Johnson's House enter through a side door into the dining room. The house has several cupboards designed for specific purposes tucked away (note the cupboard for candlesticks on the stairway) – one of these, a cellarette cupboard behind whose main door are six smaller wood-panelled compartments for bottles, can be seen behind the reception desk. Above the mantelpiece is a copy of a self-portrait by Joshua Reynolds, one of Johnson's closest friends. The fortress-like front door – secured by a strong chain with a bar across the fanlight to prevent small children from climbing through to open the locks – demonstrates the lengths to which even people of Johnson's modest means had to go to protect their worldly goods. Johnson and his friends were sure to be armed with stout sticks when they wandered the dimly lit streets at night (Johnson's and Garrick's can be seen in the will room on the second floor), hugging the safety of the walls as they walked.

The parlour is a pleasantly proportioned, squarish room with windows on two sides. Like the rest of the house it has exposed wide floorboards with Turkey carpets, original, delightfully simple door fittings and is sparsely furnished with no attempt at spurious recreation. The entire ground floor is painted a murky brown the latest batch of experts believe to resemble the original decor. The atmosphere is warm and welcoming – no doubt more so than in Johnson's day, according to Barber, who professed himself 'disgusted in the house' following Tetty's death. Pride of place over the mantelpiece is given to a portrait of Barber himself and among the other pictures are an unflattering but lively likeness of James Boswell, Johnson's biographer and travelling companion whom he met three years after he moved from Gough Square. Johnson would no doubt have approved the print of Chesterfield which shows a small, bird-brained head perched on a body bloated by the flowing robes that

alone confer status. In the display cabinet is the only image of Tetty, looking slightly disapproving – a response, it is tempting to believe, to her utter marginalisation in a house filled with images of her husband's male and female friends.

On the table in the centre of the room is a facsimile of the *Dictionary*, conceived as Britain's response to the national academy-authored dictionaries of Italy and France. Johnson employed six assistants to help him with his task and keep him company; he would read books he considered appropriate for quotation and mark the relevant words and passages which his assistants would copy and arrange in alphabetical order (friends who loaned him books complained they were returned 'so defaced as to be scarce worth owning'). Though the *Dictionary* was criticised for its omissions, sometimes laboured definitions (net is defined as 'anything reticulated or decussated at equal distances with interstices between the intersections') and partiality (see patron, above), the scope of Johnson's achievement can be measured by comparison with Nathan Bailey's 1721 dictionary, essentially a list of synonyms, in the small display case. Virtuous ladies praised him for his omission of rude words ('What, my dears! Then you have been looking for them', was his response) but a quick check (visitors can rifle through freely) revealed plenty of words absent from a common spellchecker, including turd ('excrement') and whore ('a fornicatress; an adulteress; a strumpet'), appositely illustrated with a quote from Dryden:

Tis a noble general's prudent part,
To cherish valour, and reward desert;
Let him be daub'd with lace, live high, and whore;
Sometimes be lousy, but be never poor.

At the base of the stairs is a 1915 watercolour of Johnson by Max Beerbohm, one of the house's first governors. The first floor, painted pale green throughout, attains a wonderful flexibility by having the walls of the rooms to either side of the spacious landing made up of panels that can be closed to make three discreet spaces, opened to make one large one or used to create a one-third/two-thirds arrangement. The room above the dining room has over the mantelpiece an amateur-looking picture of John Wesley (see page 71) preaching in Old Cripplegate church, with Johnson, Boswell and Williams in the congregation. Other images include engravings of a mop-haired Garrick posed dramatically, sword aloft, as Richard III and of Johnson in his travelling clothes for his expeditions with Boswell. The drawing room opposite has a portrait of the near-blind Williams (by Reynolds' sister Frances) looking patient and expressionless and an idealised after-the-event portrait after Reynolds of Johnson as an infant, as though the painter wished to endow his sickly friend with the glow of perfection of the children of his rich patrons. In the display case is a telling page of accounts including several IOUs and a letter in Johnson's surprisingly clear, unpretentious hand to the young Hester Thrale, one of his closest friends for the last two decades of his life.

The library on the second floor is dominated by a portrait of a regal-looking Elizabeth Carter, a blue-stocking poet and classical scholar who contributed two editions of *The Rambler*. In the will room opposite is a rare image of Johnson when young – a change from the two famous portraits of the bewigged scholar by Reynolds and Opie repeated *ad nauseam* in various forms throughout the house. The recreation of a literary party at Reynolds' house shows Boswell in the shadows, Johnson as if pausing to find words, Reynolds with an ear trumpet, Garrick, the elegant Edmund Burke, Oliver Goldsmith *et al* – members of the Literary Club Johnson founded in 1764 which is still in existence today.

The garret where the work on the *Dictionary* took place spans the width of the house. Johnson was said to have worked at an 'old crazy deal table', precariously balanced on an even older wooden armchair which eventually lost an arm and a leg. The room is dominated by *Johnson Doing Penance in the Market Place at Uttoxeter*, which depicts the bizarre incident when he stood bareheaded in the rain for an hour to atone for a 'sin' committed 50 years earlier when, swollen with pride from his

Oxford student life, he had refused to open his father's bookstall – one of the house's few insights into the darker side of his personality.

Dr Johnson's House is worth visiting for the charm of the building alone, a rare example of a town house in this area. Given its subject's strained circumstances and the fact that he lived before the Victorian mania for collecting took hold, few of his personal possessions have been preserved, so it's a case of soaking up the atmosphere rather than delighting in objects touched by his hands. Captions are virtually non-existent, so unless you already know something about Johnson the house can be something of a mystery – as was obviously the case for the American at my last visit, who asked with some bewilderment where the great man's typewriter was. Even so, there are times when less might have been more, as in the repeated portraits of the great man, and the brick on the first-floor landing – presumably stolen from the Great Wall of China – presented to the Johnson Club in 1922 to illustrate a quote from Boswell's biography in which Johnson expresses his desire to visit this marvel.

ADDRESS 17 Gough Square, London EC4A 3DE (020 7353 3745; www.drjh.dircon.co.uk)
OPEN May to September: Monday to Saturday, 11.00–17.30; October to April, 11.00–17.00

ADMISSION £4/£3/under-10s free/ family ticket £9
ACCESS many unavoidable steps
UNDERGROUND Chancery Lane

18 FOLGATE STREET

The late 20th century may be a fascinating place to visit, but surely… nobody would want to live in it.
Dennis Severs

18 Folgate Street was bought by Californian Dennis Severs in 1979. At the time Spitalfields was still a wholesale fruit, vegetable and flower market rather than a conglomeration of crystal and handmade-soap stalls, and the surrounding area housed newly arrived immigrants and downmarket printers rather than refugees from the City. Severs scavenged food along with the area's many tramps and camped with his chamber pot, candle and bedroll in each of his house's ten rooms, trying to discover the key to its particular atmosphere. Eventually he invented a family called the Jervises, Huguenot silkweavers who fled France soon after Louis XIV repealed the law allowing Protestant worship in 1685, bought the house when it was built in 1724, and whose descendants lived here until 1914. Over the course of 20 years until his death in 1999 at the age of 51, Severs created and furnished the rooms they lived in, each frozen at the moment when the inhabitants, startled by the intrusion of modern-day visitors, beat a hasty retreat. Anyone who has seen Alejandro Amenábar's spine-chilling 2001 film *The Others* will recognise the conceit.

Visitors are asked to remain silent for the duration of their visit, and certainly the absence of embarrassed sniggers at the stale urine in the chamber pots or irrelevant exclamations at the beauty of some of the house's objects helps keep the 21st century at bay for those willing and able to suspend their disbelief. The most intrusive element for me was the haranguing, pretentious notices asking you not to touch anything or explaining why children are unwelcome, presumably erected by the keepers of Severs' flame to bludgeon visitors into experiencing the house

as they believe he would have wished. For instance, such nonsense as: 'It is – quite simply about beauty. Art is a high plane where beauty and balance triumph over practicality… A visit here requires the same style of concentration as would a visit to an Old Masters exhibition… A most absurd but commonly made error is to assume that it might be either amusing or appropriate for children'. There's no doubt Severs' achievement is remarkable, and his installations deserve the status of 'art' rather than theme park, but the exhortations only detract from the sensual experience so much effort has gone into creating.

The three-storey flat-fronted three-bay house with basement and attic is built to a standard L plan. The ground-floor front room – in which a programme for the coronation of William and Mary in 1689 hints at the occupants' Protestantism and the date of their arrival in the country – is set up as a dining room. A heavily italicised notice explains the plot: 'Eighteenth-century silk master Isaac Jervis – his family and descendants – are all still around you somewhere in the house. As you approach – they depart, as you depart – they re-enter, but all so that by not actually seeing them your Imagination might paint a series of pictures: of the various domestic scenes your arrival has forced them to abandon.' And indeed if you listen, look and feel rather than read, the smells of food that waft around the abandoned dining table, the soundtrack of domestic exchanges, street noises and cock-crows combined with the chirping of the real caged bird produce an atmosphere that at the least could be described as uncanny.

The most spine-chilling room for me, however, is the first-floor back, where Severs has painstakingly created the scene that might have followed the drunken male party depicted in Hogarth's 1733 painting *A Midnight Modern Conversation* (which hangs above the mantelpiece here) once the protagonists had left. The abandoned jackets and newspapers, the disordered furniture, the overturned glasses and decanters, the overpowering smell of cloves from the empty punchbowl, the fire's dying embers and the morning-after-the-night-before gloom are eerie enough, but what is most disturbing is the feeling that the myriad details have been provided with such precision and completeness that the space is in fact fully inhabited, and the visitor an unwelcome intruder. The notice asking 'Would you recognise art if it fell out of the frame at you' seems supremely irrelevant.

On the landing stands a beautiful tiered dish bearing sugared almonds below a stunning crystal chandelier, introducing the more genteel atmosphere of the drawing room. But the most potent indication that we are entering the domain of the woman of the house is the change in smell – from the punch dregs of the Hogarth room to a refined lavender. Presided over by a portrait of Mrs Edward Jervis (presumably the daughter-in-law of the Mrs Isaac Jervis whose picture hangs in the dining room below), the symmetrically arranged, orderly dark-green room is set for tea, with a fan draped on what one presumes is the mistress' chair, the tea locked in a caddy at her feet, and the startled departure of her guests indicated by the upturned sugar bowl and a broken cup. On the table is a book of entertainments dating from 1740, a point at which the halt on imports following the start of the 1740-48 war with France led to a surge in demand for locally produced silk and the prosperity of Spitalfields reached its zenith.

The second floor seems to belong to a less affluent age. Abandoned wooden toys gather dust at the top of the stairs and the back room is a combined bedroom and sitting room where the dank smell of stale urine from the half-filled chamberpot mingles unpleasantly with the odour from the half-eaten mince pies and cups of lukewarm tea on the central table. The clanking and creaking soundtrack – footsteps, servants emptying slops, or perhaps simply the house groaning around us – is more evocative than any words. The date is 1821, a time when the number of silk weavers dramatically outnumbered demand for their product, the neighbourhood of Spitalfields was going steeply downhill and the influx of veterans from the protracted war with France that ended in the Battle of Waterloo in 1815 had led to social instability and unrest.

The front bedroom has a magnificent display of Delft above the mantelpiece but somehow our attention is diverted to the clockwork monkey hanging from the bedpost, which clicks as it swings from side to side. Another Mrs Jervis dominates the room through her portrait, clothes, toiletries and the chair that seems to hold the impression of her body and might still feel warm to the touch. Disconcertingly, beside the fireplace are a pair of modern men's shoes and socks and tucked away behind a screen are a jumper and sweatshirt. It's a discrete reminder that this was also Severs' room and that he chose deliberately, masochistically, to efface his own needs and personality wholly and to live in obeisance to a woman created by his imagination.

The attic landing is hung with greying underclothes, and a quotation from Dickens' *Oliver Twist* – 'The House to which Oliver had been conveyed was in the neighbourhood of Whitechapel. It was very dirty' – hints that we are now in the late 1830s. Padlocks on the doors indicate that the rooms are occupied by lodgers and in contrast with the ordered symmetry of the drawing room below, the oddments of dusty, threadbare furniture are arranged pragmatically with no pretence at beauty or elegance. Several people obviously sleep, cook, eat and live in each of the rooms – a pan of cabbage warms by the fire; the table is littered with plates of empty mussel shells.

The basement kitchen is by contrast warm and bright, with a blazing coal fire and griddle cakes done to a turn. The congealed cat food – a rare anachronism – was eaten in the course of the visit by an alive and visible black cat. The cluttered ground-floor back parlour is late Victorian, by which time gentility has reasserted itself. In the hall hangs a fine display of black leather jackets of the kind once found in abundance in the area's gay pubs and clubs.

ADDRESS 18 Folgate Street, London E1 6BX (020 7247 4013; www.dennissevershouse.co.uk) **OPEN** first Sunday of the month 14.00–17.00; first Monday 12.00–14.00; every Monday evening by candlelight, times vary according to season **ADMISSION** Sunday £7/Monday lunchtime £5/Monday evening (booking advised) £10 **UNDERGROUND** Liverpool Street

HANDEL HOUSE MUSEUM

The Brook Street buildings occupied by the Handel House Museum boast blue plaques commemorating two famous musicians: George Frideric Handel, who lived at No. 25 Brook Street from 1723 until his death in 1759, and Jimi Hendrix, who lived at No. 23 in 1968-69. At No. 25 experts have restored the rooms that formed the major part of Handel's home to their presumed condition in the 1720s using paint scrapes, an inventory made after the composer's death and the evidence still available in the less tampered-with house next door. Unfortunately the top-floor flat Hendrix occupied in No. 23 isn't open to the public, but museum director Jacqueline Riding assured me that its rooms have been restored to their late-1960s condition of white-painted woodchip walls and scarlet carpet, based on information supplied by the musician's former girlfriend and traces of fabric found between the floorboards.

Handel moved to London in 1712 at the age of 27 and proceeded to dominate the English music scene for almost half a century. Little is known of his life outside the music world – he didn't marry and had no recorded sexual relationships with men or women, left few letters and kept no diary. Contemporary accounts indicate that he was strikingly handsome in his youth, while his meteoric rise to prominence in Hamburg, Italy and Hanover before the move to London suggests a charismatic personality as well as a prodigious musical talent. As he grew older he became more corpulent, thanks to a 'culpable indulgence in the sensual gratifications of the table', as a biographer put it. Abraham Brown, the lead violinist at performances of *Messiah* in the 1750s, describes how at one dinner party Handel claimed sudden inspiration and retired to the room next door; when one of the guests peeped through the keyhole he was seen quaffing a new delivery of Burgundy vastly superior to the wine served to his guests. But such apparent meanness was tempered with public generosity, in particular to the newly established Foundling Hospital (a favourite charity of his contemporary William Hogarth, see page 228, who was also childless) for which he raised the vast sum of £10,000 in the 1750s through annual charity performances of *Messiah* and his own considerable donations. Biographers also comment on his dry humour, explosive temper and gift for storytelling.

When Handel moved to fashionable Mayfair he must have felt that his position at the pinnacle of the London music scene was secure: he had an annual pension of £400 as music master to the royal family, was music director of the opera company the Royal Academy of Music and was composer to the Chapel Royal. Brook Street itself was planned and built between 1717 to 1726 and No. 25 was part of a residential development of four buildings put up by speculative builder George Barnes. Handel was its first occupant and his neighbours were a Mrs Catherine Johnson, soon followed by Sir John Avery and MP John Monckton. Hanover Square to the east was laid out in 1714, with several of its houses leased to Whig generals, while Grosvenor Square to the west, developed in 1737, accommodated George I's mistress the Duchess of Kendal. As a foreign national, Handel would have been unable to buy the house when he moved in, but even after his naturalisation in 1727 he elected to continue to rent. The brick houses were flat-fronted, four storeys high with the two rooms on each floor arranged around the staircase in a standard L plan with a closet at the back. Following Handel's death, the house was taken over by his servant John Du Burk, who may have run it as a boarding house until 1772. In 1905 it was converted into a shop by art dealer C J Charles, who replaced the façade of the first two floors and virtually gutted the interior. Since 1971 the freehold has been owned by the Co-operative Insurance Society, which leases the rooms occupied by the museum to the Handel House Trust.

Handel arrived in England through his connection with George I (whose portrait hangs above the mantelpiece in the second-floor dressing room), whom he had courted in Hanover when the future king was the elector and Handel was *Kapellmeister*. With *Rinaldo* (1711) he had intro-

on a religious theme. He suffered a stroke in 1737 – possibly brought on by the strain of writing and producing three new operas and staging numerous other works in just eight months; in 1739 he moved to the more modest Lincoln's Inn Fields Theatre where he capitulated to public demand by giving his first all-English season. He left London for Dublin in 1741-42 to stage two new works, *Messiah* and *Samson*.

Following his return to London Handel abandoned opera to concentrate on oratorios. In 1744 he hired the King's Theatre for the first complete English oratorio season with tickets sold by subscription, at which he presented *Hercules* and *Belshazzar*. The season was a disaster, and Handel suffered a nervous breakdown. Thereafter he limited his ambitions to Lenten seasons at Covent Garden with tickets sold for individual performances. Meanwhile he was garnering great public popularity with such patriotic pieces as a *Te Deum* celebrating George II's victory over the French in 1743 in the war over the Austrian succession and *Judas Maccabaeus* (1747), an allegory of the Duke of Cumberland's rout of the Scots at Culloden with a libretto by Hogarth's great friend Thomas Morell. The rehearsal in Vauxhall Pleasure Gardens for the *Music for the Royal Fireworks* (1749) commemorating the end of the war attracted a crowd of 20,000. But whatever the work's subsequent popularity, the first performance – held in Green Park and conceived of as an extravagance on an unprecedented scale – was a fiasco, with drizzle turning many fireworks into damp squibs, one of the pavilions set alight and the display's architect arrested for drawing his sword on the event's organiser.

In 1752, following another stroke, Handel lost his sight almost completely, putting an end to composing. With the help of J C Smith the younger (whose portrait hangs in the first-floor composition room) he was able still to revise his works and direct oratorio seasons, while he continued to perform organ concertos from memory. Despite the many ups and downs in his career he was able to leave an estate of £20,000 – 400 times the annual rent of his desirable Brook Street residence.

The journey through the museum begins disorientingly with a trip in a high-tech metal lift to the second floor. Here you are directed straight

duced Italian opera to the London stage and the Royal Academy of Music, which he founded in 1719 with his Italophile patrons Lord Burlington (see Chiswick House, page 209, and the somewhat unflattering print in the dressing room) and Lord Chandos, briefly established London as Europe's opera capital. London's art world at the time was divided between those who wanted to establish a strong, homegrown British culture for the newly formed United Kingdom with its newly imported Protestant dynasty and those in thrall to the superiority of Italian and French models (the continental grand tour was still virtually mandatory for upper-class young men). In music terms, this translated into a battle between the supporters of Handel's Italian opera and those like Alexander Pope (see portrait in the dressing room) and Jonathan Swift, who deemed the fashion 'wholly unsuitable to our northern climate, and the genius of the people, whereby we are overrun with Italian effeminacy and Italian nonsense.' The rivalry culminated with the staging of *The Beggar's Opera* in 1728 at Lincoln's Inn Fields Theatre. The libretto by John Gay (another portrait in the dressing room) was both a political satire and a parody of the Royal Academy's extravaganzas, and the opera's unprecedented popularity (exploited by Hogarth, who painted at least five versions for various patrons) proved the last straw for Handel's beleaguered enterprise, by now beset by internal wrangling and financial difficulties. The Royal Academy folded and Handel went to Italy to find more singers, returning to form a new venture with John James Heidegger (also portrayed in the dressing room), manager of the King's Theatre.

In 1733 the rival Opera of the Nobility was formed by a group of aristocrats headed by Frederick, Prince of Wales. Led by the castrato Senesino (see engraving and caricature in the first-floor rehearsal room), whom Handel had brought to London for the launch of the Royal Academy, most of Handel's singers defected to the new enterprise, tired of his autocratic zeal. Handel moved to the smaller new Covent Garden Theatre where he continued to put on operas but also experimented with the new semi-dramatic form of the oratorio, usually sung in English and

into a room showing a video (largely an affirmation of the contemporary relevance of the composer's music from a range of talking heads including a singer, producer and taxi driver) arranged with the audience facing the closed door – as they gaze curiously or impatiently at each new arrival, it's a bit like suddenly finding you've wandered on stage. This pleasant room with a large three-bay bow to the side replaced the original closet in about 1790. It leads into the rear room on the second floor, which Handel used as a dressing room. As in the rest of the house, the panelling is replicated from that still in existence in Nos 27 and 29. The ubiquitous grey (like a modern undercoat) is thought from paint scrapes to have been the colour Barnes used for the whole of the development. Areas such as skirtings and doors that got more wear are believed to have been repainted chocolate brown, as here.

Each room is sparsely furnished and hung with portraits based on a theme (in the case of the dressing room, the London music scene). Unfortunately these are simply what the museum has been able to get hold of, so their relevance to the composer's career is uneven, with important characters absent and less significant players represented. The three-bay room at the front of the house was Handel's bedroom, its bed and hangings recreated for the museum from descriptions in the posthumous inventory. Though state-of-the-art in 1723, the paired curtains would have been noticeably old-fashioned by 1759, when ruches were all the rage. But Handel was apparently more interested in food, drink, good company and art (he owned some 80 canvases including Dutch, Flemish and Italian old masters, two Rembrandts and a Watteau) than in interior decoration, or at least that's the impression given by these somewhat austere rooms. The lively 1756 portrait of the composer with his fleshy face, protruding lower lip and bushy eyebrows in its extravagant frame of gilded bulrushes seems distinctly at odds with the atmosphere of calm restraint that otherwise prevails.

The room below takes up the theme of rehearsal and performance. We know that Handel held rehearsals here after he moved to Covent Garden in 1734, perhaps because the new theatre's varied programme meant the auditorium was not always available. The 1759 inventory lists no curtains for the room, possibly because this improved the acoustics. Friends' and neighbours' diaries record being invited to attend rehearsals of new works; violinist Brown recalled 'being heated by a crowded room and hard labour'. The room is dominated by a 1734 portrait of the some-what severe-looking Faustina Bordoni, a soprano who joined Handel's company in 1725. Her increasing rivalry with the more established Francesca Cuzzoni (caricatured here with Senesino), whom Handel had threatened to defenestrate in 1722 when she had refused to sing an aria in *Ottone*, culminated in a public brawl on stage on 6 June 1727 which Gay satirised in *The Beggar's Opera*. A modern reproduction harpsichord (Handel owned a 1612 model made by Hans Ruckers of Antwerp) is used during opening hours by students from the Royal College of Music for rehearsals and lessons. Unfortunately the pine cones on all the chairs and window seats (presumably to stop visitors from sitting down) discourage the kind of quiet contemplation in a room filled with Handel's music that is presumably the point of a shrine like this.

The rear room on the first floor is probably where Handel composed most of his music of this period. Alongside a 1730 portrait of the com-poser without his wig in which the charm of his younger years is readily discernible hangs that of Charles Jennens, librettist for several of the great oratorios including *Messiah*. The portrait shows the composer unconcernedly awaiting his muse; in fact, his best-known work was composed in this room in late summer 1741 in just 24 days.

ADDRESS 25 Brook Street (entrance from Lancashire Court), London WIK 4HB (020 7495 1685; www.handelhouse.org)

OPEN Tuesday, Wednesday, Friday, Saturday, 10.00–18.00; Thursday, 10.00–20.00; Sunday, 12.00–18.00
ADMISSION £4.50/£3.50/£2
UNDERGROUND Bond Street

HOUSE OF ST BARNABAS-IN-SOHO

The House of St Barnabas-in-Soho today provides 39 single homeless women with temporary accommodation, meals, 'life-skills training' and advice on healthcare, legal issues and resettlement. As such, a visit to the premises to admire, free of charge, what Nikolaus Pevsner described as 'easily the finest [interior] in Soho' is an ambivalent experience. Certainly, the staff's well-developed interpersonal skills make the visitor comfortable and welcome, and the compulsory guided tour is brisk and efficient. But there's something incongruous and unsettling in the mix of visually sumptuous rococo ceilings and the smell of institutional cabbage.

The shell of the house was erected in 1746 by speculative builder Joseph Pearce and its interior was fitted out in 1754 by Richard Beckford. Beckford, whose family fortune derived from plantations in Jamaica, soon afterwards became MP for Bristol and an alderman of the City of London. His stay here in Greek Street was brief; in 1756 ill-health led him to move to France where he soon died. His more famous elder brother William, an outspoken Whig who was twice lord mayor, refurbished the interior of Mansion House at his own expense, and it's likely some of the same master craftsmen were employed here.

The plain three-storey brick exterior gives way to an imposing entrance hall and stairwell with a richly stuccoed ceiling and wall panels whose motifs include goddesses, lions' masks and swags. The three first-floor rooms open to the public – the council room (originally the drawing room), adjacent withdrawing room (an anteroom) and records room at the rear (the master bedroom) – retain several original features including decorative ceilings, elaborate door and window surrounds and carved overmantles. Though somewhat shabby, the council room and withdrawing room at least are free of clutter and their scale and grandeur can still be appreciated.

After Beckworth's death the house passed through two private owners before being taken over in 1811 by what was to become the Metropolitan Board of Works. (It was here that the masterplans for London's 82 miles of sewers and 102 miles of surface drainage were drawn up.) In 1863 it was acquired by the House of Charity, an organisation supported by prime minister William Gladstone and *Water Babies* author and Christian socialist Charles Kingsley which sought to help families made destitute through circumstances that were not 'the manifest result of idleness or vice'. The charity raised money (some of it through the sale of the house's original fireplaces) to build the adjacent chapel. Designed by Joseph Clarke and inspired by a Romanesque abbey building at Arles in France, its ungainly plan had a central nave with chairs for the nuns and trustees who ran the charity flanked by aisles each opening into two side apses in which the 'inmates' sat on hard stone seats.

The 100 or so women who pass annually through the House of St-Barnabas-in-Soho are no longer required to attend services in the chapel twice daily, though Wednesday-evening prayers are open to all-comers. With some 40 per cent of those it helps identifying themselves as African or Caribbean, a house whose beauty was made possible through the exploitation of slave labour is perhaps at last repaying some of its debts.

ADDRESS 1 Greek Street, London
WID 4NQ (020 7434 1846)
OPEN usually first Monday of the
month, but telephone to confirm
ADMISSION free

ACCESS limited, telephone for
details
UNDERGROUND Tottenham Court
Road

THE SHERLOCK HOLMES MUSEUM

Master detective Sherlock Holmes and his stalwart friend and biographer Dr Watson rented rooms on the first and second floors of 221b Baker Street from their landlady Mrs Hudson between about 1881 and 1904. The flat-fronted four-storey house was built c. 1815 – not long after the Dickens House Museum (see page 27) and at the same time as John Nash was developing the area around nearby Regent's Park. Like the Dickens House, it's built on a standard L plan, though it's noticeably smaller in scale. Like the Dickens House too, the patina of age, to put it kindly, is everywhere apparent: here the risers of the stair carpet are holed from all those clumping male feet, while the rug in Holmes' bedroom is practically threadbare.

It's known that 221b Baker Street was registered as a lodging house from 1860 to 1934, and indeed the location – in easy walking distance of the West End and virtually overlooking Regent's Park, which was opened to the public in the 1830s – could hardly be bettered. Today the ground floor, predictably, is a souvenir shop with a separate entrance. However, the original front entrance (somewhat unnecessarily guarded by a policeman in period dress) has been retained, and the mean, gloomy hallway and stairs to the first floor – cold, ill-lit and distinctly grimy – are among the most evocative spaces of any of the houses described here. The cramped front room, a study the two men shared, has two comfortable armchairs on either side of a low table in front of the blazing fire, a dining table set for two in the corner opposite the door and Watson's desk with his medical textbooks and doctor's bag filled with a gruesome array of implements. It's obviously several notches down in terms of scale and taste from the lifestyle enjoyed by contemporary Linley Sambourne (see page 101) and as such gives rise to reflections about the relative earning powers of pre-NHS doctors, detectives and cartoonists. Unusually for

a heritage museum, you're allowed to touch the objects, sharpen your reflections with the aid of Holmes' trusty violin and try on the duo's well-worn hats. The costumed maid will take photographs if asked.

Holmes occupied the back bedroom on this floor, and the uncomfortable-looking iron bedstead in which he slept and washstand with its pitcher and ewer have miraculously been preserved. The completeness and relative poverty of the furnishings again give an almost eerily vivid idea of what life must have been like. The second-floor front room (occupied by Mrs Hudson) contains several of the objects that provided vital clues in Holmes' detective work – for instance a piece of plaster smeared with blood that led to the denouement of *The Norwood Builder*. ('With dramatic suddenness [Inspector Lestrade] struck a match and by its light exposed a stain of blood upon the whitewashed wall. As he held the match nearer I saw that it was more than a stain. It was the well marked print of a thumb.') Here also is a tragic scrapbook of recent letters begging Holmes for help – Stéphanie Duverger in France asks him to trace a missing friend and the Japanese Kanal asks him to prove a friend's death was murder, not suicide.

Watson's bedroom at the rear of the house and the two rooms on the top floor are given over to chilling displays of waxworks depicting some of the more dramatic episodes from Holmes' investigations. The top-floor bathroom has a remarkable (still functional) porcelain toilet and basin decorated with rampant blue flowers.

ADDRESS 221b Baker Street, London NW1 6XE (020 7935 8866; www.sherlock-holmes.co.uk) **OPEN** daily, 9.30–18.00

ADMISSION £6/under-16s £4 **ACCESS** none **UNDERGROUND** Baker Street

SIR JOHN SOANE'S MUSEUM

Sir John Soane was one of England's most influential and original architects, his projects including such prestigious commissions as the remodelling of the Bank of England, the Houses of Parliament and Westminster Law Courts as well as a string of country houses for the aristocracy of his day. But we have his sons John and George and their time-honoured rebellion against an autocratic, pushy parent to thank for this museum, in a story that bears out the truism 'from rags to riches and back again in three generations'.

Born in 1753 to a provincial bricklayer, Soane *père* came to London at the age of 15 to seek fame and fortune as an architect, beginning as a messenger boy in the office of George Dance the Younger. He soon made his mark and in 1784 married Eliza Smith, the niece and ward of City builder George Wyatt, thereafter dreaming of founding an architectural dynasty along the lines of the Dances. His country house Pitshanger Manor in Ealing (see page 242) was purchased in 1800 with the idea that it would be an ideal home for a budding architect, but John and George refused to play ball. Both married women who brought no wealth or social connections (George by his own admission out of spite towards his parents) and George, a grimly unsuccessful novelist and later intermittently acclaimed dramatist, began a lifelong feud with his father. Soane's bitterness and disappointment is given full rein in a paper he wrote in 1812, in which he imagines a future antiquarian speculating on the museum's origins and concluding that it was the work of a great architect who suffered for his originality and integrity, was abused by his kin and died of a broken heart.

The museum is a fantastic labyrinth studded with treasures. Its history began in 1792 when Soane, using a legacy from his wife's uncle, bought and demolished the 17th-century house that stood at 12 Lincoln's

Inn Fields and built a new family home with his office on the site of the stables at the back. In 1808 he bought No. 13 and rebuilt the stables to form a single extension with the rear of No. 12; in 1812 he rebuilt the front of No. 13 as a residence; in 1824, nine years after his wife's death, he bought and rebuilt No. 14, the back as an extension of the former stable blocks, the front as a residence which he subsequently sold. By this time the building was clearly intended as a display case for his growing collection of paintings, architectural drawings and looted antiquities, a museum that would surpass the nearby British Museum, for which the commission for rebuilding had annoyingly been given to one of his rivals, Robert Smirke Jr. In 1833, by Act of Parliament, Soane disinherited George (the sickly John had died in 1823) and bequeathed his house and its contents to the nation as a museum 'for the inspection of amateurs and students in painting, sculpture and architecture'. But he didn't quite renounce his dynastic aspirations in that he requested John's son to take on the role of curator and hoped that once a national institution to teach architecture had been established, the museum would revert to the family line and an architect would be born.

Soane made many enemies and was involved in many controversies in the course of his career. Described by a pupil as having 'an acute sensitiveness, and a fearful irritability, dangerous to himself if not to others; an embittered heart, prompting a cutting and sarcastic mind; uncompromising pride, neither respecting nor desiring respect; a contemptuous regard for the feelings of his dependants; and yet himself the very victim of irrational impulse; with no pity for the trials of his neighbour and nothing but frantic despair under his own', he was not easy to live with. His marriage to Eliza – a popular, lively, intelligent and well-informed woman with a good head for business – was a love match and she acted willingly as his emotional support and confidante. But the marriage became increasingly strained in the decade before her death in 1815 as relations between Soane and his sons worsened and Soane was reported to be seen too frequently in the company of a certain Norah Brickenden. Following Eliza's death, Mrs Sally Conduitt took over as housekeeper at

Lincoln's Inn Fields, replacing Soane's wife as hostess and to some extent as his companion until his death in 1837. His cruelty to George and to John's widow Maria continued unabated: in 1827 he refused George's pleas for money to buy medicines for his 16-year-old daughter, who subsequently died, and didn't even answer his letter asking that she might be buried in the family vault.

In 1792 Lincoln's Inn Fields was a good address, with easy access to shops and markets, galleries and theatres, the Bank of England and the Royal Academy. But Eliza found the unhealthy climate and lack of outdoor space for the children, aged seven and four when they moved, oppressive. Soane was often away overseeing jobs and she and the boys spent most of the holidays with his family in Chertsey or at Margate, where they socialised with the high society that frequented the then-fashionable Isle of Thanet. (Eliza moved with ease between her roles as hostess for her architect husband's wealthy clients and friend and supporter to the impoverished family of his bricklayer brother.) Though Soane had begun Lincoln's Inn Fields with the enthusiasm of a 40-year-old architect who at last had the chance to design a house that would express his own tastes and act as a showcase for his abilities, subsequently he was to bury himself in the project as a distraction from the many unhappy periods in his professional and family life.

The museum is immediately recognisable by its façade – a revolutionary departure for a Georgian terraced house – which boasts a three-storey loggia in painted stone decorated with Greek key patterns and topped by statuary. (It has been suggested that the elevation was a mocking response to the portico of the Royal College of Surgeons at No. 41 – another commission for which Soane was gallingly overlooked, this time in favour of Dance, with whom Soane had fallen out seemingly irrevocably in 1805-06 after he had allegedly schemed to take the professorship of the Royal Academy from his mentor.) Once you've got inside and managed to block out the overhelpful elderly gentlemen who for the most part run the place, wander and wonder.

The library and dining room at the front of No. 13 are painted Pompei-

ian red – possibly to match a sample of plaster Soane stole from the ruins during his formative three-year travelling scholarship to Italy from 1778. It's a colour that has since graced many an Islington drawing room. These rooms appear comfortably spacious and uncluttered – despite being home to some 50 urns and vases – thanks in part to the architect's trademark use of mirrors, particularly the one between the front windows which gives the impression of a continuous wall of glass and those above the bookcases on the west wall, which reflect the ceiling paintings. The furniture (invitingly curved leather chairs and a simple leather chaise of the type coveted by architects to this day) was made for Soane. A portrait by Thomas Lawrence shows the master looking benign and kindly – a bizarre contrast with Joshua Reynolds' *Love and Beauty* opposite, which depicts a woman with naked breasts and a *putto* pulling demandingly at her clothing in a manner that will strike a chord of despair with many a mother.

The study and dressing room leading to the rear of the house are so small there's an Alice in Wonderland feel about them, as if it's you who has grown, not the scale that has shrunk. There's a pleasing continuity, though, in the beautiful polished wood used for the desk and the built-in washbasin, while the Roman fragments stretch up to the ceiling. They're the rooms of a sensualist. The view of the sculpture courtyard from the east window gives the impression of an exotic Roman temple discovered among London's prosaic brick-faced backyards, an incongruous mix of worlds that perhaps reflects the way the heady idealism inspired by Soane's scholarship to Rome – a time he described as the happiest of his life – was crushed by the disappointing realities of London architectural practice.

Squeeze through a narrow corridor and suddenly the space changes from calm elegance to chaos. At this point turn right for the picture room at the rear of No. 14, where the stars of the show are undoubtedly the paintings by Hogarth (see page 228) of *A Rake's Progress* and *The Election*. Again the clash of cultures is visible in the contrast between these very English portraits of debauchery and corruption and the serene

Rafael cartoon fragments above – from the sublime to the ridiculed. Ask a steward to open out the panels and don't take no for an answer. The north wall swings open to reveal a series of Piranesi drawings of Paestum and the south wall is hinged twice, first for J M Gandy's watercolour perspectives of Soane's fantastic vistas and the second time for a view into the yard and monk's parlour below.

The monk's parlour (also in No. 14) satirises the contemporary passion for all things gothic. Soane invented the character of Padre Giovanni – allegedly buried in the yard in a tomb which in fact holds the remains of Eliza's dog Fanny – and created a melancholic atmosphere for his rooms through restricted space, sombre colours and stained glass. You emerge into the light of the crypt at the rear of No. 13, which houses a disturbing collection of prototype tombs, predominantly for women and children, designed by Soane's close friend John Flaxman. In the sepulchral chamber is the sarcophagus of Pharaoh Seti 1 which Soane bought in 1824 for £2000 after the British Museum refused to cough up, an acquisition he celebrated by throwing a three-day party with some 900 guests including the prime minister, Samuel Taylor Coleridge and his great friend J M W Turner. Poorly displayed and yellowed by the London air, it's another candidate for forcible repatriation along with the Parthenon frieze. Above it in the double-height space float dismembered bodies like an episode of *Casualty* set in stone. The experience becomes increasingly ghoulish – past the eerie wooden mummy case is a model of an Etruscan tomb with an exposed skeleton. The many sculptural fragments above the sarcophagus can best be appreciated from upstairs, where a colonnade leads to the dome beneath which a bust of poor old Soane faces forever a plaster cast of the Apollo Belvedere, considered the most perfect representation of male beauty. The cramped viewing conditions offer an unparalleled opportunity to examine what's under the figleaf as long as you look up at the right moment.

The new picture room (actually a shop with a couple of Canalettos thrown in) on the ground floor of No. 12 was not designed by Soane. The breakfast parlour of No. 12 – decorated in a much lighter and more modest style with a *trompe l'oeil* trellis on the ceiling to give the impression of a garden room – has been restored to conform with a painting by Gandy of 1798 that shows Soane and his wife taking tea while their two young sons, dressed with stifling formality, do their best to amuse themselves. The breakfast parlour of No. 13 is almost a résumé of the mature Soane style – a beautifully proportioned, near-square room with a trademark pendentive dome inset with mirrors, a central lantern, a mirror reflecting the window with its view of sculptures and fragments, highly polished wood, books, and drawings of a Roman villa (a bizarre contrast with the portraits of Fanny the dog).

The oval staircase leads to the first-floor drawing room of No. 13, painted a fashionable yellow and sparsely furnished, giving a feeling of spaciousness and light. Until 1834 the loggia was an open balcony. Typically for this patriarchal household, Eliza Soane is represented by a small pencil sketch by Flaxman while Soane and his two sons have full portraits. The elder son's obvious physical resemblance to his father must have made his inability to follow in Soane's footsteps all the more difficult to swallow.

ADDRESS 13 Lincoln's Inn Fields,
London WC2A 3BP
(020 7405 2107/7430 0175;
www.soane.org)
OPEN Tuesday to Saturday,
10.00–17.00; also first Tuesday of
month, 18.00–21.00
ACCESS limited
ADMISSION free
UNDERGROUND Holborn

SPENCER HOUSE

The part of Spencer House open to the public is a glittering recreation of the state rooms of one of London's most ambitious private palaces. Built in 1756 by the 1st Earl Spencer, the house was stripped during World War II of most of its chimneypieces, doors, skirting mouldings and architraves, which were installed in the family seat at Althorp. Restored in the late 1980s by its current occupants, J Rothschild Capital Management, virtually everything on display is thus a fake, copied painstakingly from originals made available by the family.

The 1st Earl inherited his immense wealth while he was still a minor. At a ball to mark his coming of age in 1755 he secretly married 18-year-old Georgiana Poyntz and almost immediately set about building a London house to display his art collection, hold lavish entertainments and as a 'paean to connubial bliss'. (The diamond buckles on his honeymoon shoes were valued at £30,000.) He chose as his architect William Kent's pupil John Vardy, who designed the external elevations and ground-floor rooms using motifs from imperial Rome. In 1758 Vardy was replaced by James 'Athenian' Stuart, possibly at the suggestion of Colonel George Gray, who like Spencer was a member of the Society of Dilettanti, a group of aristocrats dedicated to promoting 'Roman Taste and Greek Gusto'. Stuart had been sponsored by the society to compile the first accurate survey of the antiquities of Athens and the *piano nobile* at Spencer House thus became one of the first informed applications of Greek ornament to an English domestic interior. Subsequent alterations to the ground floor were made for the 2nd Earl by Henry Holland, fashionable architect of the Prince Regent's palace Carlton House. The 2nd Earl's sister Georgiana was the wife of the 5th Duke of Devonshire, owner of Chiswick House (see page 209).

The Palladian elevation of Spencer House to St James's Park is stun-

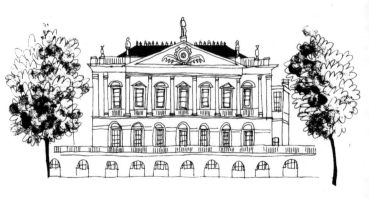

ning: a rusticated ground floor topped by a plain upper storey of seven bays separated by Doric columns supporting a five-bay pediment crowned by statues of Bacchus, Flora and Ceres – 'the embodiment of hospitality, supported by those of beauty and fertility'. Next door, presumably on an infill site created by bomb damage that highlights Spencer House's lucky escape, towers a robustly brutalist block of flats by Denys Lasdun. Spencer House's austere entrance hall with its frieze of swags and ox-skulls has original fittings left behind in the 1942 move.

The tour begins in a room intended by the 1st Earl as a family dining room. Relatively modest in scale, it is entered through double doors into an apse with a gilded coffered ceiling inspired by the Temple of Venus in Rome. This was originally designed to hold the sideboard, with smaller doors on either side; Holland transformed it into the entrance to the circuit of grand ground-floor rooms and installed the mahogany doors copied here. His alterations are also to the fore in the adjacent library – another modestly elegant room, with a delicate acanthus-leaf frieze – designed to house the 2nd Earl's book collection.

The dining room – the central space in the west front overlooking the park – is a magnificent contrast in style and scale. In Vardy's original design the walls were embellished with 12 pilasters and niches but Holland replaced these with the grand gesture of a central space screened at each end by massive scagliola Ionic columns. Vardy's adjacent palm room surpasses even this. A rectangular space opens into a trefoil-plan alcove with a statue of Venus at its centre. The coffered central dome and the half-domes of the apses are exquisitely gilded but the main impact derives from a series of gilded columns in the form of palm trees – symbol of marital fertility – with fronds spilling out to fill the upper walls.

The change of mood on the first floor is signalled by the way Vardy's unadorned lower stairwell gives way to Stuart's upper storey of Ionic pilasters linked by garlands. The music room (above the private dining room) is relatively restrained, the geometric simplicity of its architraves and chimneypiece a contrast to the swagger of the ground floor. Above the library is Lady Spencer's room. The panels in the pink, blue and gold

ceiling were intended to receive paintings, but Stuart, a painter by training who was said to prefer 'an easy and convivial life to the exacting routine of a busy architects' office', failed to get round to them in the eight years he spent on the project. In his defence, it should be noted that the replica marble chimneypiece took 5800 man-hours to carve and was not in place until three years after the rest of the restoration was completed.

The great room above the dining room was used for receptions, balls and as a picture gallery. The four medallions in the cove of the ceiling – supported by *putti* and the Spencer griffins – represent Bacchus, Apollo, Venus and the Three Graces, symbolising the pleasures for which the space was intended. Here all restraint disappears and the elaborate green and gold coffered ceiling and intricately carved door surrounds and chimneypiece make for an uninhibited display of wealth, all the more dazzling because of the newness of the restoration. It is the painted room beyond, however, that is Stuart's masterpiece. Almost every surface is decorated with urns, nymphs, wreaths, flowers and scenes on the themes of love and marriage including a Venus whose features are believed to have been modelled on Lady Spencer's.

The Spencer family lived for at least part of the year at Spencer House until the end of the 19th century when it was let to tenants by the 5th Earl as an economy measure. The 6th Earl moved back in 1910 and in 1926 the 7th Earl had the house redecorated before leasing it to the Ladies' Army and Navy Club. Though the talk given by the guide I was allocated was remarkably disorganised and uninformative, at least no effort was made to exploit any sentimental connection to the family's most famous recent member, the late Diana, Princess of Wales, daughter of the 8th Earl.

ADDRESS 27 St James's Place, London SW1A 1NR (020 7499 8620) **OPEN** Sunday, 10.30–17.30, 45-minute guided tours only

ADMISSION £6/£5/under-10s not admitted **ACCESS** limited **UNDERGROUND** Green Park

JOHN WESLEY'S HOUSE

Founder of Methodism John Wesley (1703–91) lived in this house for only the last 12 years of his long life – or more accurately, the last 12 winters, since even in his late 80s he spent some ten months of the year on the road, having clocked up some 250,000 miles and 40,000 sermons in the course of his lifetime.

Wesley's first London base was a ruinous cannon foundry 200 metres down the road; after 40 years the lease was running out and the Corporation of London was keen to acquire the land for development. The proposed new complex, designed by George Dance the Younger, the mentor of John Soane (see page 244), was located opposite an existing nonconformist burial ground but otherwise surrounded by fields. It was to consist of a terrace of five dwellings with an entrance to a courtyard and chapel running under the central house. Wesley found Dance's designs for the dwellings too elaborate and asked him to scale down the ornamentation and materials to the 'perfectly neat but not fine' aesthetic of the chapel. Only one house and the chapel were built, between 1778 and 1779, by local preacher and builder Samuel Tooth.

The hushed atmosphere of the house today is misleading: in Wesley's time it accommodated several preachers, sometimes with families in tow, a housekeeper (sometimes the wife of one of the preachers), a manservant and a live-out maid and cook (Wesley's wife had left him in 1751). After his death it became the residence of the superintendent ministers of the chapel and their families. Later residents had to endure a constant stream of pilgrims, many of whom asked to see Wesley's bones, so in 1891, when funds became available, a new superintendent minister's house was built on the opposite side of the courtyard and in 1898 the first floor of Wesley's house was opened as a museum. In 1934 artist Frank Salisbury and minister George McNeal instigated an ambitious renova-

tion plan and Salisbury donated the portrait to be found at present in the front room of the basement. A great deal of structural work was undertaken over the next half century and after an extended period of closure the house was reopened in 1981 by Margaret Thatcher – to the disgust of many Methodists who reasonably enough saw her policies as an attack on the working-class congregations from which the movement had since Wesley's time drawn its support. The museum's first professionally trained curator was engaged in 1991 and after much research the house was restored to the condition it is in today.

Visitors enter the complex into a cobbled courtyard dominated by a statue of Wesley. The neoclassical chapel at the rear has a museum of Methodism in the basement; Daniel Defoe, William Blake and John Bunyan are buried in the cemetery opposite. You enter the simple four-storey house, built of brick with stucco and stone dressings, via the trade entrance, down steps into the flagged basement kitchen with its huge fireplace and dresser. The front room contains displays of communion ware (Wesley was determined Methodism should remain a movement within the Church of England) and hymnals and other books published by Wesley Bros (Wesley installed printing presses on the site and published more than 450 works in the course of his lifetime including his journals, extracts from the classics and biographies, netting a hefty annual income from which he took a wage of only £40 to £50). Among his assembled personal possessions are a diminutive gown (he was only 5 feet 4 inches tall) and shoes (size 4½), a sturdy umbrella, spurs, a night-cap, a travelling writing case and communion set and a pair of spectacles. More dubious items include a stump and leaf from the tree under which he gave his last outdoor sermon, at Winchelsea in 1790.

Ascend the narrow stairs to the ground floor. The dining room at the front, its table laid with a simple meal of bread and cheese, has an engraving of Wesley preaching to 'Northamerican Indians' in 1745 – the incongruous black-frock-coated preacher surrounded by a befeathered tribe adorned with nose- and earrings. The room is at the same time simple and pretty, its stone-white colour believed from records and paint scrapings to be near the original. Though visitors, particularly Americans, are impressed by the austerity and 'poverty' Wesley endured, the Oxford-educated scholar in fact enjoyed an income and standard of living in line with those of his middle-class contemporaries. The smaller back parlour was where the preachers would have spent the evenings reading and chatting – as in a latterday episode of *Father Ted*. The unusual semi-glazed built-in cupboards are thought to have been requested by Wesley.

The first floor was occupied by Wesley when he was in residence. The drawing room/study at the front has a wonderful glazed bookcase full of his own books and a Queen Anne bureau with secret drawers in which he is said to have hidden letters from his wife. Wesley used the 'electrical machine' in the corner to administer a primitive form of electric-shock therapy to patients seeking treatment for depression from the free dispensary at the foundry. The portrait of Wesley aged 62 – note the slender hands, upright posture, lean features, stringy hair – was described in his journal as 'a most striking likeness'; its lack of vanity and pretension is in contrast with the regal patriarch in the basement commissioned posthumously by Salisbury and in fact modelled on arts-and-crafts architect Charles Voysey, the great-great-great-grandson of Wesley's sister. The bedroom where Wesley died and in particular the prayer room leading off it – a small space added by Wesley himself and simply furnished with a chair, a kneeler and a low bureau on top of which are a candle and a Bible – are strangely moving. Wesley would rise at 4 in the morning and spend several hours here thinking and praying, hence the room's nickname 'the powerhouse of Methodism'. On the second floor are one of the rooms in which visiting preachers were accommodated and a room commemorating the work ongoing in the house following Wesley's death.

John Wesley's House is a shrine of a quite different order from the houses of, say, Dickens or Dr Johnson. Though some might ask whether the huge cost of creating and maintaining a bricks-and-mortar memorial to a founder who preached largely out of doors, disdained material comforts and introduced what amounted to a social-welfare programme is appropriate, lesser mortals seem to need graven images, and the many thousands of believers who flock to Wesley's altar no doubt derive a thrill and some comfort. And despite my disdain for religion in general, I found the sense which pervades the house of lives lived to a purpose that transcends the material, intellectual or sensual surprisingly alluring.

ADDRESS 47 City Road, London ECIY IAU (020 7253 2262) **OPEN** Monday to Saturday, 10.00–16.00; Sunday, 12.00–14.00 **ACCESS** ground floor only

COST £4 for house and museum; free on Sunday **UNDERGROUND** Moorgate/ Old Street

[battersea/chelsea/ fulham/kensington]

Carlyle's House   79
Fulham Palace   86
Kensington Palace   89
Leighton House   94
Lindsey House   100
Linley Sambourne House   101
Old Battersea House   107

CARLYLE'S HOUSE

> To see how they live and waste here… Flinging platefuls of what they are
> pleased to denominate 'crusts' into the ashpits!… In Scotland we have no such
> thing as 'crusts'.
> Jane Welsh Carlyle, quoted from Thea Holme's *The Carlyles at Home*

Some four weeks after his marriage to Jane Welsh (1801–66) the 31-year-old Thomas Carlyle (1795–1881) patronisingly described his wife in a letter to his mother as 'a good little girl… asking, as it seems, nothing more whatever of her destiny, but that in any way she could make me happy.' Eight years later Jane, a middle-class doctor's daughter who had married a poor if promising stonemason's son, persuaded her writer/historian husband to abandon the remote Scottish farm of Craigenputtock she had inherited from her father, and in which they had lived for the previous six years, for London, settling in Cheyne Row where they were to stay until they died. And indeed much of those 32 years for Jane was spent trying to secure the conditions – chiefly absolute silence and food prepared to strict instructions – that would enable the fussy (or sensitive) Carlyle to write his masterworks *The French Revolution* (1837), *The Life and Letters of Oliver Cromwell* (1845) and *Frederick the Great* (1858–65). From an annual budget of £200 increased in 1855 to £230 after she presented her husband with an ingeniously argued parliamentary-style budget pleading her case, she managed all their financial affairs including the contracts with successive landlords and Carlyle's income tax, for which she appealed in person for reductions to the Inland Revenue commissioners. Quick-witted, cultured and determined, Jane entertained a circle of friends independently of her husband that included revolutionary-in-exile Mazzini, biographer John Forster and novelist Charles Dickens. Her vivid letters have a wit and elegance that outshine most of her contemporaries; she too could have been a writer, but instead she turned her considerable intelligence to running her home as efficiently and economically as possible in much the same way as the frustrated housewife at the heart of Marilyn French's 1970s classic *The Women's Room* tackled the housework with the research tools of a PhD graduate.

The Carlyles chose Chelsea because, as Carlyle wrote to Jane during his initial house-hunting mission, it was then 'unfashionable; it was once the resort of the Court and great, however; hence numerous old houses in it, at once cheap and excellent'. Their red-brick three-storey Queen Anne house, a standard L in plan with a small projection at the rear, was built in 1708 on a site owned by Lord Cheyne and rented to the couple for £35 per annum. The ground-floor parlour – described accurately by Carlyle as 'unfashionable in the highest degree but in the highest degree serviceable' – is endearingly tatty and intimate. Here Jane fitted the drawing-room carpet from Craigenputtock, filling in the gaps with dyed blanket. The piano at which she would play and sing Scottish ballads was brought to London in 1842 after the death of her mother. The fireplace was installed in 1843 after Carlyle decided the existing grate could not be endured 'for another twenty-four hours'.

In 1865, after Carlyle finished *Frederick the Great* in his attic work-room, the parlour was repainted for him to use as a study. Since the freehold of the house was purchased by public subscription only 14 years after Carlyle's death, to be restored by arts-and-crafts designer C R Ashbee, much of the furniture here is original including the small chaise, Jane's armchair, the central table from Craigenputtock and the dining chairs which – like most of their possessions – once belonged to Jane's parents. The degree to which the room still resembles the Carlyles' living space can be gauged from Robert Tait's 1857 *A Chelsea Interior*, of which Jane remarked: 'The dog is the only member of the family who has reason to be pleased with his likeness'. (And indeed while Carlyle, standing writing in his floor-length dressing gown, cuts a handsome, improbably youthful figure, Jane looks bitter and pinched in comparison with the nearby miniature painted some 30 years earlier that depicts her as a carefree Jane Austen heroine with bouncy ringlets.)

In the smaller back dining room, separated from the parlour by big double doors, hangs a crude likeness of Frederick the Great bought for Carlyle by Jane for 6 shillings the day before her death. In the china closet behind, Mary Russell, a maid who had been with the household for about 18 months, gave birth in 1864 to an illegitimate child who was smuggled out of the house wrapped in Jane's best table linen by the other servant, Helen. Incredibly, Jane didn't find out about the incident until some months later, and derived a certain degree of wry amusement from the idea that her husband was at the time entertaining novelist Geraldine Jewsbury in the dining room with 'just a thin small door between!' However, both Mary and Helen were summarily dismissed. In the display case to the left of the door are a number of pathetically touching valentines and keepsakes that belonged to Charlotte Southam, a maid from 1858 to 1860 whose aunt blew the whistle on Mary. In the rear display case are Jane's much less frivolous mementoes including a dying gift from her garrulous mother, whose visits to Cheyne Row inevitably ended in tears.

The 18th-century pine panelling in the entrance hall and stairwell was papered over by the Carlyles. Carlyle's trademark hat hangs by the door to the garden, for the ever-practical Jane a source of food as well as flowers which Carlyle transformed from a jungle shortly after they moved in, digging after lunch as an antidote to writing. Here he used to walk, sit and smoke – as depicted in the etching in the parlour – keeping ready-filled clay pipes in niches in the walls.

The basement kitchen, home to a succession of 34 servants in 32 years, is a miserable place. The stone sink and dresser were installed when the house was built; in 1852, after Jane had secured a 31-year lease on the property with no increase in rent because of the substantial improvements the couple were planning, the Carlyles fitted a new range, water was laid on and gas lights arrived – one above the front door for visitors and one above the range so food wouldn't be burned and wasted. At first the maid slept on the bottom shelf of the dresser and kept her belongings in the back scullery; later the spartan iron bedstead was provided. In the back kitchen was a bath lowered from the ceiling by a complex arrangement of ropes and pulleys in which Carlyle would stand every morning pouring buckets of cold water over himself. The bedrooms were furnished with chamber pots and there was an earth closet in the garden.

Outside the first-floor drawing room is a portrait of Carlyle's mother which bears a striking resemblance to Jane. (Some idea of Jane's romantic feelings towards her father can be gained from the engraving in her bedroom of the Roman soldier Belisarius, whom she thought he resembled.) Like the parlour downstairs, the drawing room is comfortable rather than imposing, the most expensive-looking item a green leather armchair given Carlyle on his eightieth birthday by John Forster. The space was originally Carlyle's sparsely furnished workroom and library; in 1843, while her husband was away, it became the subject of the first of what Jane called her 'domestic earthquakes' or remodelling projects, during which it was enlarged by removing the closet to the left of the chimney breast to give the room a third window, redecorated and refurbished with more bookcases and more elegant furnishings including legacies from Jane's mother and the sofa which she persuaded a dealer to trade for £1 and some old curtains.

Jane was justifiably proud of the economy and efficiency with which she had created 'a really beautiful little drawing room' but Carlyle was tense about having to start on his biography of Cromwell and so embarked on what sounds like a series of displacement activities. After three days he was in a rage 'for want of a closet or some equivalent to fling one's confusion in' ('Best to accumulate no confusion' was Jane's reply). Then the Misses Lambert, who had moved next door in 1839 with what Jane called 'all the things to be guarded against in a London neighbourhood, *viz.*, a pianoforte, a lap-dog, and a parrot', began to play the piano in contravention of an agreement she had reached with their father some months earlier to make no music until 2 pm so Carlyle could work undisturbed. Carlyle decided to move his study into his second-floor dressing room in which a fireplace was installed (at the same time as the removal of the offending fireplace in the parlour). This meant abandoning his adjacent bedroom for the spare room on the second-floor front, which also became unusable when the builder suggested enlarging it by removing a partition. Jane describes her husband as 'a sort of domestic wandering Jew' searching the house for places to work and sleep, all the while 'wringing his hands and tearing his hair, like the German wizard servant who has learnt magic enough to make a broomstick carry water for him, but had not the counter spell to stop it'. A letter to her cousin Jeannie Welsh bemoaning 'the inconvenience of having one's spare room as it were annihilated' reveals something of her attitude towards her husband: 'Could you for instance sleep in a double-bedded room with Carlyle?'

In 1852, Carlyle's increased means and status necessitating a more comfortable space for entertaining, the drawing room was enlarged by taking three feet from Jane's bedroom. At the same time the panelling was removed, a new fireplace and new windows were installed and the room was redecorated. Jane's description of the builders' behaviour strikes a familiar chord: 'Workmen spend three fourths of their time in consulting how the work should be done, and in going out and in after "beer"… The builder promised to have all done in six weeks, painting included; if he gets done in six months is as much as I hope.' However, with Carlyle safely removed to Germany to research Frederick and a pair of loaded pistols under her pillow, there was a certain satisfaction to be gained in 'superintending all these men. I… am infinitely more satisfied than I was in talking "wits" in my white silk gown with feathers on my head.' And Jane didn't limit her efforts to supervising: during the first 'earthquake' she wrote to Carlyle that when work was delayed she had fallen 'immediately to glazing and painting with my own hands not to ruin you altogether.'

Two years after Jane's death Carlyle's niece Mary Aitken came to stay, living at Cheyne Row until her uncle's death. One of the few changes she made was to redecorate the drawing room, and the present William Morris paper is similar to the one she chose. Mary married her cousin

Alexander Carlyle in 1879 and as Carlyle now lived more-or-less full time on the first floor, the second-floor front room (now part of the custodian's flat) became a nursery for their children. The secretaire bookcase in the drawing room was a present to the pair from Erasmus Darwin; the screen, originally made for the dining room, was decorated over a period of several months in 1849 by the indefatigable Jane with a collage of pasted-on pictures of people, landscapes and especially horses. It's the kind of thing my grandmother, a couple of generations younger than Jane and never one to leave anything plain that could be made fancy, used to do, and a method we as teenagers turned on our bedroom walls. Jane was also probably responsible for the naive inlaid decoration on the box that stands on the table, which once contained Goethe's wedding presents to the pair. Three cards on the wall that accompanied subsequent gifts bear verses in his florid hand. The veneration in which Carlyle was held by the end of his life is apparent in the eightieth-birthday testimonial on the landing wall signed by the likes of Tennyson, Darwin, George Eliot, Thackeray, Trevelyan and Trollope.

The bedroom at the back of the first floor was probably the guest room in the early years, the Carlyles occupying the second floor. Later it became Jane's bedroom, and it is extraordinary to realise that the bed on display here is actually the four-poster 'red bed' she was born in, which she used for most of her life and which Carlyle used at the end of his. (The hangings are those made for Carlyle's bed by Jane shortly before she died.) The family's strained means can be guessed at by the fact that Jane didn't have a washstand until 1850 when her husband bought her the marble-topped mahogany one in the dressing room here, presented with a note (displayed upstairs in the study) saying: 'Prophecy of a Washstand to the neatest of all Women/Blessings on her bonny face, and be it ever blithe to me, as it is dear, blithe or not'. The other washstand and the hipbath would have stood in Carlyle's dressing room above.

In 1853, with Carlyle still irritated by noisy neighbours, the couple embarked on an ambitious plan to build a new study at the top of the house: 'silent as a tomb, lighted from above'. The room was to cost £169, and architect John Chorley, working with Cubbitts, promised it would be finished in six weeks from a start date of mid August with the workmen using the outside of the house to minimise disruption to the interior. It didn't quite happen as planned and after the fifth Irish labourer fell through the ceiling the Carlyles felt compelled to move out to stay at a cottage belonging to their friend Lady Ashburton; the work was eventually finished towards Christmas. But all was not well. First, Carlyle found the quality of the workmanship and the proportions of the space disappointing. The stove wouldn't burn and the skylight let in the sounds of the outside world which resonated to the extent that Jane declared: 'The silent room is the noisiest in the house'.

Nevertheless Carlyle used his study for his 12 years' work on *Frederick the Great* after which he moved down to the parlour and the study became a maid's bedroom. Today the ascetic, functional-looking space houses his desk – again made originally for Jane's father – and mementoes including a set of engravings of notable Germans, crammed pages of manuscript, a walking stick, a shaving-soap box and the like. But it's worth planning to spend some time here, for on the table are not only copies of Carlyle's letters to various friends and relatives but Jane's too. Listen to the sounds of the outside world no architect could exclude and delight in a wit no hardship could blunt.

ADDRESS 24 (formerly 5) Cheyne Row, London sw3 5HL (020 7352 7087)
OPEN 23 March to 3 November: Wednesday to Friday, 14.00–17.00; Saturday, Sunday and bank holiday Mondays, 11.00–17.00

ADMISSION £3.60/£1.80
ACCESS not suitable for wheelchairs
UNDERGROUND South Kensington, then bus 49/Sloane Square, then bus 19

FULHAM PALACE

Fulham Palace – until recently the country retreat or sometimes main residence of the Bishops of London – is a case where the whole is less than the sum of its parts. Successive occupants – usually men of substantial means enriched by revenues from the diocese – added wings, half-heartedly remodelled rooms or ruthlessly butchered the work of their predecessors to conform with their own taste, their particular practical requirements or what they believed to be the fashion of the day. The result is somewhat dispiriting – vast amounts of money squandered on an end result that is interesting for its historical trajectory rather than for any aesthetic pleasure it might give. The building has been leased to the council since 1973 and now houses a small museum.

Though the earliest part of the exisiting palace is the great hall, which dates from 1480, it's known a palace was in place here as early as 1141. The plan of the present conglomeration consists of two courtyards – the large western (entrance) quadrangle and the smaller, purely internal eastern court – both surrounded by ranges of rooms. The great hall sits between the two. The guided tour begins in the picturesque western quadrangle, most of which dates from the late-15th and early-16th centuries. Three sides have original brickwork with a diaper pattern picked out using black, twice-baked bricks; their quality can be appreciated by comparison with the refacing of the south range undertaken in the mid-19th century by Bishop Blomfield whose machine-made bricks and painted diamonds lack the charm or durability of the rest. During Blomfield's time the quadrangle was a service area including a bakehouse, brewhouse, dairy and laundry (for washing sent from the bishops' townhouse in St James's Square). The porch of the palace dates from the time of Bishop Howley (1813–28); the entrance porch to the quadrangle is closed off by massive gates that probably formed part of the medieval building.

Bishop Sherlock (1748–61) described Fulham Palace as 'a very bad old house'. He modernised the great hall and added a parlour to the north-east corner. Bishop Terrick (1764–77) was more ambitious. A former vicar of Twickenham and an admirer of Walpole's Strawberry Hill (see page 195), he employed the surveyor of St Paul's, Stiff Leadbetter, to build him three single-storey ranges of rooms around the eastern quadrangle. Topped with battlements, the eastern, garden front featured chunky square corner towers and a central square porch; the northern elevation (adjoining Sherlock's elegant Georgian addition) had gothic windows that can still be seen. Bishop Howley, who was later to make his mark as Archbishop of Canterbury at Addington Palace (see page 322), was horrified by the 'gothicky nonsense' he inherited and hired Samuel Pepys Cockerell to remodel the eastern range into a suite of grand rooms with a uniform flat seven-bay façade, add a second storey throughout and rid the building of its towers and crenellations.

The guided tour takes in the great hall, the chapel, Bishop Sherlock's parlour and the suite added by Bishop Howley. The great hall is exceedingly modest, with none of the drama of its near-contemporary in the Old Palace at Croydon (see page 332). It originally had a large room on the ground floor and a great chamber or several smaller rooms above. Sherlock removed the first floor and installed the present coved ceiling; the mock-17th-century windows date from the time of Bishop Porteus (1787–1809). The hall was converted into a chapel by Howley, who was reportedly offended by the stench of beer from the cellar below the chapel then in use. Bishop Tait (1856–68) restored the hall to its original function of grand dining and reception room, adding the present late-17th-century screen and panelling, and hired William Butterfield to build a new chapel to the south of Howley's new wing.

Butterfield's chapel – its exterior red brick with true diaper patterning – was similarly messed about by Bishop Wand (1945–55). The original interior had the architect's trademark bold horizontal bands of polychrome brick on the lower walls topped by elaborate tiled patterns and exposed rafters. Wand had the rafters replaced by a barrel vault and the walls painted over with a series of murals by Brian Thomas. The marble flooring, probably recycled from the great hall, remains.

The integrity of Sherlock's neo-Palladian parlour was destroyed when it was turned into a kitchen by Howley after he built his new suite of rooms. A century and a half later, when the room was converted into the home for a computer, a false ceiling was installed, obliterating the rococo plasterwork. This has now been revealed, and the room, currently used as a venue for children's activities, is awaiting restoration. The elegance of Howley's reception rooms, meanwhile, is largely obscured by the museum's many panels and showcases, though something of the library designed to accommodate the books bequeathed by Bishop Porteus can still be appreciated.

ADDRESS Bishop's Avenue, London SW6 6EA (020 7736 3233)
OPEN museum only: Wednesday to Sunday, 14.00–17.00; guided tours (90 minutes), second and fourth Sunday of each month, 14.00
ADMISSION museum £1/tour £3
ACCESS call in advance
UNDERGROUND Putney Bridge

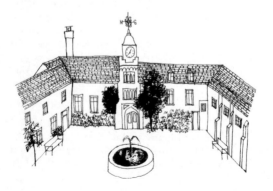

KENSINGTON PALACE

Recently given a new lease of life as a tourist venue through its association with Britain's favourite dead princess, Kensington Palace is very much a poor relation to Buckingham Palace (see page 18) and Hampton Court (see page 219). Much like many of its former inhabitants, in fact, since it functioned as a residence for the monarchy only for William III and Mary, Queen Anne and Georges I and II, thereafter housing a succession of royal spongers including several of George III's children, whose upkeep was described by the Duke of Wellington as 'the damnedest millstone about the necks of any government that can be imagined'. Most persistent was George's fourth son Edward, Duke of Kent, who lived at Kensington from 1798 until he fled to Brussels in 1812 to escape his creditors. Five years later, following the death of Charlotte, the future George IV's only legitimate daughter and the only surviving legitimate child of George III's numerous children, Edward returned to Kensington married to Charlotte's widower's sister, who some months later gave birth to the future Queen Victoria. She and her mother continued to live at Kensington until her accession in 1837 at the age of 19 alongside such minor royals as Edward's younger brother Augustus, Duke of Sussex (from 1805 to 1843), and from 1808 to 1821 the future George IV's estranged wife Princess Caroline of Brunswick, who also had a house at Blackheath (see Ranger's House, page 273); young Charlotte was allowed to visit her once a fortnight. Victoria's sixth child Louise, a sculptor, took over Augustus' apartments following the death of his widow in 1867 (her statue of her mother stands outside the east front); from 1867 to 1883 the apartments formerly occupied by Princess Victoria and her mother were given to the Duke and Duchess of Teck whose eldest daughter Mary was to marry the future George V; from 1901 to 1940 Victoria's youngest daughter Beatrice inhabited the rooms that today house the royal dress collection. Diana was assigned rooms in the palace from 1981 to her death in 1997.

The original house was a Jacobean mansion built c. 1605 for Sir George Coppin, possibly by John Thorpe, who was also probably the architect of Charlton House (see page 258). In 1689 William III and Mary II bought it from secretary of state Lord Nottingham as an alternative to Whitehall Palace. In the 13 years of William's reign his surveyor of the kings works Christopher Wren and his clerk of the works Nicholas Hawksmoor added several new wings including the queen's gallery extending off to the north and the king's gallery flanking the south façade; these together with the original house, comprehensively rebuilt in 1718-22 probably to the design of the future George II's architect Colen Campbell (see Marble Hill House, page 189), constitute the state apartments whose restoration from the taxpayers' purse was reluctantly authorised by parliament in 1897 on condition they be opened to the public.

The entrance is through the red saloon at the north of the building via the institutional and slightly grubby Teck room into the royal dress collection which occupies several rooms on the ground floor. An uninspiring staircase leads via two further rooms of collections to the first of the great spaces of the *piano nobile* – the king's grand staircase with *trompe l'oeil* murals painted in 1725-27 for George I by William Kent. The dramatic simplicity of the black marble staircase with its chequerboard landings and iron balustrade contrasts with Kent's illusionist painting which transports the decidedly unglamorous British court to an Italianate setting its creator would have regarded as the height of civilisation (he and his mistress, surveying the scene from the ceiling, look understandably self-satisfied). Among the other recognisable figures are Kaspar Hauser-prototype Peter the 'wild boy', discovered outside Hanover and presented to the king as a curiosity, and one of the pages of Marble Hill House's Lady Henrietta Howard, who balances nonchalantly on the wrong side of the balcony balustrade.

The square presence chamber, part of one of the pavilions Wren added to the corners of the original house, has a ceiling decorated by

Kent in an Etruscan/Pompeiian style that looks refreshingly modern – stylised figures and plant forms in startlingly bold reds and blues set with geometric regularity on a white ground. The less radical privy chamber, also with a ceiling painted by Kent, leads to the gloriously lofty cupola room, the principal state room of the palace. Here Kent's love of *trompe l'oeil* extends to the feigned coffering of the ceiling, the 'fluting' of the giant Ionic pilasters that dominate the decor and the 'moulding' of the bases of the columns supporting the massive marble doorway surrounds, as well as some armoury on the walls. The room was his first major commission for interior decoration, gained in 1722 after he undercut by almost 50 per cent the price quoted for the ceiling by the royal serjeant painter James Thornhill, an event that signalled the decline of the fashion for the baroque and the ascendancy of Palladianism. Thornhill never really recovered, and his future son-in-law William Hogarth (see page 229) satirised Kent in his engravings, commenting: 'Never was there a more wretched dauber that soonest got into palaces in this country'.

The king's drawing room is almost as lofty and imposing, with the added advantage of uninterrupted views over the park. Kent's ceiling boosted the royal ego with its depiction of the all-powerful Jupiter with the cowering Semele, the lover he inadvertently destroyed with his divine power. According to diarist and courtier Lord Hervey, Queen Caroline dispensed with some of the pictures – which include Vasari's *Venus and Cupid* and two voluptuous female nudes – while George II was away; on his return he insisted on having his 'fat Venus', as indeed she is, reinstated.

The next three rooms were converted for the Duchess of Kent and Princess Victoria in 1834–36. Queen Victoria's bedroom (originally the king's state bedchamber and arranged in the 1930s by Queen Mary as it might have been in the princess' time) is a surprisingly modest affair hung with family portraits and furnished with remarkably inelegant pieces including cabinets crammed with nick-nacks such as dolls' tea-sets and commemorative mugs. An anteroom leads to the Duchess of Kent's dressing room, furnished as a mid-19th-century sitting room.

The 30-metre-long king's gallery has been restored to the scheme Kent devised for George I, though the extraordinary wind-dial above the fireplace with its telling representations of the four known continents showing European elegance, Asians as Europeans with turbans, nude African 'savages' and a European traveller conversing with feathered 'Indians', was made for William III. The original picture hang was by Kent, though George II's predilection for plump female bottoms is again in evidence in many pictures including Tintoretto's *The Muses*.

The queen's apartments are on a noticeably smaller, domestic scale. More evocative than the drawing room, which suffered bomb damage in 1940, and bedchamber are the dining room – which retains its original delicately carved panelling – and the intimate, if not cramped, closet. The queen's gallery is a somewhat dismal, unfurnished affair, leading to the queen's staircase which in turn leads to the shop, dismally overfurnished with examples of Dianamania.

ADDRESS Kensington Gardens, London w8 4px (020 7937 9561)
OPEN March to October: daily, 9.30–17.00; November to February: daily, 9.30–16.00
ADMISSION £10/£7.50/£6.50/ family ticket £30
ACCESS limited; no lift to state apartments
UNDERGROUND Queensway/ High Street Kensington

LEIGHTON HOUSE

Built just a decade before the nearby Linley Sambourne House (see page 101), Leighton House is as idiosyncratic as its neighbour is stereotypical, its occupant as reclusive as Sambourne was gregarious. Frederic Leighton's vision of his home as a retreat in which he could work and recuperate away from the society in which he was so much in demand is visible from the outside – this is a buttoned-up house that shuts its face to the street in a way that belies the fluidity of the plan and the openness of the rear façade to the light and garden views.

Leighton started work on his house with his friend, the architect George Aitchison (1825–1910), in 1864. The son of a doctor whose father had amassed a considerable fortune as physician to the Czarina in St Petersburg, the 16-year-old Frederic moved to Frankfurt with his family in 1846 because of his mother's ill-health, and enrolled at the art institute. After a European journey that involved some three years each in Rome and Paris he returned to London in 1859. Though he had met with early good fortune when his *Cimabue's Madonna Carried in Procession through Florence*, exhibited at the Royal Academy in 1855, was bought by Queen Victoria, he had subsequently fallen from favour, his success deemed too easily gained. But the sale of *Dante in Exile* in 1864 to the dealer Gambert for 1000 guineas signalled a rise in his reputation and financial prospects; in 1878 he was elected president of the Royal Academy and at the end of his life was created a peer, the only British artist so honoured. Handsome, cultivated and with a private income, he was much sought after in London society and was a firm favourite with the Prince and Princess of Wales. The tranquillity of Leighton House was necessary for his work, health and sanity.

The house as originally built was an L-shape encompassing the present entrance hall, staircase hall, dining room and drawing room with a main axis running from the front door (located where the western window of the entrance hall now is) through the entrance hall, staircase hall and dining room to the garden. The only rooms upstairs were the studio, bedroom and bathroom – Leighton had no intention of disturbing his working routine by accommodating visitors overnight. The ante-room or hall of Narcissus, Arab hall and library were added between 1877 and 1879 and the silk room above the library in 1895, the year before Leighton's death. In 1889 he constructed the glass, wood and iron winter studio to the east of the studio proper, originally supported on four cast-iron columns with a void below. There are plans to demolish the present ugly post-World War II infill to reveal the structure in its former glory.

Nothing in the elegant red-brick façade or unimposing entrance hall prepares the visitor for the wonder of the continuous open space of the double-height staircase hall, ante-room and domed Arab hall, to which you are irresistibly drawn by the sound of a tinkling fountain. Intended to evoke the world of the *Arabian Nights*, the Arab hall was created by Aitchison as a setting for the tiles Leighton and his friends had 'acquired' from Rhodes, Damascus, Cairo and Tangier, which he first visited in 1852. All use a similar palette of blues and greens, but their content ranges from inscriptions and abstract patterns to leaves, birds and flowers. The jigsaw effect of fitting the various collections together adds to the appeal. Aitchison's design was inspired by the banqueting room at the Moorish palace of La Zisa at Palermo, where a black marble table with water running down a central channel for the diners to rinse their hands in stood in place of Leighton House's black marble basin. Leighton commissioned his friends Walter Crane to design the gilt mosaic frieze of birds and deer, Randolph Caldecott for the capitals of the marble columns at the entrance and Edgar Boehm for the capitals of the columns flanking the sofas. Aitchison designed the copper and wrought-iron chandelier, a modern-day crown of thorns. But the team knew where to stop: the floor is a simple pattern in black-and-white mosaic and the functional fountain is remarkable for its sound rather than its appearance.

It seems a shame to quibble about such a fabulous, magical space. And

if the theft involved in this Victorian temple to sensuality and beauty had been purely intellectual there would be no need. But the 16th- and 17th-century tiles here are cultural and religious artefacts – the large panel above the entrance, 'brought' by traveller and *Arabian Nights* translator Richard Burton from a hill temple at Sind (then in northern India), contains a passage from the creation myth in the Koran ('He has created man and taught him speech/[He hath set] the sun and the moon in a certain course…'); the brown 14th-century tiles in the west wall have had the faces erased, and the images of birds on the south wall their throats slit by chipping a line in the glaze, to conform with Islamic edicts against the representation of living things. And while the elaborate Ottoman-style grilles on the windows were an effective way of protecting Leighton's privacy, their connotations of the harem where women were to be heard but not seen introduce sinister overtones into the sensual pleasure of the space.

The library was used by Leighton as a study and the low bookcases are the original fittings. The fireplace positioned seemingly nonsensically beneath the window echoes that in the drawing room opposite, its flue rising to the left of the glass. Since Leighton's entertaining was restricted almost exclusively to male company, a withdrawing room was rarely required and the space functioned instead as a gallery for his art collection. The effect of the positioning of the fireplace, its surround of wispy grasses designed by Leighton himself, and the unusual semi-circular bay in the west wall, with a circular sketch by Delacroix (a copy of the original) inset into the ceiling, is thoroughly unpredictable, as if Leighton and Aitchison had taken nothing as given, reworking assumptions from scratch. The doors are made of the ebonised woodwork found throughout the house, with stylised plant forms picked out in gold and mouldings, in another bizarre joke, derived from picture frames. The chandelier, a little-girl's fantasy of pink, blue and clear glass baubles and flowers, offsets the gloomy Burne-Joneses and Leighton's laughably sentimental *The Widow's Prayer* in which a widow swathed in black is prostrated in grief while her chubby daughter, bathed in light, plays on the stairs. The dining room is larger and more pleasantly proportioned, its bay over-looking the garden. The door to the right of the chimneypiece led to the servants' stairs and the basement kitchen.

From the staircase the ingenuity of Aitchison's enfilade of rooms to the Arab hall becomes apparent. The livid, vivid bright blue tiles designed by ceramicist William De Morgan (see page 107), ebonised wood and gilt combine to stunning effect. The design of the black-and-white mosaic floor becomes more complex where the wall tiles become simpler. The space is sparsely furnished – a stuffed peacock, echoing the colours of the tiles, a table with flowers and a statue of a dancing faun. Leighton's interpretation of the Orpheus myth in which the songster appears to be pushing his wife Eurydice from him could be taken as an expression of homosexual revulsion, especially compared with the com-passion of Elisha raising a small boy from the dead.

The spacious top-lit landing above the ante-room leads to a day-bed, also 'brought' from the Middle East, which projects over the Arab hall. With its grille filtering views of the golden dome and tiles and the sound of the fountain, it has fuelled many an erotic fantasy. The windowless silk room, top-lit by a dome that matches the one above the landing, extends that space to make it a usable and pleasant room rather than just a pas-sage. Created to display paintings given to Leighton as a mark of respect by his contemporaries, today its many portraits include Leighton's cross-looking Desdemona, modelled on Dorothy Dene whom he befriended and encouraged towards the end of his life (their platonic relationship may have been the source for Shaw's *Pygmalion*), and a sensual, bronzed Pan with the proportions of a Michelangelo nude. Leighton's bedroom, above the entrance hall, is closed to the public.

The studio – which to judge from contemporary photographs was once overflowing with materials, props and the beautiful objects that served as Leighton's inspiration – is now regrettably unatmospheric. The walls are painted with Leighton's preferred colour for displaying pic-tures; the small archway on the south wall led to the service stairs by which models would arrive to undress behind the screen. Among the many paintings are the dramatic *Death of Brunelleschi* with its Piranesi-like background of classical ruins embarked on shortly after Leighton's arrival in Rome and *Michelangelo Nursing his Dying Servant*, a sensitive and human portrait of grief so much more moving than the stylised symbolism of *The Widow's Prayer* downstairs.

A copy of Leighton's self-portrait shows a handsome man with an aquiline nose, sensitive face, kiss curls and a heavy beard dressed in the garb of a Roman senator, reflecting his love for a country and an era he regarded as his spiritual home. His actual home, along with his art and what can be gleaned here of his life, reflect the contradictions of this fantasy of a more glorious age filtered through Victorian constraints. In his home, at least, we should be grateful the fantasy won out.

ADDRESS 12 Holland Park Road, London W14 8LZ (020 7602 3316)
OPEN Wednesday to Sunday, 11.00–17.30

ADMISSION free
ACCESS none
UNDERGROUND High Street Kensington

LINDSEY HOUSE

Only partially and rarely open – providing you can attract the attention of its inhabitants via the not-always-reliable entryphone at the front gate – Lindsey House is Chelsea's sole surviving 17th-century mansion. It was built c. 1674 for Robert Bertie, 3rd Earl of Lindsey, as a plain three-storey 11-bay house with a central pediment and two corner pavilions of unequal size. Major alterations including the heightening of the attic floor and addition of the mansard roof were made in the 1750s by Moravian architect Sigismund von Gersdorf after the house was acquired by religious leader Count von Zinzendorf. Von Zinzendorf had been exiled from his native Saxony because of the zeal with which he conducted the colony of Moravian Brethren, a Protestant cult founded in the 1720s by Moravian exiles inspired by the teachings of 14th-century theologian John Huss. The house was sold and divided into five dwellings in 1775; subsequent occupants include painters James Whistler and John Martin and engineer Isambard Kingdom Brunel.

Access today is limited to the hallway and back study of No. 100. The entrance and bay were added in 1890, though the staircase dates from von Gersdorf's alterations of 1752. The hall, with its chequerboard floor, marble fireplace and black and white marble columns, is certainly handsome, but hardly worth the effort.

ADDRESS 95–100 Cheyne Walk, London SW10 0DQ
OPEN No. 100, four times annually by written appointment

ADMISSION free
UNDERGROUND South Kensington, then bus 49/Sloane Square, then bus 19

LINLEY SAMBOURNE HOUSE

Linley Sambourne House is a time capsule – a Victorian/Edwardian home preserved almost unchanged since the death of the *Punch* cartoonist in 1910. Unlike the former dwellings of more famous figures, often acquired several decades after their occupants' deaths and then filled by curators with contemporary furniture and mementoes, here a house and its contents are displayed intact as once used by the Sambourne family, even, allegedly, down to the unseen contents of the drawers.

Stafford Terrace was built between 1868 and 1874 – the high point of Victorian domestic development in northern Kensington – as the final phase of construction on the Phillimore estate, once attached to Campden House. According to the 1871 census, the estate's inhabitants included retired officers, senior civil servants, a barrister and several tradesmen. The four-storey stuccoed house, with a bay on the ground and first floors, is distinguished from its neighbours only by the glazed window boxes that interrupt the clean lines of the façade.

The 30-year-old Linley Sambourne and his wife Marion bought No. 18 in late 1874, shortly after their marriage, with financial help from Marion's father, stockbroker and engineer Spencer Herapath. (Mrs Bentley, the house's first occupant, had died 18 months after its completion.) Maud Sambourne was born the following year and Roy three years later. This comparatively small Victorian household was supplemented by Linley's mother Frances (died 1892) and three live-in servants – a housemaid, a parlourmaid and a nanny or governess. A horse and carriage were kept in the mews. Though by no means poor (Sambourne earned a regular £38 per month for drawing cartoons and caricatures for *Punch*, rising to £100 in 1883), the family were probably less well-off than most of their friends and neighbours, and the gregarious Linley's socialising with Kensington's artistic elite had something of an aspirational quality.

On ringing the bell you're welcomed by Victorian Society members as if to their own home and given a brief introductory talk. The pleasant hall sets the tone – Sambourne was anxious to make his home a palace of art and almost every wall is covered in pictures, whether his own drawings, admired work by his contemporaries or the Old Masters he studied as source material for his cartoons. (Apprenticed at the age of 16 as a draughtsman to a firm of marine engineers, Sambourne was largely self-taught, his only formal artistic training two or three months at the South Kensington School of Art.) The decor is exquisite – the entrance lobby is papered in a delicate tulip pattern with a ceiling of ripening fruit bursting forth (William Morris' 1864 *Pomegranate*) – though there's the occasional unwelcome surprise such as the framed dead birds that hang on the walls. Typical of the whole enterprise, a full range of walking sticks, including a sturdy staff topped by a carved owl, forever await their owners.

The dining room at the front of the house has an endearingly worn carpet, stamped gilt ceiling paper and more *Pomegranate* wallpaper largely obscured by a collection of copies of paintings in which Victorian family scenes jostle uncomfortably with bloody classical dramas given an artificial, alienating effect by all being rendered in sepia at approximately A4 size. Though full, the room doesn't appear cramped, and some of the furniture – for instance the highly polished inlaid Queen Anne bureau beside the door – is charmingly delicate. The morning room behind is more claustrophobic, perhaps because in this small space the tasselled velvet that overhangs all the rooms' mantelpieces, heavy curtains and dark wallpaper become oppressive. This is a house filled with art, not books, and the modest bookcase containing mainly 18th-century poets and popular modern works is the house's largest collection. The rectangular bay at the back was a much-needed extension installed by the Sambournes. The many photographs show the ever-genial Linley, a somewhat uptight Marion and the strikingly beautiful Maud as a grandmother with her youngest child Anne (1902–92), mother by her first husband to Princess Margaret's first husband Lord Snowden, whose son bears the name Viscount Linley (for anyone who cares about such things).

The stairs are hung mainly with cartoons and drawings by Sambourne and his contemporaries surmounted by his ambitious diploma for the 1883 International Fisheries Exhibition which shows the wealth of his draughtsmanship and invention when freed from the constraints of time and space that govern magazine work. The half-landing is extended to house a water garden – a tank filled with shells and a tinkling fountain - that brings light and music into an otherwise gloomy space.

The dramatic drawing room fills the whole of the first floor, though that doesn't prevent every surface from being littered with objects – I counted eight cabinets and chests of drawers, three desks and eight occasional tables, all stacked with framed photographs and mementoes. Though a second door was installed by the developer and there are two fireplaces, it is believed the room was always a single space. The Sambournes put in the parquet floor and covered their original Morris wallpaper at a later date in a Spanish leather so expensive they didn't do behind the mirrors or large pictures. So much of it is obscured by the swathe of prints of the type found in the dining room you wonder why they bothered. As in both downstairs rooms, a shelf running at frieze level holds the blue-and-white porcelain the couple collected. The door is decorated with Marion and Linley's family crests (Linley was very proud of his association with the composer Thomas Linley whose daughter Elizabeth married Sheridan) which are also incorporated into the stained glass of the rear extension, designed by Sambourne himself as an eruption of blowsy sunflowers much less successful than the stock geometric patterns in the morning room below.

The front of the room has armchairs including two diminutive ladies' chairs set close to the ground in the popular 'Chinese' fashion and Marion's mirrored writing desk; the central zone is dominated by her baby grand piano; the extension was Linley's studio and houses his desk, easel and camera. Sambourne had to draw his cartoons for *Punch* between Wednesday and Friday, and often had only eight hours from midday Friday to complete his work, with a messenger waiting at the door. His granddaughter Anne remembered 'a little messenger boy, with pillbox hat, white gloves and bicycle, waited by the gate outside. His task was to be ever in attendance upon the whims of my grandpa – rushing all over London with last-minute drawings or messages… It was a house of perpetual motion, sometimes guests and relations, but often models coming in and out from grandpa, and now and then the little figure of the artist himself in his black-and-white plaid suit bounced down – with great gold watch in hand, to make it tinkle for the children.'

The front bedroom on the second floor was used by Anne and her second husband Lord Rosse as a London base from Maud's death in 1960 until the house was sold to the GLC in 1980 (with the proviso that it would be run by The Victorian Society). Though Anne installed the Morris wallpaper, the furniture – including an ebonised suite with white neo-grec decoration purchased from Maples in Tottenham Court Road – was chosen by Linley and Marion. The fan in front of the fireplace is the equivalent of a visitors' book, with autographed drawings by the likes of Alma Tadema and Millais. On the walls are the more ambitious illustrations Sambourne provided for *Punch* annuals, photographs including Anne as a striking 1930s flapper in her outfit for George VI's coronation and a sketch of her – cheekbones as prominent as ever – by her brother, the ballet, opera and film designer Oliver Messel. Roy's bedroom at the back of the house, which he occupied until his death in 1946, is a sad tribute to early-20th-century bacherlorhood – the stockbroker's only contributions to the decor appear to be the modern carpet, a few books and several signed photographs of the actresses he courted in his youth including belle of New York Edna May (who spurned him in favour of a series of millionaires).

The top floor was originally a nursery and from 1899 became Linley's studio, for which purpose the skylight was installed. Some of the original wallpaper with family friend Walter Crane's illustrations of nursery rhymes has been revealed. The basement, which once housed the kitchen and copious wine-cellar, has been converted into a caretaker's flat.

Sambourne was a keen amateur photographer and used the mezzanine bathroom as a darkroom – hence the coffin-shaped marble bath, its surface impervious to chemicals. His cartoons were based firmly on real life and on the wall hang surreal portraits and self-portraits staged as reference material: policemen arresting a mannequin, hunters engaged in ballet, the irrepressible artist snapped in the garden wearing a dress and holding a fan or striking deliberately silly poses in fancy hats. The biggest surprise, however, are the titillating pictures he took at the Camera Club of nude or near-nude females giggling provocatively, in softcore lesbian couplings, in black stockings, wrestling – a blatant assault on the seemingly genteel Victorian family values that pervade the rest of the house. As so often, behind the upright façade of the Victorian male, secret longings were acted out to dangerous or merely futile effect – though to judge from the number of powerfully sensual classical nudes in the drawing room, perhaps in this case sex and the beauty of the body were placed more healthily centre stage.

ADDRESS 18 Stafford Terrace, London w8 7bh (020 7602 3316 – Leighton House; www.rbkc.gov. uk/linleysambournehouse) **OPEN** closed until January 2003, then March to October: Wednesday, 10.45–15.30 (last entry); Sunday, guided tours only, 14.15, 15.15, 16.15 **ADMISSION** £3.50/£2.50/£1.50 **ACCESS** limited **UNDERGROUND** Kensington High Street

OLD BATTERSEA HOUSE
(THE DE MORGAN FOUNDATION)

As it stands today, Old Battersea House (built as Terrace House in 1699 perhaps for Samuel Pett, controller of victualling to the navy to whom the globe and instruments in the freize above the central doorway of the west front may refer) is in places so heavily restored it looks like a Quinlan Terry-style recreation of what a two-storey seven-bay red-brick William and Mary mansion might have been. The reason it's open to the public is similarly oblique: it was lived in for some 35 years by Wilhelmina Stirling, sister of painter Evelyn De Morgan (1855–1919) and sister-in-law of ceramicist William De Morgan (1839–1917) both of whose works, now the property of the De Morgan Foundation, are on display. Visits consist of a brief talk on the house, the trust and the artists, after which you can spend as much time as you wish wandering freely in the three open rooms and questioning the ever-patient guides. But visitors can't fail to notice the prominent display of signed photographs of the likes of Elizabeth Taylor, Ronald Reagan and Bill Clinton on the table beside the signing-in book and on the doors of the cloakroom, highlighting the fact that the house today is the London base of American publishing dynasty the Forbes family, Liz Taylor's UK home-from-home and was one of the places where Ronald Reagan and Margaret Thatcher pursued their special relationship.

The house was inhabited by various wealthy merchants and lawyers until the late 1830s when it became the residence of the principal of St John's teacher-training college. At the beginning of 1930 the college site was acquired by Battersea Council with the intention of demolishing the buildings to put up housing. A press campaign in which it was claimed – with no supporting evidence – that the house was designed by Christopher Wren to mark the fiftieth wedding anniversary of Sir Walter St John resulted in a preservation order. Soon afterwards Mrs Stirling persuaded

the council to give her and her husband a life tenancy on condition they would display their collection of De Morgan art to the public by appointment, an arrangement that lasted until her death in 1965, a few days before her hundredth birthday. By now in poor repair, the house was rescued by multimillionaire Republican business-magazine owner Malcolm Forbes, who restored it in the 1970s for the private use of the Forbes Foundation and to display the De Morgan collection on the ground floor.

Old Battersea House's heavy-handed exterior gives little hint of the delicate sensuality that lies within. The spacious entrance hall is dominated by a copy of the life-size sculpture *Athlete Wrestling a Serpent* by Lord Leighton (see page 94) that stands at the foot of the fine oak staircase and by Evelyn De Morgan's luscious female figures. It has the pleasant feeling of being lived in – you hang your coat in an already half-full closet and are invited to sit wherever you please, while the welcoming dim lighting and eclectic range of objects including a grand dolls' house add to the sense that this is a home. The drawing room beyond, occupying the three central bays of the garden façade, is also lined with paintings; in the panelled dining room that takes up the two bays to the east are a display case of William's pottery and some paintings by Evelyn's maternal uncle John Roddam Spencer-Stanhope who studied at Oxford with Burne-Jones and to whose Florence villa she was a frequent visitor.

Much of our information on Evelyn comes from Wilhelmina Stirling, whose biography *William De Morgan and His Wife* spins a web of romantic wishful thinking around the facts. Ironically, by assiduously buying up most of her sister's art and thus limiting its public display, Stirling almost killed her reputation. Though Evelyn (one of the first women to train at the Slade) was recognised by the prominent Victorian artist G F Watts as 'the first woman artist of the day' and her work – influenced first and foremost by the Italian renaissance, in particular Botticelli, and only later by Burne-Jones, Millais and Rossetti – was praised for the rich use of colour, bold compositions and fine draughtsmanship she brought to her largely visionary and allegorical subject matter, she is today far less known than her often inferior male contemporaries. (Her drawing technique, illustrated also in a collection of female heads in the entrance hall, outshines Burne-Jones', for instance.)

In 1887 Evelyn married William, a ceramicist whose pottery is recognised as having a richness of colour and pattern unequalled in England before or since. William had been designing tiles for William Morris (see page 286) since 1863; in 1870 he had rediscovered the lost lustre technique first used in Persia in the 13th century for which he became famous and by the middle of the decade his tiles were the fashionable accompaniment to Morris' wallpaper in affluent middle-class homes. The years of his marriage saw him produce his most achieved work, some of which is displayed here, as the delicate Morris-like floral designs were replaced by bolder depictions of fantastic animals and ships and deep-ruby glazes inspired by medieval tiles joined the iridescent Islamic blues and turquoises of tiles such as those at Leighton House. A poor businessman (Evelyn's 1909 portrait shows a frail-looking bearded aesthete who is almost a caricature of our image of Morris and co.) whose studio was supported generously by his wife's small personal fortune, he retired in 1907 and in the same year published *Joseph Vance*, the first of a series of now-forgotten Dickensian bestsellers that were to make him more money than the ceramics for which he is still revered.

Evelyn and William's relationship has been described as a marriage of minds, and certainly Evelyn in her paintings seems interested almost exclusively in women – whether the sensual nudes of *Night & Dawn*, the English roses of *Flora* and *Lux in Tenebris* or the more sombre figures of *In Memoriam* and *The Dryad*, for which the sitter was Wilhelmina's nurse Jane Hales. Her few men – as in *The Poor Man Who Saved the City* or *Mercury* – are smooth-skinned, androgynous creatures while the heterosexual couple at the heart of *Love's Passing* are disquietingly alike. It's tempting to trace a trajectory from the female victims of her early work (the pallid, sexless serpent-entwined nude of *Cadmus and Harmonia*; the bare-breasted figure roped to the moon in *Luna*; Ariadne disconsolate on the beach after being abandoned by Theseus in *Ariadne at Naxos*, painted when she was 20 and exhibited to great acclaim at the inaugural show of the avant-garde Grosvenor Gallery) to later paintings where women are strong and in control: the confident witch of *The Love Potion*; the lightning-cracking avengers of *The Storm Spirits*. Postdating a series of less impressive allegories of the evils of war inspired by World War I, *The Gilded Cage*, unfinished at her death, depicts the young wife of an older man (William was her senior by 16 years) who gazes enviously at the freedom embodied by a party of gypsies dancing outside.

Whether or not Evelyn was a lesbian, the embracing showgirl mer-maids of *The Sea Maidens*, one of whom gazes defiantly from the canvas as if to challenge anyone to disapprove, and the hand-holding nude nymphs of *Moonbeams Dipping into the Sea* proved too much for the powers-that-be at Norman Shaw's Northumbrian Cragside, who asked for them to be removed to a more liberal London setting.

ADDRESS 30 Vicarage Crescent,
London SW11 3LD (De Morgan
Trust 020 7495 3393)
OPEN usually once a week by
appointment with Susan
Seagrave, De Morgan Trust,
56 Bradbourne Street,
London SW6 3TE
ADMISSION £2.50
RAIL Clapham Junction

[wimbledon]

Southside House   114

SOUTHSIDE HOUSE

When Major Malcolm Munthe died in 1995, a handwritten codicil to his will commanded 'do not decorate' Southside House. Whether the prohibition extended to cleaning isn't revealed, but the swathes of cobwebs, flaking plaster and ropy-looking wiring in the garden room at the start of the tour tell you this is no pristine National Trust property. According to our guide, himself a member of this extraordinary family, the Tudor farmhouse that became Southside was bought in 1685 by Robert Pennington so he could move out of London following the death of his son from the plague. Pennington, the product of some 300 years of marriage among first cousins, allegedly stole a horse from his republican grandfather at the age of 14 and went on the run with the future Charles II. Following the restoration in 1660 he was rewarded with a post in the chancery, married his cousin Elizabeth Wharton, of course, and eventually set about refurbishing Southside using Dutch architects he had met during his years in exile. The house today – despite dirt and lack of decoration – is very much about show and showmanship, whether in the one-brick-thin skin of the would-be grand façade tacked on to the asymmetrical Tudor walls, the wood-imitating-stone monumental hall, or the fantastic stories of the guide about royalty rescued, befriended and bedded.

Southside looks more like an overgrown cottage than an imposing manor. Two storeys high, the ten bays of its Dutch brick façade are relieved by two shallow pedimented projections each three bays wide set with central niches at ground-floor level containing statues of 'Spring' and 'Plenty' modelled after Pennington's wife and daughter, their everyday English proportions a welcome contrast to the usual classical idealism. The entrance door, next to a strange projecting bay, is off centre, presumably to coincide with the only room of the farmhouse that could be modelled into a suitably impressive double-height entrance hall.

The tour begins in the garden room at the back of the house which sports some dubious *trompe l'oeil* and a number of canvases by Peter Munthe, Malcolm's elder brother who died in 1976. A door leads to a narrow corridor lined with 17 small family portraits by Theodore Rouselle commissioned by Robert's cousin Philip, the 4th Lord Wharton. (Since many of the boys of this inbred family died young or went mad, inheritance tended to pass through the female line so all the women here look alike while the men are in-laws.) In the hall is a portrait by Angelica Kauffmann of the Chevalier d'Eon de Beaumont, a cross-dressing French spy. Helped to escape from revolutionary France by John Pennington, who was an inspiration for the character of the Scarlet Pimpernel, he lived out the rest of his life in England as a woman.

The gloomy breakfast room – its only windows in the bay that protrudes beside the front door – may once have had a certain charm, but today the rose brocade looks tired and grey and the gilded horsehide frieze, installed by Robert Pennington, is worn and flaking. Still, it must be one of the few rooms in Britain that hasn't been decorated for more than 300 years. Among the family portraits are those of John Pennington and Axel Munthe (1857–1949), the Swedish-born author, doctor and philanthropist. When in his 40s he fell in love with the 17-year-old heiress Hilda Pennington Mellor (John's great-granddaughter and the mother of Peter and Malcolm), whom he eventually married against her parents' wishes. Hilda's father, John Pennington Mellor, and Axel both look strikingly like Freud. Other paintings include a 'sketch' by Constable, a one-time family friend, for *The Cornfield*.

The dining room behind – its rear projection part of the old cross-wing of the former farmhouse – looks too much like two disparate spaces cobbled together to impress. The original Tudor fireplace with its elaborate Stuart surround is off-centre; squeezed unceremoniously between it and the door, just discernible in the gloom, is Burne-Jones' *St George*. The wonderful portrait by Hogarth of Sir Charles Kemeys-Tynte, great-grandson of Philip the 4th Lord Wharton and the financial supporter of the Chevalier d'Eon, makes the other portraits that line the walls – however colourful the tales of their subjects' bravery or wickedness – look flat and two-dimensional. Pride of place in terms of notoriety goes to another Philip, who became involved with the Stuart pretenders to the throne, black magic and the Hellfire Club, leading to his banishment in 1729.

The absurdly monumental doorway dominating the breakfast room leads to a galleried entrance hall which reveals the full extent of Robert Pennington's pretensions. Into a relatively small space is squeezed a fireplace with an enormous baroque surround (the smoke-blackened mantelpiece testifies to the fact that here form preceded function), a gallery supported by oversized columns and two elaborate doorways. The house suffered bomb damage during World War II and with the support of London County Council planner Patrick Abercrombie, a family friend, it was awarded a grant to restore it as nearly as possible to its 1687 condition. The entrance hall was remodelled in wood; a walk around the cramped gallery reveals the inadequacy of Peter Munthe's attempts to recreate the original ceiling.

The upstairs library is as Axel Munthe made and left it – a huge desk with such mementoes as shells, china ornaments and family photographs, the worn furniture torn by the dogs he refused to discipline, the Corona typewriter. The claustrophobic Prince of Wales' bedroom was decorated for Frederick, Prince of Wales (1707–51), son of George II, who used to stay here when reviewing the troops on Wimbledon Common – an arrangement encouraged by the family to dispel rumours of their allegiance to the Stuart pretenders (Frederick subsequently fell out of favour and was banished from court after he backed the parliamentary opposition). The bed with its original crimson counterpane and headboard decorated with sequinned fleur de lys was also used by Edward VII (1841–1910), who installed the gold hangings, painted ceiling and a secret staircase to a bedroom occupied by his mistress Alice Keppel (great-grandmother of today's royal mistress Camilla Parker-Bowles). In a glass cabinet is further evidence of the family's tendency to back the losing horse: Anne Boleyn's ivory comb and vanity case (Philadelphia Carey, the beheaded queen's niece, was the mother of Philip the 4th Lord Wharton) and the pearl necklace worn by Marie-Antoinette at her execution, presented to John Pennington by Josephine Bonaparte to thank him for conducting many of her relatives to safety in England.

The music room downstairs was created from two smaller rooms to provide a space in which Edward VII's entourage could dance. Among the many pictures is one of a former Swedish king and queen who are both said to have been lovers of Axel Munthe.

The bombs that largely destroyed Southside's hall and dining room forced the family to retreat to their home in Herefordshire, taking many valuables and documents with them. Within weeks Birmingham was targeted and bombs destroyed the tin box in which the documents were stored. So none of the above can be verified – but that's entertainment.

ADDRESS 3–4 Woodhayes Road, Wimbledon, London SW19 4RJ (020 8946 7643)
OPEN January to 21 June: Wednesday, Saturday and Sunday, guided tours at 14.00, 15.00 and 16.00. Group visits by arrangement with the administrator
ADMISSION £5.50
ACCESS very limited
UNDERGROUND/RAIL Wimbledon, then bus 93

[hampstead]

Burgh House   **121**

Fenton House   **123**

The Freud Museum   **126**

Keats House   **132**

Kenwood   **138**

Lauderdale House   **148**

2 Willow Road   **155**

BURGH HOUSE

The front half of this imposing five-bay, three-storey red-brick Queen Anne house, nestled among council flats in a quiet Hampstead lane, was built in 1703, probably by wealthy Quakers Henry and Hannah Sewell. The spa at Hampstead Wells, whose foul-tasting, iron-impregnated waters were bottled at the nearby Flask Tavern, was beginning to be developed and the spa's physician Dr William Gibbons lived at Burgh House in the 1720s. He doubled the size of the property by extending it to the rear. Subsequent occupiers include Whig politician Nathaniel Booth (in residence 1743–59), upholsterer Israel Lewis (1776–1822), who was a friend of Keats (see page 132), and the Reverend Allatson Burgh (1822–56), from whom the house takes its name. Burgh – author of *Anecdotes of Music, Historical and Biographical* and like neighbour James Fenton (see page 124) actively involved in the successful 1829 petitioning of parliament for the withdrawal of a private bill that would have permitted the lord of the manor to develop Hampstead Heath – let the house fall into a state of extreme disrepair. Following his death it was used by the Royal East Middlesex Militia as a headquarters and officers' mess. In 1884 it was rented out to Thomas Grylls, an acclaimed stained-glass designer responsible for the rose window in the poets' corner at Westminster Abbey. In the 20th century the house was lived in by art expert George Williamson, Captain Constantine Benson, a director of Lloyds bank who purchased it at auction for £4750 in 1925 (less than double the price paid by Burgh a century earlier), and retired diplomat George Bambridge, husband of Rudyard Kipling's daughter Evelyn. It was bought by the council in 1946 and used as a community centre; following a public campaign in the mid 1970s to prevent it from being turned into commercial premises, it was restored and leased to the

Burgh House Trust which runs it as an exhibition centre and local-history museum.

Today the front door leads directly into a reception area that occupies the two right-hand bays of the Sewells' house; originally this would have been a narrow hallway and a self-contained, squarish room. Lined with 18th-century panelling probably from nearby Weatherall House, the music room to the left – which occupies the two bays on the other side of the door plus a three-bay single-storey extension – was created in the 1920s on the site of the larger officers' mess. To the rear (in the Gibbons addition) are a library, decorated in Georgian style, and art gallery.

The pleasingly simple staircase with its original barley-twist balusters leads to panelled bedrooms containing displays about the history of Hampstead. Alongside the expected stories of Constable and Keats is a corner devoted to the Isokon flats in Lawn Road designed in 1934 by Wells Coates, with a bar created by Walter Gropius and Marcel Breuer that became a popular meeting place for the modernist artists and architects who gravitated to Hampstead in the 1930s, many of them German refugees (see 2 Willow Road, page 155). Now empty and vandalised, this too has been a worthy focus of a public campaign to preserve an equally significant part of the area's history.

ADDRESS New End Square, London NW3 1LR (020 7431 0144) **OPEN** Wednesday to Sunday, 12.00–17.00

ADMISSION free **ACCESS** ground floor only **UNDERGROUND** Hampstead

FENTON HOUSE

A two-storey, red-brick house, Fenton was built in about 1686, possibly by the bricklayer father of its first owner William Eades. Subsequent inhabitants were typical of Hampstead's professional middle-classes: lawyer Sir George Hutchins (in residence 1689–1706); Quaker linen and iron-ore merchant Joshua Gee (1706–30), one of the original mortgagees of Pennsylvania and part of a consortium of six British businessmen who raised £6000 to get William Penn out of debt, using the state of Pennsylvania as security; admiral's widow Mary Martin (1857–65), who added a clock to the east front, giving the house for a time the name of Clock House; and tobacco importer John Hyndman (1765–86). In 1793 the house was bought by merchant Philip Fenton who with his nephew James had made a career in Riga exporting goods to England; James, his wife Margaret and their seven children lived at Fenton until James' death in 1834. Later occupants include merchant Richard Hart Davies (1834–42), lawyer Thomas Turner (1842–56), gas engineer George Trewby (1884–1920) and electrical engineer Robert Brousson (1922–36). The last private owner, Lady Katherine Binning, left the house to the National Trust in 1952. It now holds a collection of porcelain and pictures assembled by herself, her mother Millicent E Salting and her uncle George Salting, and the early-instrument collection of George Benton Fletcher.

The house was originally designed to be entered via the elegant south front – seven bays, the outer two blind on the ground floor and the central three projecting slightly and capped by a pediment. The asymmetrical pitch of the roof suggests the house was the work of a master builder rather than an architect; the bold carved wooden cornice under the widely projecting eaves is almost identical to that at nearby Burgh House (see page 121). Moving the main entrance to its present position on the five-bay east front and marking it with an imposing colonnaded loggia slung between the two projecting end bays was probably the idea of James Fenton.

The room that now runs the length of the south front was once a separate morning room and dining room divided by the entrance passage. The bay that occupies the projecting wing on the east front was originally a closet and as elswhere the tiny windowless room leading off it would have housed a close-stool or toilet. The ghastly striped orange wallpaper, along with most of the decoration in the house, dates from the National Trust's 1970s refurbishment of the property. In the north-west corner of the roughly square, four-room plan is the smaller porcelain room (named for its collection of Meissen and English 16th-century figurines), used at various times as a study, smoking room, sitting room and doctor's surgery during the tenancy of Dr Abercrombie (1937–39). The oriental room to the north-east with its collection of early Chinese ceramics is furnished much as it was when it was Lady Binning's library. Like the other rooms on the east front its basic rectangular plan is enhanced by opening up the former closet, here to create a bay that provides light and a degree of seclusion for a desk and chair.

The staircase – lit by an enormous window that dominates the west front – retains its original 17th-century twisted balusters. The prickly-pear wallpaper clashes hideously with the heavily patterned carpet taken from a design at Hardwick Hall. The Rockingham room (named from the collection of ceramics from that factory) in the north-east corner has a fascinating assembly of 17th-century stump- or raised-work needle-work pictures – in *King Solomon and the Queen of Sheba* (possibly a tribute to Charles 1 and celebration of the restoration of the monarchy) the heads are three dimensional and the chain-mail is worked in relief.

The blue porcelain room (named for its collection of blue-and-white Chinese china) in the south-east corner was enlarged by James Fenton by replacing the wall of the corridor that led to the mechanism for the clock on the east front with a screen of Ionic columns. From at least 1884 this room was linked to the drawing room in the south-west corner by

[hampstead]

double doors. The drawing room – decorated in depressing two-tone yellow – retains the panelling and arched alcoves flanking the deep chimney breast installed by the Fentons. The small green room in the north-west corner contains more needlework pictures and pottery.

The attic rooms were probably used originally as bedrooms for the family, with the servants sleeping in outbuildings (Joshua Gee had nine children and James Fenton and George Trewby seven each). To add a further layer to what is already a baffling mix of interests, one room is devoted to a display of illustrations, cover art and toys from James Roose-Evans' 1970s 'Odd and Elsewhere' children's books, which use Fenton House as the setting for an equally baffling series of adventures.

ADDRESS Windmill Hill, London NW3 6RT (01494 755563)
OPEN 2 to 17 March: Saturday, Sunday, 14.00–17.00; 23 March to 3 November: Wednesday to Friday, 14.00–17.00; Saturday, Sunday, bank holidays, 11.00–17.00
ADMISSION £4.40/£2.20
ACCESS ground floor only
UNDERGROUND Hampstead

THE FREUD MUSEUM

More than any other of London's great men's houses, the Freud Museum has the unsettling quality of a place of pilgrimage to which initiates come to pay homage, communing with their long-dead prophet to bolster their faith. The impression is reinforced by the lack of information provided – no-one coming through the door out of curiosity will learn anything here or have their interest kindled. On the other hand, there's also none of the curatorial nonsense that assembles anything the great master has touched and then tries to justify its presence. The strategy was laid bare in the museum's celebration in 2000 of the centenary of *The Interpretation of Dreams*. Objects – some added, such as a bowl of cherries on a table, some already there, such as a cupboard – were captioned with cryptic, allusive dream descriptions taken from Freud's *magnum opus*. Slippage, ellipsis – the onus of interpretation is on you.

20 Maresfield Gardens was the home of father of psychoanalysis Sigmund Freud from 27 September 1938 until his death at the age of 83 on 23 September 1939 and of his youngest daughter Anna (born 1895), known for her controversial work in child psychology, and her lifelong companion Dorothy Burlingham until their deaths in 1982 and 1979 respectively. It opened as a museum, in accordance with Anna's wishes, in 1986.

The red-brick double-fronted two-storey Edwardian house with big dormer windows in the roof – thoroughly English and from the outside disarmingly cottage-like – opens like Freud's explorations of the mind into an unexpectedly extensive and complex array of spaces. Beyond the small entrance lobby in the central bay is an imposing double-height hall that runs half the depth of the house. Freud's study occupies the space running the full depth of the house to the right; behind the hall is a spacious dining room with a conservatory beyond part-designed by Freud's architect son Ernst. (It's now a shop that sells Freud-modelled

'brainy beanies' alongside learned texts.) Above the dining room is a room devoted to the life and work of Anna Freud; above Freud's study are exhibition and video rooms. The left-hand side of the house is now office and administration space.

Freud was released from Vienna following the Nazi invasion of Austria in March 1938 mainly because the German authorities realised he was too big a fish to fry. Works by Freud and other psychoanalysts had been publicly burned in Germany in 1933 and now the Gestapo demanded as conditions of his release that a copy of his complete works stored for safekeeping in Switzerland should be returned and ceremoniously burned and that he should sign a statement declaring he had been treated 'with all the respect and consideration due to my scientific reputation, that I could live and work in full freedom… and that I have not the slightest reason for any complaint' (he signed, insisting on adding: 'I can heartily recommend the Gestapo to anyone'!). In addition he was required to pay large amounts of so-called fugitive tax to prevent his library and collections from being seized, some of which was put up by his pupil Marie Bonaparte, who through her connections with the Greek royal family had already arranged for his stock of gold, then a common insurance against inflation, to be transferred to London by the Greek king. Freud's permitted retinue included his wife Martha, Anna, Martha's sister Minna, two maids and his dog Lün; he was never to know that the four sisters he left behind were incinerated five years later.

London welcomed him with open arms: he was fêted in *The Lancet* and *BMJ*; visitors included H G Wells, Chaim Weizmann and a delegation from the Royal Society. According to his biographer and disciple Ernest Jones, he thought the house 'really beautiful' ('too good for someone who would not tenant it for long') and was particularly fond of the garden, which he would enter through the French doors in his study to sit in a comfortable swing couch shaded with a canopy from the unseasonable autumn sunshine. Later, as he succumbed to the cancer of the palate that had dogged him since 1923, involving 33 operations, he had his sick bed moved here and enjoyed the views of the flowers.

Freud's study today – its blinds shut in the interests of conservation – gives a mistaken impression of stereotypical Viennese gloom and dark, impenetrable secrets. But it's still less austere than might have been imagined: the famous couch, on which even towards the end of his life he conducted up to four sessions a day sitting himself on a green tub chair out of sight, is draped in a richly textured Persian carpet (the stuff of dreams, indeed); Freud's well-worn swivel desk chair takes the playful form of a human figure. An extensive library lines the walls and the collection of some 2000 objects including antiquities from ancient Greece, Rome, Egypt and the orient – arranged by his son Ernst and maid Paula Fichtl to replicate as closely as possible the Viennese apartment in which he had lived for 47 years – is crammed into cabinets and scattered over surfaces rather than displayed, as if the enjoyment was in possession not contemplation. (Freud confessed that his passion for collecting was second in intensity only to his addiction to cigars.) In many ways the room seems distinctly Edwardian – the heavily draped table in front of the window, the relentless clutter – especially in comparison with its modernist neighbour and direct contemporary at 2 Willow Road (see page 155).

Freud's Viennese study is captured in photographs in the dining room which also show Vienna's swastika-festooned streets and the familiar severe, bearded face of the master. The 18th- and 19th-century peasant furniture painted with scenes and stylised plants is from Anna and Dorothy's Austrian country cottage. A tacky Alpine holiday-souvenir painting in a gold frame shows a surprising streak of kitsch sentimentality.

The mezzanine landing in the light-filled bay above the lobby – whose table displays a Biedermeier elegance characteristic of much of the assembled furniture – was presumably another favourite place to sit. On the top landing is a remarkable portrait by Salvador Dali, for whom Freud's fascination with myth was a major influence, that conflates Freud's head with a fingerprint. Dali was brought to the house in July 1939 by writer Stefan Zweig. Freud commented afterwards: 'Until now I have been inclined to regard the surrealists, who apparently have

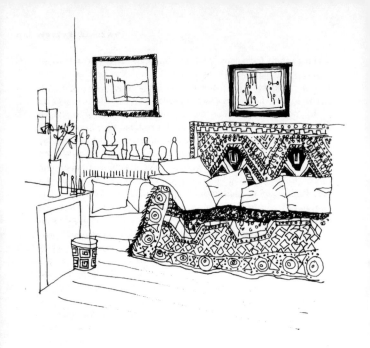

adopted me as their patron saint, as complete fools... That young Spaniard... has changed my estimate.'

In the Anna Freud room, behind a green baize door, are assembled the couch and desk from her study, the loom she kept in her bedroom (she used to knit when conducting sessions) and various certificates and family photographs. The father-daughter relationship is described by Jones as 'peculiarly intimate' – from 1918 she was psychoanalysed by her father, while he admitted to becoming increasingly emotionally and physically dependent on her as his illness progressed. (Freud's wife is conspicuous by her absence.) After her father's death, Anna opened the Hampstead War Nursery which provided foster care for children whose relationships with their parents had been disrupted by the war and later she worked with orphans from concentration camps. But whereas the aim of Freud's analysis was arguably to help his patients better understand themselves, Anna believed people could be encouraged to become model citizens by strengthening the rational side of their ego, enabling them to control their unconscious impulses. She experimented first with Dorothy Burlingham's children following their parents' divorce – Rob, whom she had tried to dissuade from being gay, died of alcoholism; Maddy returned to commit suicide at Maresfield Gardens in the 1960s. But there's little hint of this darker story at the Freud shrine bar the testimony of a member of staff from the Hampstead Clinic for Children, established by Anna in the early 1950s, who hints that emotion and professionalism were as linked here as they must have been in her initiation into psychoanalysis with her father: 'The Hampstead Clinic is sometimes spoken of as Anna Freud's extended family, and that is how it often felt, with all the ambivalence such a statement implies.'

ADDRESS 20 Maresfield Gardens, London NW3 5SX (020 7435 2002) **OPEN** Wednesday to Sunday, 12.00–17.00

ADMISSION £4/£2/under-12s free **ACCESS** very limited **UNDERGROUND** Finchley Road/ Belsize Park/Swiss Cottage

KEATS HOUSE

You could not step or move an eyelid but it would shoot to my heart – I am greedy of you – Do not think of any thing but me. Do not live as if I was not existing – Do not forget me… If we love we must not live as other men and women do – I cannot brook the wolfsbane of fashion and foppery and tattle. You must be mine to die upon the rack if I want you…

No – my sweet Fanny – I am wrong. I do not want you to be unhappy – and yet I do, I must while there is so sweet a Beauty – my loveliest my darling! Good bye! I kiss you – O the torments!

Such was the letter the 24-year-old John Keats (1795–1821) wrote to his 20-year-old fiancée and neighbour Fanny Brawne (1800–65) a few days after he left for the last time this Hampstead house where he was the tenant (paying £5 per month) of his friend Charles Brown. Plagued by financial worries, family problems, doctor's instructions not to work, the absence of friends and above all an acute awareness of his advancing consumption, he looked to Fanny as an emotional lifeline while at the same time suffering torments at the idea that she might be enjoying the company of others. The tragic ironies of Keats' situation – heir to an unobtainable legacy and reduced to borrowing from friends; a writer whose first two books were so unpopular they lost money but whose *Odes*, published just months before his death, would be claimed as the most perfect poems in English; a consumptive whose medical training gave him an inescapable awareness of his condition – pervade Keats House. Yet the 18 months he spent here included happy times with friends, some productive months of work and the dawn of a love affair that was as passionate and unreasonable as might be expected from any young love.

The eldest of a family of four surviving children, whose father had died when he was nine and mother when he was 15, Keats moved into Went-

worth Place in December 1818 following the death from consumption of his younger brother Tom. He had nursed Tom in the lodgings in nearby Well Walk which the three brothers had shared until George's emigration to the United States earlier in the year. As Brown, a 32-year-old merchant who had retired to spend more time on his writing, recalled: 'Early one morning I was awakened in my bed by a pressure on my hand. It was Keats, who came to tell me his brother was no more... At length, my thoughts returning from the dead to the living, I said – "Have nothing more to do with those lodgings – and alone too. Had you not better live with me?" He paused, pressed my hand warmly, and replied – "I think it would be better." From that moment he was my inmate.'

The pleasant stuccoed Regency house was built as a two-family dwelling in 1815–16 by Brown and his schoolfriend Charles Wentworth Dilke, a literary critic and civil servant. The appearance of a symmetrical three-bay detached house was maintained by having Dilke's entrance in the centre of the main façade and Brown's on a side wall. The house was surrounded by fields and the Heath, and Hampstead was a village favoured by such writers and artists as Shelley, Coleridge and Keats' first champion Leigh Hunt, publisher of the radical *Examiner* who following years in exile moved to Chelsea and was a friend of the poet's exact contemporary Thomas Carlyle (see page 79). In 1839 Wentworth Place was made into one house and the single-storey extension comprising the Chester room and a conservatory (replaced in 1975) added by retired actress Eliza Chester. In 1921, threatened with demolition, it was bought by the Keats Memorial House fund and offered to the council; four years later it opened to the public. The Corporation of London started a conservation and restoration programme in 1999, due to be completed by 2004.

The recommended route begins in the light-filled Chester room, decidedly more decorative and delicate than the rest of the house. The main interest (apart from the print of the actress – nicknamed 'Prinny's last fling' because of the Prince Regent and future George IV's interest in her – as Lady Teazle in Sheridan's *School for Scandal*) is a collection of facsimiles of Keats' letters. As you walk round the room the tone darkens from the lighthearted merriment of the missives to his sister Fanny (eight years his junior) or to Dilke from the walking holidays he and Brown enjoyed (one of which suggests the far-from-angelic poet was using mercury, a remedy for gonorrhoea) to despair as recognition of his consumption becomes unavoidable. The lifemask of 1816 by his friend Benjamin Robert Haydon, with its fine cheekbones and aquiline nose, looks haughty and confident; the deathmask, five years later, drawn and wasted.

The door back into the rest of the house was the front door to Brown's residence; the hall, lined with his amateurish watercolours, contained his staircase. On the left is Keats' sitting room, a squarish space with French windows to the garden whose tranquillity after the noisy conditions and distress of Well Walk enabled him to write such masterpieces as the odes 'To Psyche', 'To a Nightingale', 'To a Grecian Urn' and 'To Melancholy', completed in a month in April 1819. The two slender bookcases contain volumes he is known to have owned – Burton's *Anatomy*, Chesterfield's *Letters*, the works of Molière and Spenser, the *Illiad* and the complete Shakespeare he always carried. The somewhat priggish posthumous portrait by Joseph Severn, who accompanied Keats to Italy in September 1820 and stayed with him until his death in February 1821, shows the room as Keats inhabited it; more heartrending are the likenesses of his sister Fanny in late middle age – a reminder of what might have been – and the print of Severn's watercolour of Tom, dead at the age of 19.

Brown's sitting room opposite, slightly larger and used for entertaining, once looked out on the Heath and it was here that Brown made up a sofa bed for Keats during his illness of February and March 1820. The most intriguing item is Brown's anaemic copies of some 70 heads from Hogarth's *A Rake's Progress* mounted against a black background. Keats described it as 'A damn'd melancholy picture… during the first week of my illness it gave me a psalm singing nightmare, that made me almost faint away in my sleep.' Though Brown's clowning and comic verse occasionally became wearisome, he supported his friend emotionally and financially until the latter's death. In the summer of 1820 Brown and his maid Abigail O'Donaghue had a son, Carlino, and in 1822 he moved to Italy.

The damp and depressing basement kitchens house Brown's wine cellar and bread oven. Both the kitchens and the ground-floor Brawne rooms in Dilke's side of the house – originally two rooms with communicating doors – are more generously proportioned than Brown's spaces. Keats met the Brawne family – Fanny, her widowed mother and her younger siblings Samuel and Margaret – after Brown rented them his rooms while he and Keats were on a walking holiday in Scotland in the summer of 1818. Keats, troubled by a sore throat, returned early (having covered 642 miles in a couple of months) and met Fanny on visits to the Dilkes. Preoccupied with nursing Tom and beginning work on *Hyperion*, he didn't properly register her presence until November. It was hardly love at first sight, though he was intrigued, describing her as 'beautiful and elegant, graceful, silly, fashionable and strange.' Intelligent, diligent and quick-witted, interested in languages and fashion and with no pretensions to literary appreciation, to Keats' relief she 'liked me for my own sake and for nothing else.'

The Brawnes moved to a nearby cottage on Brown's return and in May or June the following year Dilke – whose portrait here shows a robust, jolly young man in contrast to the air of abstracted asceticism which colours the likenesses of Keats – rented them his side of Wentworth Place. Keats' love letters to Fanny begin in July 1819, when he was forced by Brown's summer letting of his home to stay with his sick friend James Rice in the Isle of Wight and then with Brown in Winchester. The source of the famous 'season of mists and mellow fruitfulness', this summer and autumn were a low point in Keats' life: his brother George was writing from America asking for money; none of his friends could or would repay him the total of £230 he had generously loaned out and he was penniless; his sore throat was getting worse and Rice and he got on each other's nerves; as well as writing *Lamia* and struggling with *Hyperion* he was turning a play by Brown, *Otho the Great*, into comic verse as a potential money-spinner. After considering putting his medical training to good use by signing up as a ship's surgeon, he decided instead to try his hand at journalism, moving in October to rooms in Westminster. After a dispiriting few days tramping the streets in search of a position he returned helplessly to Brown. Fanny and Keats were engaged in December.

Though enlarged following the removal of Brown's staircase and containing no original furnishings, Keats' bedroom is surprisingly atmospheric. It was here he retreated in February 1820 when after travelling home from London on the outside of a coach – to save money – he caught a chill and experienced the first haemorrhage which told him he had pulmonary tuberculosis. Though he was to make a brief recovery in spring – enough for Brown to continue with his plans of letting the house out for the summer – following a stay with the Hunts in Kentish Town Keats returned to Wentworth Place where the Brawnes nursed him until the journey to Italy which it was hoped would restore his health. Alongside views of the Heath hang a copy of Keats' medical-training certificate from Guy's and St Thomas's and a replica of a portrait by the loyal Severn of the poet less than a month before his death inscribed: 'Drawn to keep me awake – a deadly sweat was on him all this night.'

In Brown's bedroom is a small display of material relating to Fanny Brawne. A miniature painted in 1833 at the time of her marriage to Louis Lindo shows an unremarkable face with pale eyes. (Perhaps in a telling attempt to relive her first love – whose engagement ring, displayed here, she wore all her life – she chose a man 12 years her junior whom she wed as soon as he came of age.) Among the other relics of a life that included three children and was spent largely on the continent are a scrapbook of travels, a charm bracelet and a book of fashion plates. As much as anything else in Keats House, there's a poignancy to our interest in this unremarkable woman whose only claim to fame is that she inspired an unconsumated passion in an aspiring poet who died tragically young.

ADDRESS Keats Grove, London NW3 2RR (020 7332 3820) **OPEN** Tuesday to Sunday,

12.00–17.00 **ADMISSION** £3/£1.50 **UNDERGROUND** Belsize Park

KENWOOD

> While he aimed at elegance within, he covered the outside of his buildings with frippery… Most of the white walls, with which Mr Adam has speckled this city, are no better than Models for the Twelfth-Night Decoration of a Pastry Cook.
>
> Robert Smirke, painter and illustrator and father of the architect, in a pamphlet attacking Adam, 1779

Until it was bought in 1754 by newly appointed attorney general William Murray (1705–93) and considerably aggrandised by Robert Adam between 1764 and the publication of Smirke's pamphlet, Kenwood was a simple brick Queen-Anne-style house two rooms deep and seven bays wide with an orangery to the west. It was built between 1694 and 1704 by surveyor general of the ordnance William Bridges on the site of (and perhaps incorporating) a dwelling built by king's printer John Bill around 1616. Murray had left his native Scotland for England at the age of 13. Though his father and one of his brothers had been imprisoned during the Jacobite uprising of 1715 and another brother was the tutor to the Young Pretender (Bonnie Prince Charlie), William threw himself firmly behind the Hanoverians.

Kenwood, meanwhile, had been in Scots hands since it was bought by John Campbell, 2nd Duke of Argyll – one of several Scots who flocked to London to seek preferment at court following the Act of Union of 1707 – from William, 4th Earl of Berkeley, who moved to the more fashionable Twickenham. By 1746 the house had passed to Campbell's nephew John Stuart, 3rd Earl of Bute, soon to become tutor to the future George III and from 1762–63 the new king's chief advisor and one of England's most unpopular prime ministers, not least because his government supported the supremacy of the royal prerogative. At about this time Bute moved to Luton Hoo, where he was later to employ Robert Adam, whom in 1761 he had persuaded the king to appoint as architect of the king's works. It is therefore probably to Bute – Murray's friend and mentor – that we owe Adam's transformation of Kenwood.

Murray himself – who took the title Earl of Mansfield in 1756 – is regarded as one of the greatest British judges and law reformers of the 18th century, credited with ruling against the rights of slavers over slaves in England. In 1738 he had joined the aristocracy by marrying the 34-year-old daughter of the 2nd Earl of Nottingham and 7th Earl of Winchilsea; his transformation of Kenwood must in part have been inspired by the need for a house suitable for entertaining the public figures it was in his interest to cultivate. For whatever his abilities, Mansfield was never forgiven for being a Scot (at a time when his fellow countrymen were perceived to hold undue power and influence) and was repeatedly accused of Jacobite leanings, of being a closet advisor to the king and even a papist. Matters reached a head during the anti-Catholic Gordon riots of 1780 when a mob burned down his Bloomsbury Square house (including his prized library) and pursued him to Hampstead, armed with the townhouse's iron railings. Kenwood escaped a similar fate in part because the landlord of the nearby Spaniard's Inn plied the rioters with free ale, supplemented by barrels set out by the roadside by Mansfield's steward.

Mansfield and his wife had no children of their own but they brought up Anne and Marjory, the sisters of William's nephew and heir David, 7th Viscount Stormont, and then Elizabeth, David's daughter by his first wife, and the 'mulatto' Dido, illegitimate daughter of Mansfield's other nephew Sir John Lindsay, a captain in the Royal Navy who had taken her mother prisoner in the West Indies and brought her to England where she gave birth. David – a former ambassador in Paris and Vienna – survived his uncle by only three years, during which time he hired George Saunders to enlarge Kenwood with the addition of the two brick wings that flank the entrance front. His son, who owned the house from 1796

to 1840, employed William Atkinson, a pupil of James Wyatt, to oversee an extensive programme of restoration and refurbishment, using many of the same cabinet-makers as the future George IV employed at Carlton House. His heir, the 4th Earl, spent only three months a year at Kenwood, preferring the family seat of Scone, but the 5th Earl – dubbed the most eligible bachelor in London – made the house for eight years around the turn of the 20th century once more the backdrop for a glittering social melee. Under the 6th Earl it was let to tenants including Grand Duke Michael Michaelovitch (in residence 1910–17), the great-great-grandson of Catherine the Great, who had been exiled from Russia in 1891 following his morganatic marriage to Pushkin's great-great-granddaughter. During World War I the service wing was used as a barracks; from 1917 to 1920 Kenwood was the home of Nancy Leeds, the wealthy widow of an American tin-plate manufacturer, who also rented Spencer House (see page 66).

In 1925 Kenwood was acquired by Edward Cecil Guinness, 1st Earl of Iveagh, who bequeathed it to the nation on his death. (Despite such gifts, the exchequer reaped £11 million in death duties from the estate, enabling chancellor Winston Churchill to lower the basic rate of income tax.) In 1886 Guinness Breweries had become a public company and the multi-millionaire had set out to form an art collection, buying some 240 drawings and paintings in the space of four years. Some 60 of these are on display at Kenwood today – a mix of late-18th-century British portraits, 17th-century Dutch and Flemish old masters and French rococo art.

Adam regarded Kenwood as one of his most significant achievements and the brothers devoted the entire second part of their calling-card *Works in Architecture* to its design. In Mansfield he found a supportive client, who 'gave full scope to my ideas', and the house's relative modesty allowed him a freedom impossible at Syon (see page 249) or Osterley (see page 235). He transformed the nine-bay entrance or north front through the addition of a massive full-height portico spanning the central three bays, its pediment supported on four Ionic columns. At the time the Highgate-to-Hampstead road ran just outside and the portico ensured that the house – no isolated country seat but a suburban villa designed to impress – would have a suitably imposing profile. Saunders' two projecting single-storey wings are each one bay wide and three deep, their white Suffolk brick (used by Henry Holland at Carlton House) a deliberate contrast with Adam's stucco. The 2nd Earl also commissioned landscape architect Humphry Repton to draw up plans for the grounds, with the result that Hampstead Lane was diverted to the other side of North Wood so the approach to the house, as today, was via a picturesque serpentine drive that raises expectations of a romantic secluded residence rather than the neoclassical formality of Adam's frontage.

Adam again used stucco on the south or garden façade to disguise the varying colours of the existing brick. This front was designed to be appreciated by family and friends from the terrace or lawn rather than to impress from a distance, and the architect topped a rusticated base with a delicate confectionery of swags, medallions, Greek-key patterns, honeysuckles and arabesques typical of his interiors. Adam described Kenwood's setting as 'magnificent, beautiful, and picturesque' and insisted that 'the decoration bestowed on this front of the house is suitable to such a scene'. But Kenwood's façade was also to be the perfect advertisement for stucco, for which Adam and his brother James had bought the patent from its Swiss clergyman inventor and had even obtained an act of parliament giving them the exclusive right to manufacture the material (in 1778 they prosecuted a Mr Johnson who had obtained a patent for an improved version; the case came before Mansfield, who unsurprisingly found in favour of the brothers).

As Julius Bryant points out in his excellent guide to the house, Mansfield may have regretted his decision, however: Kenwood's façade deteriorated rapidly, and according to Repton, 'The Great Lord Mansfield often declared, that had the front of Kenwood been originally covered in Parian marble, he should have found it less expensive'. (The present façade is faced with fibreglass mouldings copied in 1975 from Adam's drawings.) Further evidence that Adam was more concerned with style than substance is found in a letter from Atkinson defending himself against the 3rd Earl's complaints about delays to the schedule of works. According to the architect, 'the ignorance or inattention of the former Architects to the House' had resulted in dry rot (from failing to give the walls time to dry before plastering) while the perishable timber they had built into the walls had to be replaced by new solid brickwork.

Adam's transformation of the south front also involved building a single-storey library extension to the east (an appropriate choice of 'grand room' for a bibliophile with no family portraits to display), mirroring the existing orangery to the west. And he added a third storey, roofing it before he took down the old roof so the house remained habitable throughout the alterations. The sprawling brick service wing to the east, which today houses a café and restaurant, was an addition by Saunders for the 2nd Earl to replace much less extensive facilities behind the orangery.

Adam's innovation was to introduce the ornamental vocabulary of Roman domestic architecture to his work (unlike the Palladians, who drew inspiration from public buildings), supplemented by elements from 16th-century Italy and from contemporary France. Certainly the scale and ornament of the entrance hall at Kenwood – decorated in blue and green with motifs that reflect its dual function as a dining room – are thoroughly domestic in comparison with the grandeur sought at Osterley or Syon. The relative modesty of the 'great stairs' is in part attributable to the layout of the house: because the main reception room (the new library) was on the ground floor, guests simply passed by the staircase – admiring the honeysuckle-motif balustrade (identical to that at Osterley) on the way – rather than ascending it to a *piano nobile*. The delicate oval lantern replaced a dramatic Adam ceiling when the landing window was filled in to accommodate Saunders' new wing. In the hall hangs a replica of a 1775 portrait of Mansfield decked out in full regalia beside a bust of Homer bequeathed to him by his friend and mentor Alexander Pope (who tried, unsuccessfully, to help his protégé lose his Scottish accent). Opposite it hangs a picture of Mansfield's

future wife Elizabeth and her sister Henrietta painted two years before the marriage.

The antechamber and library form an easterly extension to the south front built entirely by Adam. A basically unaltered realisation of a 1764 design by James Adam that typifies the brothers' early style, the antechamber consists of a screen of two marble Ionic columns opposite a Venetian window with a panoramic view over the lake and woods beyond. The unexpected sequence of spaces – the imposing portico, the domestic entrance hall, the lofty great stairs, the short passage cut through the exterior wall of the original house – is the embodiment of Adam's desire to introduce the movement found in nature into architecture: 'the rising and falling, advancing and receding... have the same effect in architecture, that hill and dale, foreground and distance, swelling and sinking have in landscape.' The drama of the antechamber today is enhanced by the splendid vista through high double doors to the dining-room wing added by Saunders.

The library – regarded by aficionados as the finest example of Adam's late style – is a riot of pink, blue and gold confectionery that might just epitomise Adam at his worst. Like the antechamber, it uses screens of columns – set in front of semi-circular apses at each end of the double cube of the main room – to give drama to the space, but any plasticity of form is obscured by the marshmallow colours and elaborate piping that covers every surface. The style reaches its apogee in the mirrored recesses opposite the windows (sensibly Adam chose not to fenestrate the side facing the road but rather to reflect the romantic views from the tall windows overlooking the park). Here mirrors decorated with gilded urns and framed by uprights that seem to cobble together the gamut of Adam's decorative motifs are topped by arc upon arc of different patterns with above them the gilded frieze of lions and heads of deer and the coved ceiling with panels painted by Venetian artist Antonio Zucchi, who was later to marry Angelica Kauffmann, one of whose paintings hangs in the antechamber.

The change in scale from the original house and Adam's additions to

Saunders' more imposing new wing is immediately apparent in the dining-room lobby where the high coffered ceiling is topped by a balustraded lantern resting on four thin segmental arches. The sequence of two consecutive antechambers also gives the sense of a much larger house than Kenwood actually is. The dining room beyond – which contains two gems from the Iveagh bequest, a Rembrandt self-portrait of c. 1663 and Vermeer's *The Guitar Player* (c. 1672) – is impressive in scale but relatively free of decoration.

Running along the south front of the original house from the library and antechamber are Lord Mansfield's dressing room, the breakfast room, Lady Mansfield's dressing room, the housekeeper's room and the orangery. With the exception of the last, all are intimate and domestic in feel and Adam's intervention is restricted to designs for chimneypieces, cornices and architraves. Lord Mansfield's dressing room – a plain, squarish space – would have served as a study and reception room in which to see morning visitors, and was the library until Adam added his new wing. The much larger breakfast room was until 1815 a separate drawing room and parlour or private dining room, both with direct access to the entrance hall. Lady Mansfield's dressing room is about half the size of her husband's; the similar-sized housekeeper's room is dominated by an incongruously large Venetian window placed to retain the symmetry of the façade rather than to correspond with any internal function. The light-filled orangery – originally a freestanding building which would have concealed the service wing from the terrace and lawn – was used like a traditional long gallery, for recreation in wet weather. Orangeries became a popular symbol of political affiliation (and wealth) after the accession of William of Orange in 1689.

The orangery provides a splendid vista through the length of Saunders' other wing, which consists of an antechamber framed by two screens of Ionic columns (echoing but not directly imitating Adam's antechamber), the green room and the music room. Though these lofty chambers are relatively unadorned, the most striking decorative motif being a frieze of gilded harps, the music room at least was to have had decorated panels by Julius Ibbetson, of which only the borders were completed. The walls today are hung with 18th-century portraits – mostly of such female icons as Emma Hamilton (depicted by George Romney as St Cecilia), courtesan Kitty Fisher (depicted by Joshua Reynolds as Cleopatra), and actress Mrs Jordan (depicted by John Hoppner as Viola in *Twelfth Night*). The house has continued to attract collections, and displays of miniatures, shoe buckles and jewellery are on show in the upstairs rooms.

ADDRESS Hampstead Lane, London NW3 7JR (020 8348 1286) **OPEN** April to September: daily, 10.00–18.00; October to March: daily, 10.00–16.00 **ADMISSION** free **ACCESS** ground floor only **UNDERGROUND** Hampstead

LAUDERDALE HOUSE

An unattractive pebbledash building with an uninspiring five-bay Georgian entrance front, a surprisingly unthought-out arrangement of windows on its long south-east side and a fine Doric colonnade at the back, Lauderdale House is nevertheless endowed with a history – both architectural and social – that's one of the most interesting in this book.

One of the few surviving large timber-framed London houses, Lauderdale was built in 1582 by Sir Richard Martin, warden and master-worker at the Royal Mint, for his younger son Richard, probably with the rich bounty of 'Spanish gold' earned from financing Sir Francis Drake's circumnavigation of 1577–80. The Martins' home was built on a U-shaped plan around a central courtyard. The long south-east flank (the base of the U) was probably divided into three rooms with a traditional great chamber on the first floor; the present entrance hall in the north-east (right-hand) wing was probably a dining room. A single-storey building at the open end of the courtyard, connected by a corridor to the dining room, contained the kitchens. As at Whitehall (see page 335), the construction is timber frame infilled with wattle and daub, with the larger upper-floor frame resting on projecting joists, a method known as continuous jettying. The slight projection of the upper floor today and the asymmetrical fenestration on the long front are the clearest clues to the building's Tudor origins.

Subsequent owners include merchant Sir William Bond (in residence 1599–1625), who was the brother of the younger Martin's wife Anne, and lord chief justice Sir Henry Hobart (1625–35), who had built Blickling Hall in Norfolk. The house received its first makeover in the early 1640s when wealthy widow Lady Home transformed it into a residence befitting an aristocrat by widening the single-room-deep long flank with the addition of a corridor on the courtyard side to provide independent

access to the rooms in the two shorter wings, extending the entrance wing to the north to create a servants' hall in the empty corner between the dining room and kitchens, and adding a third storey to the opposite wing (which I will call the café wing in reference to its present function).

On Lady Home's death in 1645 the house passed to her younger daughter Anne, who just over a decade earlier had married John Maitland, 2nd Earl of Lauderdale. A staunch royalist, Maitland spent nine years in prison during the interregnum and from 1649 was forced to lease out his Highgate house to John Ireton, brother of Cromwell's son-in-law. After the restoration he was rewarded with the post of secretary of state for Scotland and from 1667 was one of the five members of Charles II's inner circle of advisors, the Cabal ministry. When Lauderdale's daughter Mary married at Highgate in 1666 it was the king who gave her away. It is perhaps unsurprising, then, that when Lauderdale separated from Anne to pursue Elizabeth, Countess of Dysart (see Ham House, page 182), a wife more suitable to his enhanced status, the king should ask that Lauderdale House be let to his own mistress, actress Nell Gwynn. Though there is no direct evidence to support persistent claims that Gwynn lived at Lauderdale House – or the story that she held her infant Charles out of one of its windows and threatened to drop him unless the king made him an earl – an inventory of the house and its contents made in 1685 (see below) describes the first-floor rooms tucked away in the corner of the café wing, accessed by a separate staircase, as 'the kinges chamber and closett'.

Anne retired to a Calvinist community in Paris and died in 1671; shortly afterwards Lauderdale and Elizabeth married and the newly created Duke and his wife embarked on the ambitious refurbishment of Ham. Some idea of the state of Lauderdale House, meanwhile, can be gained from a letter from the exiled Anne to her husband in which she complains that the house 'is likely to fall down – particularly that part my mother built. I was already afraid that all that weight [of Lauderdale's books] at the top of the house would bring the old house on my head… Remember that it is only mine for my lifetime and then goes to your heirs; I have not the power to take it from them. So I look to you for the repairs.' (Quoted in its 'translated' form from Barber, Cox and Curwen's fascinating study of the house.)

In what must have been a contrast with the royal shenanigans of the previous years, the house was bought in 1677 by Quaker merchant William Mead, who married Sarah Fell, the step-daughter of Quaker founder George Fox. Among Mead's alterations were the reconstruction of the staircase and the installation of an elaborately carved recess in the dining room known by the improbable name of Nell Gwynn's Bath.

The next owner, John Hinde, was a property developer who with Sir Thomas Bond, grandson of previous owner Sir William, built up the area around Old Bond Street. In September 1685 Hinde was declared bankrupt with assets of no more than £10,000 and liabilities estimated at up to £200,000. The inventory of Lauderdale House made by his auditors gives us a clear picture of the house at that time. As in the Martins' dwelling, the entrance hall probably doubled as a dining room. The long flank was made up of two parlours: the white parlour adjoining the dining room, which contained an organ and therefore may have doubled as a chapel, and the green parlour beyond (replacing two rooms of the original dwelling). In the café wing was a red parlour and brewhouse. The kitchen and servants' hall occupied the same positions as in previous schemes. Mrs Hinde's bedroom was above the dining room with a nurse's room above the servants' hall. The tripartite arrangement of the long flank was retained on the first floor: the rooms are described as a matted gallery (or great chamber), best chamber (Mr Hinde's bedroom) linked to a dressing room in the corridor extension added by Lady Home, and beyond it in the café wing the 'kinges chamber and closett', with a separate staircase, and a further bedroom. The six attic rooms were empty.

In 1688 Lauderdale House was bought by its last owner-occupier, Tory MP and philanthropist Sir William Pritchard, and in the century that followed his heirs leased it out among others to Sir Thomas Burnet (c. 1752), son of the Earl of Lauderdale's arch-enemy Bishop Gilbert Burnet. In the 1760s Matthew Knapp transformed the exterior into the neoclassical-style building we see today, adding columns at the corners of the long front to give a more 'classical' profile to the overhanging upper storey, replacing the oriel windows with Georgian sashes and concealing the irregularities of the café front by extending the upper floors forward, capping them with a pediment and supporting the extension on wooden Doric columns. It is known from his diaries that John Wesley (see page 71) stayed here twice in the 1780s, describing it as 'one of the most elegant boarding houses in England'. From 1794 to 1837 it was leased as a school.

The colonnade on the café front was extended to the north in the first half of the 19th century and a billiards room, adjoining the kitchen wing and filling in the open side of the courtyard, was added behind it. It was probably at about this time that the façades received their pebbledash render. The dining room was extended internally by replacing the wall to the white parlour with the Ionic columns still in place today and the green and red parlours were combined into a single L-shaped room by means of a similar screen. The last private occupant was James Yates (in residence 1850–71), who in 1827 had helped establish University College London. Yates had no children and it's likely he transformed the bedrooms in the long flank into the long gallery we see today.

The last private owner of the house was Sir Sydney Waterlow, the wealthy head of a firm of banknote-printers. From 1872 to 1878 he let the house rent-free to St Bartholomew's Hospital and in 1889 gave it to the London County Council, which converted the upper floor into five flats for park-keepers and the ground floor into a refreshment room. In 1961 the council decided to bring the whole house into public use and embarked on an ambitious programme of restoration thwarted by a fire in 1963. The GLC then reroofed the house and inserted a steel carcass within the Tudor structure. After a public campaign to reopen the house it was let to the Lauderdale House Society in 1978 and the money from the fire insurance was used for a partial restoration of the ground floor. It is run as a community arts venue.

The illustrious history of Lauderdale House can barely be discerned in the building as it stands today. The dining room and half the adjacent reception room are a single space devoted to exhibitions. On the right of the entrance, Nell Gwynn's Bath – probably intended for displaying plate – houses a plethora of leaflets about local activities; at the far end of the space part of the original doorway to the yard has been revealed. The Ionic columns installed in the early 19th century are still in situ here and in the café, located in the south-west wing behind the 1760s colonnade.

A doorway leads from the dining room to the staircase installed by Mead, lit by an octagonal lantern probably designed by royal serjeant painter James Thornhill in the early 18th century. (Behind one of the panels is some earlier *trompe l'oeil* decoration that indicates that the original staircase ascended in the opposite direction.) The first-floor landing (part of the linking section created by Lady Home in 1640) could belong to any institutional building if it weren't for the piece of the original external wall revealed in the corner. The 27-metre long gallery, though created post-1850, gives the best sense of the original house. All in all, a building that's perhaps more interesting to read about than to visit, unless you're inclined to participate in one of the admirable range of community activities or enjoy the terrace café.

ADDRESS Waterlow Park,
Highgate Hill, London N6 5HG
(020 8348 8716)
OPEN Tuesday to Friday,
11.00–16.00; Sunday 12.00–17.00
ACCESS limited
ADMISSION free
UNDERGROUND Archway/
Highgate

2 WILLOW ROAD

You know what importance I attach to building my first house, and one
specially for you… We must think seriously how to conceive this house so that
it does not become a weight which one drags after one for years or a chain that
attaches us to one place.
Ernö Goldfinger to Ursula Blackwell, 1931

Modernist architect Ernö Goldfinger's first house, completed just before
war broke out in 1939 as a family home and investment for his wife's capital from food manufacturer Cross & Blackwell, may not have been the
chain that attached him to this corner of Hampstead, but was nevertheless his home for almost 50 years until his death in 1987. The keys to its
success, in my view, are an exacting attention to detail, with each element
designed for its specific location and function, and flexibility – what once
was the nursery became rooms for Goldfinger's ageing mother; the servants' quarters were converted into a flat in which both his sons and their
families lived at different times.

The intimacy and elegance of Goldfinger's house and its purpose-
designed furniture may come as a surprise to those who know only the
architect's much-maligned 'concrete jungles': the Ministry of Health's
Alexander Fleming House (1962) at Elephant & Castle; the housing
schemes focused on Balfron Tower (1965) on the northern approach to
the Blackwall Tunnel and Trellick Tower (1973) in north Kensington.
However, though these developments were held up in the 1980s as prime
examples of modernist arrogance and contempt for human values,
Goldfinger (whose personal arrogance his friends readily admit) was to
some extent rehabilitated in the 1990s as the sculptural drama, construc-
tivist heroics and above all fine detailing of his schemes were appreci-

ated. Apartments in Trellick Tower – made uninhabitable because of social not architectural factors – now command high prices.

Born in Budapest in 1902, Goldfinger moved to Paris in 1920 where he participated in a near-revolution at the conservative Ecole des Beaux-Arts by asking Auguste Perret, one of the first architects to explore the artistic possibilities of reinforced concrete, to set up a studio. He and Ursula, a painter who studied with Le Corbusier's one-time collaborator Amédée Ozenfant, left for London in 1934, the year after their marriage and the birth of their first child Peter (Liz was born three years later and Michael in 1945). The family moved into Berthold Lubetkin's utopian Highpoint 1 in Highgate and Goldfinger set up a studio in Bedford Square. Business was far from brisk – his only executed building was a house in Essex for the painter Humphrey Waterfield, though he also designed a showroom and some toys for the educational toy firm Paul and Marjorie Abbatt and his only furniture designs to reach the production line, some storage cabinets for Easiwork.

In Paris Ernö and Ursula had numbered among their friends surrealists Max Ernst and Roland Penrose (whose collages hang in the dining room), so it's hardly surprising they were attracted to Hampstead, which in the 1930s had replaced Chelsea as the London centre for left-leaning artists and writers. (Goldfinger was a signatory of the English surrealist group's call for the government to lift the arms embargo to republican Spain and in 1942 held a fund-raising 'Aid to Russia' exhibition at Willow Road that included work by Hampstead artists Henry Moore, Barbara Hepworth and Ben Nicholson.) The first design for the Willow Road site, a four-storey block of flats and studios, was rejected by the LCC, and a campaign to block the design-as-built was initiated by Tory MP Henry Brooke. But the target was a poor one – Goldfinger's modest row of three brick-clad houses was far less radical than such local schemes as Wells Coates' Isokon flats (1934) and in any case, as the architect himself pointed out, was 'a modern adaptation of the eighteenth-century style... far more in keeping with the beautiful Downshire Hill houses round the corner than their [florid Victorian] neighbours in Willow Road… As for the objection that the houses are rectangular, only the Esquimeaux and Zulus build anything but rectangular houses.'

Though Goldfinger supported the modernist call for cities characterised by 'espace, soleil, verdure' – apparent in Willow Road's plentiful windows and Heath-side location – he was no fan of Le Corbusier's nostalgic Mediterranean vernacular of smooth white walls, which he dismissed as 'kasbah' architecture. Like Perret he believed in the open expression of materials and structure, so here the reinforced-concrete floor slabs and supporting columns are clearly visible on the outside. The concrete frame, which relies on the cylindrical well of the internal spiral staircase for extra strength, was calculated by Ove Arup, at the time working for J L Kier (though at the back of the house two concrete columns run from basement to second floor, at the front the top storey is supported on thin steel stanchions behind the ribbon window). Goldfinger was a great admirer of London's Georgian squares and terraces, and Willow Road, with its brick cladding, stone coping and classical internal arrangement of a first-floor *piano nobile*, can be seen as a modern reinterpretation of the traditional street. The family occupied the central house (No. 2); No. 3 was presold to civil servant Stephen Wilson and finished to his specifications; No. 1 was rented to classical scholar R P Winnington-Ingram. The contract price for No. 2 was £2751 6s 1d at a time when a suburban semi cost just £800.

Unusually for the time, Willow Road had two built-in garages, one with an inspection pit, and the guided tour begins with a well-presented video screened in one of them, now hung with Goldfinger's idealistic wartime poster designs for travelling Army Bureau of Current Affairs exhibitions on such subjects as 'Twenty-five Years of Soviet Progress', 'Planning Your Neighbourhood' and 'Planning Your Kitchen'. Photographs of Ernö at a student fancy-dress party show him to have been startlingly handsome; later cine film captures a tall, dark-haired, imposing figure with the confident bearing and glamour of a filmstar (rumour has it that notorious anti-Semite Ian Fleming took such a dislike to him he gave his name to his arch-villain). Peter and Liz talk of a childhood filled with parties and dinners; associates and friends describe a demanding nature tempered by extreme generosity, a love of argument and a fiery temper.

The small entrance hall, like the rest of the house, is hung with pictures, many of which are inscribed with personal dedications to the couple. The door at the rear led to bedrooms for the chauffeur, cook and au pair, the kitchen and the laundry (now the custodian's flat). The walls on either side of the front door are made up of textured glass panels set into a grid of wooden shelves filled with souvenirs – as well as art, Ernö and Ursula collected knick-knacks and the kind of anthropological artefacts Ozenfant and his contemporaries used as inspiration. Typical of Goldfinger's capacity to rethink every detail from scratch and produce an elegant and economical solution is the letter box: a clear glass flap (completely unobtrusive, through which you can see when mail has arrived) on the inside of one of the compartments hinged at the top for opening.

2 Willow Road has a footprint of 1000 square feet (93 square metres), though the fact that many of the rooms are interconnected, avoiding the need for corridors, and so the only space given over purely to circulation is the compact spiral stair, makes it seem larger. You climb the cantilevered reinforced-concrete cork-covered treads, holding the rope balustrade, to the semi-open-plan first floor. At the front, separated when required by folding floor-to-ceiling partitions, are the dining room and studio; at the rear (where the floor level is lower – hence the very low ceilings of the entrance hall, cloakroom and flanking garages) are the living room (separated by folding partitions from the studio) and study. For parties – as at Dr Johnson's House (see page 37) – the whole floor could be opened up.

The use of colour – a cubist palette of mustard yellow, terracotta, poster red and dirty blues that get lighter as you progress through the house – is startling: the doors off the staircase are bright red gloss; the rear wall of the dining room, on which hangs a black-and-white Bridget Riley, is terracotta. The dining-room furniture, created by Goldfinger for the Highpoint flat, is another reinterpretation of a traditional form.

There's a sideboard whose doors slide back at the touch of a finger to reveal drawers individually crafted for cutlery and other implements; a large table with a lino-clad plywood top set on a heavy cast-iron industrial base; and tubular-steel and plywood chairs with reclining backs. The only discordant note is the pair of elaborate silver candlesticks – a present from Ernö's mother. Originally the kitchen was downstairs and food was delivered by dumb waiter to an adjacent servery. Later this was transformed into a tiny fitted kitchen where Peter remembers his mother 'rustling up endless meals'. It's a windowless galley shoehorned in the leftover space between the stairwell and party wall into which, by dint of careful planning, are squeezed a washing machine, oven, microwave, coffee-maker, etc. Ernö and Ursula's children gave the house to the National Trust in lieu of paying inheritance tax, and here – as you gaze at the Ambrosia creamed rice, Cafe Hag and ketchup that still fill the shelves – the sense of the place as a time capsule is strongest.

There's little evidence in the house that Ursula used her studio much for its original purpose and it seems that Ernö took it over completely following his retirement in 1977. Alongside his desk with its pivoting drawers crammed with a mess of rubber bands, lightbulbs, a hole punch, etc., are personal files with such headings as 'Obituaries', 'Questions political and social' and 'Interviews'. Built-in cupboards contain household tools, cameras and artist's materials; beneath the raised platform leading to the living room – lit to serve as a dais for models – are enviably large plan-chest drawers. A strikingly simple Ozenfant pencil drawing of a mother and child is inscribed 'Pour mon ancienne élève Ursula Goldfinger'.

The oak-ply-lined living room, with a full-length balcony overlooking the garden, is a comfortable, homely space furnished with an assortment of chairs, some of which have needlepoint covers made by Ernö's mother to Ursula's designs. The fireplace is set into a convex-curved wall – to throw out the heat – with bookshelves ingeniously fitted into the space between the front of the curve and the party wall behind. Among the collection of personal artefacts are a tray of souvenirs, a pebble painted by Max Ernst which inspired Goldfinger to paint some of his own, an intricate mechanistic pen-and-ink drawing of a head dedicated to the couple by Eduardo Paolozzi, with whom Goldfinger worked on the iconic 1956 'This Is Tomorrow' exhibition, and a striking photograph of Ursula – as tall and handsome as her husband – by Man Ray. Around the sofa is a wooden frame holding books at the bottom and demarcating a gallery space for a changing display. Alongside a Duchamp, a Riley and a Jean Arp is a picture of a car drawn by one of the couple's grandsons. The adjoining small study contains Ernö's library.

The second floor has a top-lit landing and two bathrooms in the middle sandwiched by the nursery at the front and the main and spare bedrooms at the rear. The austere main bedroom (above the dining room) is almost filled by the low bed (Ernö believed that higher civilisations, such as the Japanese, slept nearer the ground) flanked by simple wall-mounted metal anglepoises. The party wall with the spare room is a row of fitted cupboards (incidentally providing a sound barrier) with different sections accessed from one side or the other or from the landing (the linen cupboard). The en-suite bathroom is the site of more masterful rethinking: a built-in dressing-table/cupboard with mirrors at the back and on the doors, glass shelves and an array of family snaps tacked on the walls; a washbasin bracketed to hang clear of the wall for easy cleaning; a bidet (the height of European sophistication); a separate toilet lit with its own skylight. Both the tip-up bed and the washbasin in the spare room can be concealed in cupboards when not in use. Among the furnishings here is a kitsch ashtray in the form of a pair of goggles.

The nursery could be subdivided into three – originally the two ends were for the children, with the nanny (suffering an acute lack of privacy) in the middle. A servery similar to the one on the first floor allowed meals to be eaten upstairs. The end walls were left in natural grey plaster so the children could draw on them (Peter remembers carving a hammer and sickle); their heights are marked in pencil on the partititions. Alongside the modernist, unpainted-plywood dolls' house Goldfinger designed for Liz are examples of the educational toys he produced for Abbatt.

The extent of the journey Goldfinger travelled to enable him to conceive of Willow Road is poignantly illustrated by a photograph of the
nursery when it was occupied by his mother Regine in the 1960s – claus-
trophobically stuffed with heavy, ornate Austro-Hungarian furniture
and portraits. But the evolution of the house from the 1930s to the 1980s
tells a story of changing social pressures and aspirations too. It is incon-
ceivable today that a young married couple, even with a considerable fortune, would contemplate filling a house this size with three live-in servants, expect to have their meals cooked and sent upstairs on a tray and
to be driven wherever they wished at a moment's notice. By the end of
the couple's life, however, the cooking was done by Ursula and the space
had been juggled to accommodate four generations. That it did so successfully is a tribute to the capacity of Ernö – still popularly reviled for
placing ideals above human understanding at his death – to 'think seriously', inventively and humanely about a family's needs.

ADDRESS 2 Willow Road, London
NW3 1TH (020 7435 6166)
OPEN 30 March to 28 October:
Thursday, Friday and Saturday,
12.00–17.00; 4 to 25 March and
1 to 16 December: Saturday,
12.00–17.00. Guided tour only,
every 45 minutes from 12.15
ADMISSION £4.40
UNDERGROUND Belsize Park

[hackney/islington]

9/10 Stock Orchard Street **164**

Sutton House **170**

9/10 STOCK ORCHARD STREET

'I think we're just more conceited than the rest', says Jeremy Till when asked why he and Sarah Wigglesworth have decided to open the house and office they designed and built for themselves to public scrutiny. And with good reason: whether in terms of its ecologically sound credentials, innovative range of materials, generous scale, canny exploitation of an awkward site or sheer, unbounded exuberance, 9/10 Stock Orchard Street is quite an achievement. Especially as it was the architects' first complete building, with a budget of only £500,000. Till and Wigglesworth bought the site at auction in 1994 complete with a collection of dilapidated buildings and sitting tenants – a forge making springs. The journey to the house's near-completion at Christmas 2000 was far from straightforward, and the temptation to give up and realise the site's development potential as the location for several highly profitable 'nasty little Noddy houses' must always have been there. But as Wigglesworth says, 'You've got to know this thing really well, you've walked through its spaces time and again, you've imagined your life living in there. It just becomes a part of you.'

The site – which runs the full width of a depressingly undistinguished street of houses and workshops on the wrong side of Islington – is bounded to the south-east (henceforth referred to as east) by the main London-to-Edinburgh railway line, with only a chain-link fence between the buildings and the trains. The L-shaped structure Till and Wigglesworth created is divided into a living space – behind the long, largely glazed south elevation that faces the street – and a shorter office block that runs parallel with the railway line, providing a something of a protective buffer. The couple sold their previous home, moved into temporary accommodation and raised a mortgage to enable construction to begin towards the end of 1998; having spent some months in a caravan

on site, they finally moved in properly at the end of 2000. The planned five-storey library tower is still a shell with no staircase, but Till and Wigglesworth claim to enjoy the idea that the project is ongoing. Not only have they chosen materials that will transmute and weather over time, but like the rest of us who buy houses readymade, they relish the opportunity to be able to make changes to the look and layout as and when they can afford it.

Both office and house use unexpected materials and techniques. The entire, virtually windowless wall to the house at the extreme northern edge of the site (where sunlight is least forthcoming) and a block at the opposite end to the railway line, referred to as the 'west wing', are made of straw bales, the first time this material has received planning permission in the UK. The idea came from a teasing remark by a journalist friend ('You'll be building with straw bales next!'). Till and Wigglesworth investigated and discovered 300-year-old straw-bale houses in Germany and a thriving straw-bale movement in Nebraska, USA. As well as being cheap (£825 for 550), straw bales – stacked between a timber frame that takes the roof and floor loads – are quick and easy to build with, even using unskilled labour (that is, friends). And they have the added ecological perks of recycling a surplus material that took little energy to produce while providing an insulation value three times that of current requirements. Even before the foot-and-mouth crisis of 2001, the Cotswolds farmer who took pride in the precision of his bailing was more than eager to explore a potential new source of income. These walls are clad on the outside with galvanised corrugated steel ('wriggly tin') with a window of transparent polycarbonate through which the golden straw is clearly visible, giving a conjunction of the industrial and the organic ('the slick and the hairy') that is one of the building's charms.

Only the west wing and the staircase pods are at ground level; the rest of the house is raised on slender columns with an open 'undercroft' space below where Till and Wigglesworth intend to keep chickens. (Another of the house's charms is its sense of being a rural oasis in the middle of a city.) The main street elevation is pleasingly organic and eclectic and a direct contradiction to the perceived view of modern architecture as minimal and high tech. Adjoining the chunky metal-clad west wing is an open deck, then the largely timber-clad, slightly projecting kitchen area with its seemingly random arrangement of horizontal slit windows ('the bee-hive'), then the heavily glazed walls of the living space which take advantage of the maximum sunlight afforded by the south-western orientation. The roof – covered, we are told, in grass planted with wild flowers and strawberries – slopes dramatically up from west to east.

The office block is raised on chunky piers made of recycled rubble enclosed in metal cages ('gabions'). According to Wigglesworth, an evangelical green, the construction of buildings in the developed world accounts for 50 per cent of the consumption of raw materials and 22 per cent of manufacturing energy consumption while before the introduction of landfill tax construction waste accounted for 30 per cent of all UK waste. So recycling construction materials is a dual imperative. (The effect is spoiled somewhat by the knowledge that planners insisted on the insertion of a loadbearing column in the centre of each pier in case the wire cages melted in a fire and the rubble spilled out, leading to the building's inevitable collapse.) Between the piers and the block itself are small round green boxes – secured only with a locating pin – containing springs that absorb the vibrations caused by passing trains. The defensive wall facing the railway is made of hessian bags filled with a mixture of sand, cement and lime that were watered with a watering can as they were put up. Over time the concrete will harden and the hessian disintegrate to give a highly rusticated effect. The sleepers that act as lintels for the seemingly randomly placed windows were found on site. The cladding on the house side resembles a shiny grey quilted jacket buttoned on to the structure – in fact, it is silicone-faced fibreglass with an insulating layer and an inner lining, quilted by a sail-maker. It has a life expectancy of 60 years, though it could easily be unbuttoned and replaced with something else.

The main entrance is via a porch to the west wing supported by a column made from a single yew tree (another conjunction of nature and manufacture). Inside the west wing at ground level are a utility room, bedroom, toilet and bathroom. The inner surfaces of the straw-bale walls are rendered throughout in lime plaster that allows them to breathe and accommodates movement. While the postmodern notion of deliberately exposing a building's innards (as in the polycarbonate 'window' that allows a view of the straw bales) has become something of a design cliché, the imperfect interior finish on a new house is the antithesis of the smooth base walls we have come to expect. It may have been my imagination, but the rather cheerless bedroom did seem to smell of straw. The composting toilet – 'a permanently ventilated waterless chamber which over time produces a rich liquid manure (completely sterile) and a small amount of odourless solid compost' – was not on view. Its green credentials are marred slightly by the fact that it was man-ufactured in Sweden then flown to a supplier in Canada, from whom it was purchased and flown back to Europe.

The freestanding staircase (on wheels, like the stairs that let you on and off a plane, to avoid problems from vibrations) leads to the main floor of the house, a dramatic single space that thrills after the somewhat poky west-wing rooms. From west to east this contains a kitchen, nestled under the lower end of the sloping roof, an airy double-height living space and a dining room cum meetings room. The main feature of the remarkably un-designery kitchen is a long table, its top made largely of recycled glass, that continues through a slot in the wall to the outside deck. The living space is punctured by a conical larder that projects through the roof and by the industrial steel girders that support the library tower; the tower mezzanine extends into the room, providing a platform for a spare bed. The dining area is an intermediate space that can function either as part of the house or can be closed off by big tim-ber sliding doors to become part of the office.

The colours of the house are warm and natural; the staircase leading to the office (accessed from ground level by its own front door or from the dining room) is industrial metal, signalling a transition to the serious business of work. As Wigglesworth describes it, the office is a 'modernist gem inside the Flintstone exterior of the sand bags'. The first floor is let to tenants, with Wigglesworth Architects located above on a top-lit bridge that spans the length of the building.

Wigglesworth's tour of 9/10 Stock Orchard Street avoids poetic and pretentious architect-speak or embarrassing confessions about lifestyle and personal habits in favour of an approach grounded admirably in the pragmatic and the political. Indeed, virtually every architectural decision is described in terms of its contribution to her vision of a 'sustainable building for living and working' that would use recycled materials, be energy efficient and fun. And to judge by the interest the building has aroused and the favourable comments of local people, the house not only takes little from the environment but has succeeded in giving something back to an area where the rest of the post-war architecture is for the most part decidedly grim.

ADDRESS 9/10 Stock Orchard
Street, London N7 9RW
(020 7607 9200)
OPEN details from

www.swarch.co.uk
ADMISSION £2/£1
ACCESS ground floor only
UNDERGROUND Caledonian Road

SUTTON HOUSE

Preserved in an attic room in Sutton House is a red-and-black mural of an eye, believed, according to the caption, to date from 1985 and to be 'the emblem of the rock group P.S.I.' The parlour two floors down is one of only three London rooms (including one at Hampton Court, see page 222) completely lined with 16th-century linenfold panelling. That either has survived is something of a miracle – the panelling because it was dismantled by thieves who moved in following the eviction of the squatters who painted the mural, sold, and then restored to the National Trust by a wary dealer. The mural because the policy underlying the house's restoration in the early 1990s seems to have been one of uncovering the many layers of its history rather than simply fixing on a set period to preserve.

Sutton House was built by Sir Ralph Sadleir, a privy councillor to Henry VIII, in 1535. Like Eastbury (see page 280), it follows a standard Tudor H plan, with the rear legs of the H, which flank the south-facing courtyard, skewed to accommodate existing buildings. The bar of the H was occupied by the great hall, entered via a screened passage to the east with a dais to the west and the great chamber above; the service wing was to the east and the family wing to the west. In the attic floor beneath the gabled roof were rooms for servants and children.

Sadleir had started his career at the age of 14 in the Fenchurch Street household of Thomas Cromwell, soon rising to become the king's chief advisor's right-hand man. Attracted perhaps by Hackney's reputation for clean, healthy air, Cromwell was in the 1530s rebuilding a house in nearby Clapton known as King's Place, for which purpose Henry had given him 100 oaks from the royal forest at Enfield. Though Sadleir's relatively modest house, unusually, was of red brick – hence its original name of 'bryk place' – it's likely some of this timber found its way into the frames of its heavy mullioned windows and the bargeboards of its four gables.

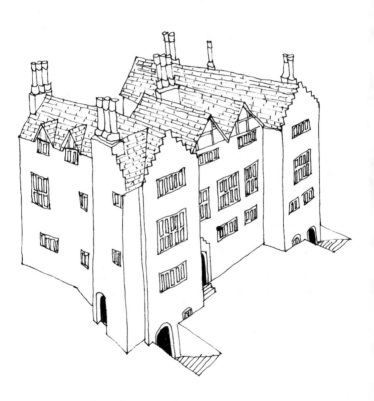

Following Cromwell's execution in 1540 for refusing to sanction the king's marriage to Anne of Cleves, Sadleir managed to disassociate himself sufficiently from his past master to survive in office until midway through the reign of Elizabeth I. Meanwhile in 1550 he sold his house to John Machell, a wealthy wool merchant and sheriff of London whose family lost possession when their acquisition of a large estate in Cambridgeshire led them into debt. From c. 1630 the house was owned by silk merchant Captain John Milward, who was also forced to surrender it following the collapse of silk prices. For almost a century from 1657 it was a girls' school (Hackney had so many of these it became known as 'The Ladies' University of Female Arts').

In 1741 John Cox took over the house with the intention of modernising it to earn higher rents. He transformed Sadleir's Tudor pile into an elegant Georgian manor, replacing the mullioned windows with sashes, concealing the gables behind a parapet, removing the large Tudor chimneys and adding a small cottage to the rear. Luckily most of his alterations were done on the cheap, so the traces of the Tudor building – including many of the original fireplaces and some decoration – were left in place behind them. On the death of his first tenant Mary Tooke, the widow of a prominent Huguenot merchant and the first of many occupants of French Protestant descent, he divided the house into two with most of the great hall going to the western house and the cottage to the eastern portion. For most of the 19th century the latter functioned as a school. In 1896 Canon Evelyn Gardiner bought both halves and reunited them into St John's Church Institute, a recreational club for local men. The house was bought by the National Trust in 1938 and was used as offices for charities, Hackney Social Services and the trades union ASTMS until the 1980s. In 1990–94, after a public campaign to prevent it from being developed into flats, it was restored to its present form.

The entrance in the eastern corner of the central recessed front is via the original front door, moved to this position by Cox. Though the façade of the east wing was rendered in the 19th century, the west side retains its Tudor brick and some diaperwork. The space that was once the great hall is still divided much as it was by Cox and is now occupied by the reception area, which retains its 18th-century panelling, and the entrance corridor. The linenfold parlour at the front of the west wing is completely lined in 204 individually carved panels, to breathtaking effect. The panels date from about 1535 and were probably moved here by Machell from his previous house, as was common practice. The simple oak furniture allows the beauty of the varnished wood to dominate – an effect that can presumably be regarded as a return to form after the excesses of Milward, traces of whose decorative scheme of corn yellow, emerald green and mahogany red can still be glimpsed. The rear of this wing is occupied by the present café.

In the damp-smelling cellar is a display of recuperated building materials including the original carved bargeboards. In the stairwell, overlooking the internal courtyard and therefore ignored in Cox's showy remake, is one of the original mullioned windows. The staircase itself was probably installed by Milward. Towards the top are fragments of his stencilled gold murals including a *faux* strapwork frieze and a pair of griffins intended to resemble elaborately carved newel posts. The remains have all the poignant romance of a ruin, as well as providing a strong flavour of how the house must have looked after his sumptuous decorating spree.

The gallery above the café (originally divided into two rooms) has also been left in a suspended state of discovery, with layers peeled back to reveal the original brickwork, a Tudor stone fireplace decorated with Milward's coat-of-arms hiding behind a staircase installed by Cox, and fragments of late-18th-century wallpaper. The little chamber above the linenfold parlour has an original stone fireplace and plainer panelling dating from the late 16th century, some of which swings open to reveal the fragile lath and plaster beneath. The majestic great chamber beyond, also fully panelled, gives a sense of the grandeur the house once possessed. Opposite a full-length painting of the swaggering Sir Ralph are portraits of his descendants by Mary Beale (1632-99), one of the first professional female portrait painters.

The room at the front of the east wing – originally the principal bed-chamber – is restored as a Victorian study. The east parlour below, originally a buttery, has panelling and a fine dentil box cornice installed by Cox. The overall effect including the grey-green colour scheme closely resembles the rooms occupied by Dr Johnson (see page 36) at much the same time. The kitchen behind – which became the entrance hall of Cox's eastern residence – has been restored as nearly as possible to its Tudor form. The courtyard was enclosed at the turn of the 20th century by the 200-seat Wenlock Barn by Lionel Crane (the son of painter Walter). The austere chapel in the east cellar was designed by Edward Maufe, later architect of Guildford Cathedral.

On the top floor with its low arches and doorways is an exhibition about Sutton House's history – including the mystery mural – most of it researched during the 1980s. Among the findings was that Thomas Sutton, founder of Charterhouse Hospital and School in Clerkenwell, after whom the National Trust renamed its possession, in fact lived next door.

ADDRESS 2 and 4 Homerton High Street, London E9 6JQ (020 8986 2264)
OPEN February to December: Friday and Saturday, 11.00–17.30; Sunday and bank holiday Mondays, 11.30–17.30
ADMISSION £2.10/50p/family ticket £4.70
ACCESS ground floor only
RAIL Hackney Central

[richmond/ twickenham]

Asgill House   **178**
Ham House   **181**
Marble Hill House   **189**
Strawberry Hill   **195**

ASGILL HOUSE

Visiting this gem is a triple delight: for the beauty and geometric perfection of the house itself; for the pleasure of seeing an architectural masterpiece actually used as a home; and for the ingenious way a holiday villa built almost a quarter of a millennium ago has been adapted for modern-day full-time occupation with minimum disruption to its plan and spirit.

Built in the 1760s towards the end of the vogue for Palladianism that was already being eroded by such gothic extravaganzas as Horace Walpole's nearby Strawberry Hill (see page 195), Asgill House is the smallest and perhaps most perfect villa designed by Robert Taylor, who preceded John Soane (see page 58) as architect of the Bank of England. It was intended as a summer and weekend retreat for merchant banker Sir Charles Asgill. Basically a Bath-stone cube with angled bays to the sides of the ground floor, the house was transformed almost beyond recognition in the 1840s by the addition of a bulky wing to the front. This provided the service areas necessary for full-time occupation once the railway made Richmond commutable from central London. After falling derelict in the 1960s it was restored as nearly as possible to its original form in 1969–70 by Fred Hauptfuhrer, who still lives in the house.

Asgill House is built on a small, awkward site, which discipline may account for its intricate geometry. Originally a narrow entrance hall was flanked by two ovals. The one on the right still contains the wonderfully sinuous staircase; in the Victorian transformation the one on the left became a rectangular inner hall, which was adapted during the 1969–70 restoration with the addition of a cloakroom. The door to the left leads to the spacious drawing room, a rectangle enhanced by the large bay. Mirroring this on the other side of the house is an identical space now used as a kitchen. Between them (originally accessed via a door opposite the entrance, where the cloakroom now is) is an octagon – the largest and

most elegant room in the house – which would have served as an entrance hall for visitors arriving by river, as at nearby Marble Hill (see page 189).

Luckily most of the interior's delicate mouldings and cornices are still intact – their restraint can be appreciated by comparing the surrounds of the three windows in the drawing-room bay with the cruder variations around the subsequently opened windows at the front and back, or the heavy cornice with its stylised plants with the spare geometry of those in the other rooms (thankfully the pelmets positioned at every available opportunity have been removed). The double-door access to the octagon is also Victorian but the fireplaces in both rooms are original – though Taylor's arrangement in the octagon of two fireplaces set on the diagonal, their chimneys cleverly concealed in the leftover triangles of the plan, has been replaced by a centrally positioned single fireplace. This now has a matching fibreglass overmantel made by the props department of the Royal Opera House from a design uncovered in a pattern book in Oxford's Taylorean Institute (endowed by the architect).

The first floor includes an octagonal study above the ground-floor octagon. The master bedroom above the sitting room has an arched screen with fluted Ionic columns to create a bed alcove, a Palladian device used also at Marble Hill. An en-suite bathroom has been ingeniously tucked into the leftover space of the antechamber. Taylor knew how to pack incident into his house's small spaces, as in the landing where a remarkable vista across the house is created using a pair of arches supported on columns similar to those in the bedroom.

Restoration – supported initially by the Historic Buildings Council and the GLC – is ongoing: recent improvements include reactivating shutters and recessing radiators to make them less obtrusive. And some of the villa's mysteries – the exact path of the stairway leading down to the basement or the original purpose of various rooms – are still up for debate.

ADDRESS Old Palace Lane, Richmond, Surrey
OPEN write for an appointment
ACCESS ground floor only
ADMISSION £6
UNDERGROUND/RAIL Richmond

HAM HOUSE

> It is so blocked up and barricaded with walls, vast trees, and gates, that you
> think of yourself an hundred miles off and an hundred years back. The old
> furniture is so magnificently ancient, dreary and decayed, that at every step
> one's spirits sink, and all my passion for antiquity could not keep them up…
> In this state of pomp and tatters my nephew intends [Ham] shall remain.
> Horace Walpole, 1770

Often referred to as 'Sleeping Beauty' or 'the house time forgot', Ham House was in fact seriously and serially meddled with during its first century before the rot of poverty set in. Built between 1608 and 1610, like its exact contemporary Charlton (see page 258) it was designed on a regular Jacobean H plan, though the symmetry promised by the façade breaks down immediately inside as the imposing entrance hall stretches off to the left with service spaces to the right in accordance with Tudor tradition. And though the north front has been rebuilt rather than redesigned, the south front was transformed in the 1670s by the addition of a grand suite of rooms filling the space between the H's two legs and spilling out at their sides.

Ham was built for former naval captain Sir Thomas Vavasour but by 1626 had passed to the dashing William Murray (to judge by the portrait in the duchess' private closet), whose uncle (like Charlton's owner Sir Adam Newton) had been personal tutor to one of the sons of James I, in this case the ill-fated Charles. William joined the royal establishment as a whipping boy who would be punished for the prince's misdemeanours. On Charles' accession he was appointed gentleman of the bedchamber and with Inigo Jones – architect of the radical Palladian Queen's House designed less than a decade later (see page 270) – was a member of a select group of collectors, connoisseurs and arbiters of taste who advised the king. In 1637 he embarked on an ambitious programme of remodelling and refurbishment at Ham cut short by the outbreak of the Civil War in 1642. Following Charles' execution in 1649 he went into exile in Holland (where he presumably knew the young Robert Pennington, later owner of Southside, see page 114); his house was transferred to his wife and following her death in the same year was willed to their four daughters, the three youngest of whom were hunchbacks.

Elizabeth, the eldest daughter, was to inherit the title bestowed on her father in 1643, becoming Countess of Dysart on his death in 1655. In 1648 she had married wealthy landowner Sir Lionel Tollemache; the couple lived mainly at his family seat of Helmingham Hall in Suffolk and their London home in Covent Garden. Highly educated and politically astute, Elizabeth cultivated Cromwell, with whom she is said to have had a liaison, while at the same time risking her life to work for Charles II's restoration through the Sealed Knot, a secret society that gathered information on behalf of the court in exile (her pseudonym was Mrs Legge). A decade after the restoration she married John Maitland, 2nd Earl (and subsequently Duke) of Lauderdale, secretary of state for Scotland and a powerful member of Charles' inner cabinet, the Cabal – with whom she had probably already had an affair. (Certainly she had persuaded Cromwell to save him from the block during his nine-year imprisonment in the interregnum and had entertained him openly at Ham after she was widowed in 1669.) The couple married soon after the death of Lauderdale's wife in 1671 (see Lauderdale House, page 150) and almost immediately embarked on an ambitious programme to extend Ham with a suite of rooms designed by Elizabeth's cousin William Bruce.

Ham's north (entrance) front is spectacular – a three-storey red-brick structure with stone dressings consisting of five bays between projecting wings with the junctions effected by rectangular cloistered blocks originally topped by turrets with ogee caps. The frontispiece above the door was removed in the 1740s; the Italianate busts in niches between the ground- and first-floor windows were moved from the garden wall c. 1800.

The great hall is enhanced by the decision of Elizabeth's son Lionel, 3rd Earl of Dysart, to take down much of the ceiling, to create a double-height well. The black-and-white marble floor probably dates from 1610; the full-height figures of Mars and Minerva on the chimneypiece may have been modelled on William Murray and his wife Katherine. Among the portraits are the women two of the family eloped with: Henrietta Cavendish, who ran off with the 3rd Earl's son, and Charlotte Walpole (whose uncle, Horace, lived across the river at Strawberry Hill; see page 195), who secretly married the 5th Earl in 1760. The family living room at the front of the eastern wing was transformed into a chapel by Elizabeth and Lauderdale in the 1670s. The great staircase behind it was remodelled by William Murray in 1638-39 as a magnificent prelude to his state-of-the-art state apartments on the *piano nobile*. It succeeds in impressing: the robust balustrades are decorated with remarkably bold carvings of arms (originally highlighted with gilding); on the walls hang copies of paintings by Miguel de la Cruz, probably gifts from Charles I who commissioned them when he and Murray were in Spain together in 1623 to search for a royal bride; the plaster ceiling is in the restrained style recently pioneered by Inigo Jones.

The museum room above the chapel was originally a bedroom. Among the paintings in the hall gallery (above the great hall and formerly the great dining room, the first of Murray's ambitious new suites) is a double portrait of the Duke and Duchess of Lauderdale c. 1679, looking like two fleshy, well-fed villains – he smug, she wanton – living off the fat of the land, as indeed they were. A highly educated and intelligent man of coarse manners and passionate furies, the fiercely royalist Lauderdale used his iron rule of Scotland – where his task was to impose the absolute power of the crown on church and state – to line his own pockets. (According to his enemy, historian Bishop Gilbert Burnet: 'The sense of religion that a long imprisonment had impressed on his mind was soon erased by a course of luxury and sensuality, which ran him into a great expense, and which he stuck at nothing to support; and the fury of his behaviour heightened the severity of his ministry and made it more like the cruelty of an inquisition than the legality of justice.') The volatile Elizabeth was, if anything, worse. (Burnet: 'The Lady Dysart came to have so much power over the Lord Lauderdale that it lessened him much in the esteem of all the world; for he delivered himself up to all her humours and passions... [She] was wanting in no methods that could bring her money, which she lavished out in a most profuse vanity.')

The centrepiece of Murray's apartments, the north drawing room (which doubled as a state bedroom before the 1670 additions), was probably designed by Franz Cleyn, who also supplied the inset paintings of cavorting *putti*. The most prominent feature is the baroque fireplace surround with its distinctive twisted and spiral-fluted columns supporting Ionic capitals topped by an overmantel featuring more chubby *putti*. The sumptuous furniture includes an Indian carpet, a set of French chairs with gilded arms and legs in the shape of dolphins and an extremely costly and complex ivory cabinet, all probably purchased by Elizabeth in Paris in the 1670s. The long gallery that runs the depth of the west wing retains most of its original panelling. Among the portraits is one of Elizabeth at around the time of the birth of the second of the 11 children she bore between 1648 and 1661 (five of whom survived into adulthood) with a black servant, a status symbol at the time. Above the cloisters is the green closet, designed as a contrast to the scale of the long gallery to display miniatures in an intimate setting, its ceiling embellished by more Cleyn *putti*. The library closet and library in the south-west corner – with direct access from the duke's closet below – represent one of the first purpose-built facilities in the country, perhaps reflecting Lauderdale's unhappy experience at Lauderdale House where the weight of his books threatened the building's structural safety.

Along the central flank of the south (garden) front run the antechamber to the queen's bedchamber, the bedchamber itself and the queen's closet. The antechamber still has what was probably the original 1672-74 swirling olivewood graining and 'blewe Damusk' hangings from about a decade later (now faded to a depressing brown). Though the queen's

bedchamber, placed pivotally at the centre of the south front, is the most magnificent of the rooms added by the Lauderdales, its scale is unimpressive. The richly decorated closet beyond retains most of its original decor including the ceiling painting by Antonio Verrio, who had worked for Charles II, the parquet floor emblazoned with the Lauderdale ducal coronet and crimson hangings.

The ground floor of the Lauderdale extension consists of enfilades of rooms for the duke and duchess on either side of the central marble dining room, its black and white floor replaced by the parquet installed along with the stamped-leather hangings by the 4th Earl of Dysart (Elizabeth's great-grandson) in the 1750s. The rooms to the east comprise a withdrawing room, the volury room (in the wing of the original house), which takes its name from the birdcages flanking the bay window, and the duchess' two private closets where she would read, write and take tea with her close friends. Both have painted ceilings by Verrio, that of the inner private closet depicting the penitent Mary Magadalen (who looks not unlike the duchess herself) – perhaps suggesting secret Catholic leanings. Alongside various family portraits including those of her parents and eldest son is a startlingly erotic overmantel of *Medea* by William Gouw Ferguson.

To the west of the marble dining room are the duke's dressing room, a bedroom (in the wing) and the duke's closet. The bedroom – hung with almost Rothko-like modern reinterpretations of the original damask – was the nursery in which Elizabeth's 11 children were raised before the 1670s additions. It was then occupied by the duchess; in 1673 she ceded it to her husband but she was back by 1677, at which point he moved to the volury room or napped in the 'sleeping chayre' in the closet. The arrangement of having to cross each other's bedrooms to reach the private closets seems bizarre – the only logic being that Elizabeth was understandably attached to her two inner sanctums but at the same time wanted easy access to the bathroom below her bedroom. The suite of two rooms – a smaller space for the bath-tub, which would have been enveloped by curtains to create a steamy atmosphere like a Turkish bath, with a larger outer room with a bed for relaxing in afterwards – can be seen in the basement along with the kitchens, whose welcome-to-touch display is one of Ham's few concessions to children.

At the front of the west wing are the steward's hall and back parlour, for the use of senior domestic staff, who also had their own bedrooms in the garret where all the servants slept. The cosy wood-panelled rooms contain photographs of more recent family (the house was presented to the National Trust in 1948) as well as a portrait of Lauderdale's brother, whom Elizabeth tried to sue for repayment of her husband's £5000 funeral expenses following his death in 1682 and who in turn contested his brother's will, which left almost everything to his wife. In any case, the Lauderdales had run up so much debt with their lavish refurbishment of Ham and various Scottish properties that even the sale of most of their assets, the mortgaging of Ham and the pawning of pictures and jewellery failed to satisfy their creditors.

Elizabeth retreated to Ham where she died in 1698 following several lonely years in which it would seem from a letter to one of her daughters that she repented at least the consequences of her ways:

> All my movable estate is sold (even to the disfurnishing of this my dwelling house)… And now what can I or what must I further do? But condemn my own mistaken measurs which have proved so fatal that should I be cutt in pieces to gratify owr Enemyes none of my children nor their children would be the better.

ADDRESS Ham, Richmond, London TW10 7RS (020 8940 1950; www.national-trust.org.uk/hamhouse) **OPEN** April to October: Monday to Wednesday, Saturday and Sunday, 13.00–17.00 **ADMISSION** £6/£3/family ticket £15 **GETTING THERE** Underground to Richmond, then bus 371; ferry from Orleans Road, Twickenham

MARBLE HILL HOUSE

Contemporary with Lord Burlington's Chiswick House (see page 209), the initial plan for Marble Hill was by Colen Campbell (1676–1729), author in 1715 of the influential survey of classical architecture in England *Vitruvius Britannicus*, architect to the Prince of Wales (the future George II) and with Burlington the foremost champion of the new Palladian movement. Whereas the baroque manner forged by Christopher Wren, who remained surveyor of works until 1718, was associated with the Tory party and the Stuarts, Palladianism was the style of the Whigs (Whig prime minister Robert Walpole chose Campbell as architect for Houghton Hall) and the Hanoverian succession. It is therefore no coincidence that one of London's finest Palladian villas should have been commissioned by Henrietta Howard (c. 1688–1767), woman of the bedchamber to the Princess of Wales and the mistress with whom vice-chamberlain Lord Hervey declared the prince would spend 'every evening of his life, three or four hours in [her] company'.

The first 43 years of Henrietta's life were dogged by financial dependency, from the age of 17 on her first husband Charles Howard, the improvident youngest son of the 5th Earl of Suffolk, in whose household she lived after she was orphaned at 13. (The household was based partly at Audley End, a Jacobean mansion of the type Marble Hill was to supersede, designed by the architect of Charlton House, see page 258.) After a spell going by assumed names in London to avoid angry creditors, the couple moved to Hanover in 1713 to 'ingratiate themselves with the future Sovereign of England' as her future friend and neighbour, Walpole's son Horace (see page 195), was to put it. Returning to England in the retinue of George I, Henrietta was given a post in the household of the Prince of Wales and Charles was made groom of the bedchamber to the king. When George I and his son quarrelled Henrietta followed her royal mistress, leading her husband to dismiss her as his wife. Her loyalty was rewarded in 1723 when the prince awarded her a settlement of £11,500. Her friend Lord Ilay bought her some land near his own home of Whitton Place near Twickenham and Palladian champion Lord Herbert reduced Campbell's plans to a more affordable scale. In June 1724 builder Roger Morris set to work, though 12 months later construction was interrupted for three years, perhaps because Henrietta's husband was demanding money. The house was finished in summer 1729 and in 1731 Henrietta was made more secure by a legacy from her brother-in-law, on whose death her husband became 9th Earl of Suffolk and Henrietta the Countess of Suffolk. Her troublesome spouse died two years later. In 1737 she married the Hon. George Berkeley and the decade until his death, spent largely at Marble Hill, was perhaps the happiest time of her life, marred only by the death in 1744 of her only son Henry at the age of 37.

Heavier and more solid than the dainty dolls' houses writ large that are Asgill (see page 178) and Chiswick, Marble Hill is nevertheless a Palladian gem of startling simplicity. A near-cube three storeys high and five bays wide, its road front has a projecting pedimented centrepiece with a rusticated base topped by four double-height Ionic pilasters. The centrepiece of the plainer river façade to the south is unadorned though the proportions of both fronts are enhanced by a slightly projecting platband between the ground floor and *piano nobile* and the banded entablature beneath the eaves.

As at Asgill House there are in effect two central halls: a lobby to the north containing the staircase and a grander space to the river, which at the time provided the safest and most comfortable means of transport. The low ceiling of the riverside hall is supported by four Ionic columns in imitation of the arrangement of the central court of a Roman house. In the south-east corner of the plan is the breakfast parlour, small but well proportioned with an elaborate arched screen designed by Herbert. The geometrical patterned wallpaper is a reproduction of samples found in the room that probably date from the tenancy at the end of the cen-

tury of Mrs Fitzherbert, ill-treated mistress of another Prince of Wales (see Buckingham Palace, page 18). On the walls hang Campbell's designs for the house: the first (c. 1723) has single-storey service wings to the sides in the manner of Palladio's Villa Emo; the second (published in the third volume of the *Vitruvius Britannicus* as 'A house in Twittenham [*sic*]') has no pilasters or pediment on the north-front centrepiece but a double staircase leading to the *piano nobile* as at Chiswick. Among the likenesses of Henrietta's friends is a bust of neighbour and exact contemporary Alexander Pope (1688–1744) who helped her design the grounds and kept an eye on the property while she was at court. His 1725 tribute 'On a certain Lady at Court' demonstrates the esteem in which he held her: 'I know the thing that's most uncommon;/(Envy be silent and attend!)/I know a Reasonable Woman,/Handsome and witty, yet a Friend.' In the south-west corner is the dining parlour, hung with boards detailing the history of the house; the 'paper room' in the north-east corner has one of the better stately-home videos.

The grand mahogany staircase is a translation into timber of a balustraded stone stair. The story of how the boards, some of which are over half a metre wide, were procured illustrates the arrogant plunder that's still having an environmental impact today – George II simply instructed an English captain in the bay of Honduras to land and cut down some trees, incidentally nearly provoking a war with Spain as he failed to seek permission from the Spanish governor. The 'great room' above the riverside hall is an 8-metre cube with a deeply coved ceiling that projects into the attic storey. Symmetry is retained by the introduction of two sham doors mirroring those leading to Henrietta's bedchamber and dressing room on either side. The elaborately carved mouldings and frieze featuring sungod Apollo are by James Richards, successor to Grinling Gibbons as master carver in wood to the king. Peacocks symbolising Juno, queen of the gods, appear in the decoration and on the base of a marble-topped sidetable designed for Henrietta by William Kent. The views of Roman ruins by G P Panini above the fireplace and doors were commissioned for the room in 1738.

Henrietta's bedroom, hung with striking green-silk damask, follows the Palladian model, with a bed alcove screened by fluted Ionic columns that echo the screen in the breakfast parlour below. Adjoining it is a smaller and simpler bedroom named after Miss Hotham, Henrietta's great-niece and companion in her later years. Mirroring Henrietta's room to the west is the dressing room, probably used to receive guests informally in the mornings as well as to get dressed, to judge by a 1767 inventory which lists it as containing seven chairs covered in green damask. The 1724 portrait of an impressively young-looking Henrietta, reclining against a classical backdrop in an attitude usually reserved for men of letters, originally belonged to Pope; she bought it in the sale following his death and gave it to Walpole to hang at Strawberry Hill. Mirroring Miss Hotham's bedchamber is the damask bedchamber, which presumably took its name from a bed hung with red damask curtains listed in the inventory.

Though the grand staircase stops at the *piano nobile*, a door on the landing open on to an elegantly simple stone staircase leading to two further storeys used to entertain intimates and as quarters for domestic staff. The staircase could also be accessed via the jib door in Henrietta's bedroom and originally led down to a service wing to the east of the house that was demolished in 1909. This was built in stages from 1741 after Henrietta's niece and nephew Dorothy and John Hobart moved in and she and her husband entertained more frequently at Marble Hill, their guests including Lord Mansfield from Kenwood (see page 139). Arranged around the upper part of the great room, this floor contains a Jacobean-style long gallery and three bedrooms used by Dorothy, John and guests which now contain a fine collection of chinoiserie.

Following Henrietta's death Marble Hill was lived in by her nephew John, after whose death it passed to her great-niece Henrietta Hotham, who rented it out to Mrs Fitzherbert and others. In 1825 it was sold to Jonathan Peel, brother of Robert, and it was occupied by his family until 1887. After standing empty for many years it was sold to property developer William Cunard; building materials had already been moved on to the site and sewers dug when a public outcry led to the house being bought by the London County Council and others to be opened as a tea-room in 1903. In 1966 it was restored and opened as the historic house we see today; since 1986 it has been run by English Heritage.

ADDRESS Richmond Road, London TW1 2NL (020 8892 5115)
OPEN 20 March to 31 September: daily, 10.00–18.00; 1 October to 31 October: daily, 10.00–17.00; closed from November 2002 until April 2003
ADMISSION £3.30/£2.50/£1.70
ACCESS ground floor only
GETTING THERE rail St Margarets/ rail and Underground Richmond

STRAWBERRY HILL

When England's first prime minister Robert Walpole died in 1745, his youngest son Horace (1717–97) decided to use part of his inheritance to buy a country house. He was lucky to find one of the last undeveloped plots of land at Twickenham, at the time only two hours' coach-ride from London and highly fashionable. (Walpole described it to a friend as having 'dowagers as plentiful as flounders'.) The house he bought in 1749 for £776 10s was a relatively modest cottage built in 1698 and known as Chopp'd Straw Hall because locals assumed its coachman owner had been able to afford it only by giving his employer's horses chopped straw and illicitly selling off the more valuable hay for his own profit. Within 50 years, Walpole – perhaps in an act of Oedipal rebellion against Houghton Hall, the house commissioned in 1722 by his father from England's leading Palladian architect Colen Campbell (see Marble Hill House, page 189) – was to use a style previously reserved largely for follies to transform his 'little plaything house' into a sprawling gothic mansion that initiated a new architectural fashion and turned the tide against classicism.

Walpole is largely remembered as a letter-writer whose first-hand accounts of politics and society are one of our most valuable sources of information on 18th-century life. The paper-thin flamboyance and aestheticism he brought to Strawberry Hill applied to the man himself: he was described by his friend Laetitia Hawkins as 'always enter[ing] a room in that style of affected delicacy, which fashion had then made almost natural… knees bent, and feet on tip-toe, as if afraid of a wet floor.' His celebrated collection of books, pictures, furniture and antiquities, plus such curiosities as Cardinal Wolsey's red hat and Charles I's death warrant, aroused the interest of many would-be visitors; the auction at which it was sold off by his descendants in 1842 took 32 days and was so hyped that spoof catalogues appeared claiming such items as a mouse that had run over Queen Adelaide's foot were included. Walpole staged lavish entertainments, at one of which – for French, Spanish and Portuguese dignitaries – he dressed in a 'cravat of Gibbons' carving, and a pair of gloves embroidered up to the elbows that had belonged to James I'. Among his close friends were poet Thomas Gray (who accompanied him on a grand tour of Europe in 1739–41), actress Kitty Clive and the Countess of Suffolk at nearby Marble Hill, whose reminiscences contributed greatly to his *Memoirs of the Reigns of George I and George II*.

The house Walpole bought – an inelegant L-shaped structure at the eastern corner of the present building – could best be described as having potential. His first job was to stamp its unpromising exterior with his personality by adding new façades and bays incorporating gothic elements drawn from the architecture of medieval castles and abbeys: battlements, finials and gothic ogee and quatrefoil windows. His attitude to borrowing, inside and out, had an air of 'make-believe' – designs for tombs were re-used as fireplaces and rood screens as bookcases with no respect for the integrity of the original. Unlike in the work of 19th-century gothicists such as A W N Pugin, these embellishments were pure confectionery, done for theatrical effect with no structural rationale and using insubstantial materials (outside lath and plaster enclosed by brick, inside wood or plasterwork) to mimic stone monumentality. Walpole and the friends who joined him in a Committee of Taste to debate and design the new work – most importantly illustrator Richard Bentley, John Chute and William Robinson of the Board of Works – wanted to do away with classical symmetry and rationality (Walpole coined the term serendipity). The effect is something like a fairytale castle stretched sideways with the expected elements rearranged at random.

In 1753–54 Walpole added a two-storey wing to the north to house the great parlour and library and in 1759 tacked the Holbein chamber on to the north-west corner. In the early 1760s he more than doubled the length of the south façade by adding an open cloister above which was the long gallery. The round tower that terminates the long gallery was

built in 1763 and the thinner Beauclerk Tower in 1776. Further rooms were added to the northern side of the long gallery, including the great north bedchamber (1770). Most of the façades of the 1750s and 1760s were designed by Chute, but the plainer, more linear offices to the south were conceived by James Essex and erected by James Wyatt in 1790. You could say Walpole had the builders in for 50 years.

Following Walpole's death Strawberry Hill passed eventually to Lady Frances Waldegrave (1821–79) whose first husband John was a descendant of Horace's brother Edward. He died a year later and she married his brother George, who took a dislike to Strawberry Hill after being imprisoned by Twickenham magistrates for 'riotous behaviour' (an event that led Frances to miscarry her only pregnancy). George decided to sell Walpole's collection and let the house rot (Frances, unbeknown to her husband, bought back various Reynolds paintings of her inlaws and some of the original Flanders glass from the sale). Following George's death – like his brother from syphilis – she made a third marriage, at the age of 27, to the much older George Granvill Harcourt. In 1856 she decided to restore and expand her derelict inheritance: after spending £100,000, she stopped counting. Her major change was the addition of a building linking Walpole's round tower and the Wyatt offices, containing a banqueting or drawing room, dining room, billiards room and accommodation for guests and servants. She was sensitive to Walpole's intentions and to compensate for the greater ceiling height of her grand new rooms she lowered the lawn, added a floor to each of Walpole's towers and some tall, highly decorated 'Tudor' chimneypots (compensating aesthetically for the removal of his gothic finials). She also filled in the cloisters to provide staff accommodation and linked the Holbein chamber and great north bedchamber.

Harcourt died in 1861 and two years later Frances married Chichester Fortescue, a Whig minister and secretary for Ireland. Strawberry Hill became the Liberal salon of the day, with guests including Palmerston, Gladstone and the Prince and Princess of Wales, and Frances, whose fame eclipsed her husband's, was known as the Queen of Dublin. In

1923 the house was bought for St Mary's Catholic Teacher Training College (which still occupies it) and Sebastian Pugin Powell, grand-nephew of A W N, designed a chapel and various accommodation. Extensive restoration was undertaken by Albert Richardson after World War II.

The tour begins in the little parlour, originally occupied by the stair-well of Chopp'd Straw Hall. The extent of Walpole's sleight-of-hand and striving for effect can be seen in the ogee windows, which look per-fect from the outside but inside have to be truncated to squeeze in beneath the low ceiling. In 1750 Walpole had 450 pieces of Flanders glass depicting peasants at work, stories from the scriptures, birds, flowers and coats of arms shipped to England; what remains of the collection – often cut up and arranged with no respect for narrative – is one of the unex-pected delights of Strawberry Hill. Originally the parlour walls were painted in a 'gothic paper of stone colour', as Walpole put it in his *Description of the Villa* printed on his own press, in line with his desire to create the atmosphere of 'gloomth' evoked in his pioneering gothic novel *The Castle of Otranto* (1764). The fireplace surround, like most of the dec-oration in the house, is based on a copy from a book of a bit of a medieval cathedral, here a bishop's tomb from Westminster Abbey. This and the bizarre rococo chimneypiece in the yellow bedchamber next door are the work of Bentley.

The main entrance to the house was from the London road, which Walpole's additions abutted, leading the more powerful Lady Walde-grave to have the thoroughfare diverted. Outside the front door is a colonnaded 'oratory' with a basin for 'holy water' and a niche in which Walpole placed a bronze saint. In this cloister (designed by Chute) is a Chinese bowl in which Walpole's cat drowned trying to catch goldfish, inspiring Gray's poem 'Ode on the Death of a Favourite Cat' with the lines: 'Not all that tempts your wand'ring eyes/And heedless hearts, is lawful prize;/Nor all, that glistens, gold.' Here both the earnest playful-ness of Walpole's vision and the flimsiness of the structure supporting it are apparent: the cloister is vaulted with papier-mâché and the rust from

the nails holding the laths in place can be glimpsed through the mock-stone rendering.

Walpole's gloomy hall – grey ceiling, grey floor, grey walls – was a ridiculously scaled-down version of a medieval great hall, just as Bentley's rococo staircase is an uncomfortably cramped replica of a stair from Rouen cathedral. For Walpole this hall was 'the most particular and chief beauty of the Castle', but Lady Waldegrave obviously disagreed. She embarked on a programme of prettification that included installing a beautiful tiled floor and a fleur-de-lys-studded blue ceiling best seen from the landing, which Walpole had decked out as an armoury. The adjacent great parlour or refectory – the first of Walpole's extensions beyond the confines of Chopp'd Straw Hall – is at the opposite end of the house from the kitchen in the round tower with no possible indoor route. Bentley's extravagant chimneypiece with its several finials is one of the few reminders of Walpole's conception here; the blue and gold wallcoverings that give the room its character are Lady Waldegrave's.

The breakfast room above the little parlour was Walpole's living room before he extended the house. The generous bay with its three windows with glass depicting the story of the prodigal son set in no particular order was originally shaded by a lime tree Walpole planted to increase the gloomth. Lady Waldegrave refurbished the room as a 'Turkish boudoir' (it was described by George Bernard Shaw as 'the wickedest room in England') and today it is her gold velvet tent-like ceiling hangings, Moorish fretwork, blue silk walls and blue velvet sofas that survive.

The library is one of the most nonsensically decorated of Walpole's rooms, its book-lined walls fronted by an unevenly proportioned, cloister-like series of gothic arches (designed by Chute after yet more ecclesiastical precedents) that swing open to give access to the books. The Holbein chamber, designed by Bentley to house Walpole's collection of 20 original and 34 copied Holbeins, reflects the royal nature of the portraiture in an elaborate papier-mâché ceiling based on that of a bedchamber at Windsor Castle. Though the room borrows the Palladian device of a screened bed alcove (modelled from Rouen cathedral), the plan, which has the entrance into the alcove rather than into the main part of the room so anyone coming in has to squeeze past the bed, leaves much to be desired.

In the long gallery Walpole's wedding-cake elaboration reaches its peak. Opposite the windows are recesses lined with mirrors edged in fretwork in a Moorish style that reflects the taste of new committee member Thomas Pitt, who had travelled to Iberia. The ceiling (designed by Chute) is a series of elaborate gilded papier-mâché swirls up to 2 metres deep that appear to spin out of the recesses like icing from a cake-decorator's nozzle. (Their origin is less fanciful – papier-mâché was made by barefoot women and children who risked their lives by treading down rags in lead solution.) Lady Waldegrave spent £20,000 (Walpole's total budget for the house including the purchase price) on shipping the floor from a Viennese villa she had visited on her honeymoon.

Walpole's 'tribune' – a small, once crammed treasure chest for the display of his coins, medals, miniatures and enamels – has a quatrefoil plan and domed ceiling. He referred playfully to this room of worldly goods as 'the chapel' – which is ironically what it became after the arrival of St Mary's. The drawing room in the round tower, designed late in the day by master confectioner Robert Adam, looks a model of restraint after Walpole's incomparably more sugary fare.

ADDRESS Waldegrave Road, London TW1 4SX (020 8240 4044) **OPEN** 31 March to 20 October: Sundays only, tours at 14.00 and 15.30

ADMISSION £5/£4.25 **ACCESS** none **GETTING THERE** rail Strawberry Hill/Underground Richmond, then bus 33

[west london]

Boston Manor **207**

Chiswick House **209**

Gunnersbury Park Museum **216**

Hampton Court Palace **219**

Hogarth House **228**

Osterley Park **235**

Pitshanger Manor **242**

Syon House **249**

BOSTON MANOR

This charmless three-storey red-brick Jacobean mansion was constructed in 1623 for Lady Mary Reade, who wanted the work finished in a hurry in time for her wedding to her second husband, Sir Edward Spencer of Althorp. Modest in scale (the original house probably comprised only the four left-hand bays of the present building viewed from the front door, and was just one room wide), her home had none of the court-inspired grandeur of Charlton House (see page 258), completed a decade earlier, or the fine proportions of Forty Hall (see page 300), built a decade later. In 1670 the house was bought by merchant banker James Clitherow, who probably added the two right-hand bays and the heavy stone window surrounds and architraves. The council bought the house in 1923.

The Clitherows were bankers with royal connections. Though many had large families for whom they made generous provision, there was still money to spare for local philanthropy. Another James (1766–1841) and his wife Jane became friendly through their good works with William IV and Queen Adelaide and in 1834 they were the first commoners to entertain the royal couple to dinner. According to James' sister Mary, Jane was appreciated because of her 'honest manner and sound judgement which she ventures to express to His Majesty'; Adelaide – married to a man almost 30 years her senior who had spent 20 years living with an actress and who had ten illegitimate children – described her as 'a friend who tells me true'.

The plain exterior of the house with its three gables and elaborate 19th-century stone porch gives way to a hall with an original plaster ceiling and 19th-century wood screen. If you ignore the municipal furnishings, the dining room at the front, used by the council as a meeting space, is light and pleasantly proportioned. The unatmospheric library at the rear – accessed through an ante-room in the massive spine wall that holds the chimney stacks, allowing for flush fireplaces – looks set up for WI coffee mornings. The elaborate Grinling Gibbons-style overmantel carved with cherubs and flowers is 17th century; the Puginesque ceiling was probably installed by General John Clitherow in 1847.

The heavy oak staircase, part of the original house, has its balustrade echoed on the wall opposite in painted *trompe l'oeil* – an effective joke. But nothing prepares the visitor for the breathtaking space of the first-floor state drawing room, hung with gold damask and with a ceiling – probably by Edward Stanyon, who created those in the long galleries at Blickling Hall, Norfolk and Langleys, Essex – that fully merits its description as a high-water mark of Jacobean elaboration. On a pale-green background, overlaid with an intricate pattern of enriched double ribs with strapwork in lower relief, are set roundels containing a remarkable series of emblematic high-relief figures, with faces like Hogarth caricatures, portraying the five senses, the elements, peace and plenty, war and peace, and faith, hope and charity. The equally elaborate overmantel has a central image of the angel stopping Abraham from sacrificing Isaac taken from a 1584 engraving by Abraham de Bruyn. The state bedroom at the rear has a similarly elaborate ceiling with nipple-like pendentives.

On the stairs to the second floor is a large stretch of 18th-century wallpaper showing Roman ruins – a folly, a sphinx, an obelisk – in greys and golds. Lightly protected but unrestored, it gives a magically romantic insight into how this everyday space must once have looked.

ADDRESS Boston Manor Road, Brentford, Middlesex TW8 9JX (020 8583 4535) **OPEN** April to October: Saturday, Sunday and bank holiday Mondays 14.30–17.00 **ADMISSION** free **ACCESS** limited **UNDERGROUND** Boston Manor

CHISWICK HOUSE

Most rueful biographical speculation follows the model: 'if only [subject] had had more education/money/connections, how much more could (s)he have achieved?' With Richard Boyle, 3rd Earl of Burlington, the inverse applies: if only the privileged aristocrat had had to work for a living, how many more Palladian masterpieces – or follies, depending on your viewpoint – would we have to celebrate?

Burlington was born in 1694 into one of the richest Anglo-Irish dynasties. He was appointed lord treasurer of Ireland under George I, and his wife Lady Dorothy Savile, heir of the 2nd Marquess of Halifax, was lady-in-waiting to the Princess of Wales. Following the accession of George II, Burlington was made a privy councillor in 1729. Three years later he opposed Whig prime minister Robert Walpole's excise bill against smuggling and fraud; unlike Lord Chesterfield (see Ranger's House, page 273), who on being ousted from office for the same offence defected to the opposition, Burlington resigned all his commissions and moved to Chiswick, which became his principal residence.

Like most contemporary nobility, Burlington had made a grand tour of Europe, spending almost a year in 1714–15 accumulating some 800 trunks of paintings and objects. In 1719 he embarked on a second tour, this time inspired by his studies of Giacomo Leoni's first English translation of Palladio's *Quattro Libri dell'architettura* and Colen Campbell's *Vitruvius Britannicus*, a survey of classical architecture in England. Campbell was the champion of the new Palladian movement associated with the Whigs and the Hanoverian succession. He was architect to the Prince of Wales, he prepared the initial designs for Marble Hill House (see page 189), home of the prince's mistress Henrietta Howard, and in 1722 Walpole commissioned him for his Norfolk house, Houghton Hall. Burlington had hired Campbell to rebuild his London residence,

Burlington House in Piccadilly (now the much-altered home of the Royal Academy), as early as 1719. And from about the same time the architect was involved with work on the original house at Chiswick, a mid-17th-century mansion bought by the 1st Earl of Burlington in 1682, for which the 3rd Earl later designed a new front elevation.

In 1725 the Chiswick house was badly damaged by fire and perhaps as a result Burlington set about designing the annexe that today is regarded as a manifesto of the Palladian movement. In an era when architecture became the province of scholars, Burlington's new building was characterised by a single-minded adherence (whatever the inconvenience to the house's users) to geometrical laws believed to govern the harmony of the universe and by a profusion of references to the architecture of antiquity redeployed – albeit in a sometimes playfully rococo way – not just as ornament but to confer meaning. (Burlington House was decorated to illustrate the virtues of chastity and marital fidelity; Chiswick incorporates an allegorical expression of the arts.) The precisely chiselled architectural gem is a variation on Palladio's Villa Rotonda transplanted to the north, its chimneys concealed in ranges of obelisks on the roof (a solution initially proposed by Campbell for Marble Hill). The absence of a kitchen (but copious wine cellar) has led to speculation that it was intended merely as a place for art and conversation, a cross between a gallery and a club. However, an inventory of 1770 shows that apart from a kitchen, it contained everything a functioning household might need, and certainly the bedrooms were used: Lady Burlington died in her chamber in the south-east corner in 1758, five years after her husband and a year after Charlotte, the last survivor of their three daughters.

Burlington's two-storey villa, built between 1727 and 1729, has a square plan with an octagon at its centre from which is accessed the procession of square, rectangular, circular and octagonal rooms that surround it. The entrance in what for clarity will be called the south (actually south-east) front is via a modest door in the rusticated sub-basement. A flamboyant double staircase leading to the pedimented portico supported by fluted Corinthian columns copied from the Temple of Jupiter Stator in Rome

gives direct access via a narrow passage to the central first-floor saloon or tribunal used for ceremonial occasions. The composition is topped by a shallow stepped dome above the tribunal modelled on the Roman Pantheon, its semi-circular windows replicas of those in the Baths of Diocletian. At the sides of the house stand statues of Burlington's mentors: Andrea Palladio (1508–80) and Inigo Jones (1573–1652), whose Queen's House at Greenwich of a century earlier (see page 270) is the London building Chiswick most closely resembles. The much plainer east and west façades are dominated by single Venetian windows; the north front has three Venetian windows and a staircase to the garden.

The visitor is most aware of the house's geometry on the ground floor, where the inward-looking rooms with their relatively low ceilings are obviously carved out of a larger envelope with the leftover spaces sometimes awkwardly visible. The octagonal lower tribune, ringed with Tuscan columns, the order recommended by Palladio for hallways, is lit only by daylight from its four approach passages. Below it is the vaulted wine cellar, lined with barrels. Documents indicate that the plainer rooms to the east (not open to the public) were probably a linen room and butler's pantry; those to the west – a square room at the front of the house in which a video is screened and a larger rectangular room behind with information about the villa's history – are described in the inventory as bedchambers and are presumed to be the apartment from which Burlington would emerge to receive guests waiting in the lower tribune. His portrait here, dressed in a pale-blue silk suit, pink coat and turban, shows him every inch the handsome aesthete, to his delicate arched eyebrows and elegant tapering fingers. The three rooms on the north front – a central rectangle with apses at each end leading to a small circular room (to the west) and octagon (to the east) – housed the earl's library.

As at Palladio's Villa Rotonda, vertical circulation is via circular stairtowers concealed behind the diagonals of the octagon. The largest and most dramatic room of the *piano nobile*, the central octagonal tribunal or saloon, is hung with most of the paintings known to have been here in 1761: a mix of stuffy portraits of royalty such as Anne of Austria, Louis

XIII and Charles I and his family and voluptuous mythological female nudes as in Schoonjans' *Rape of Proserpine*. The outstanding feature is the intricate, lace-like coffering of the lofty ceiling.

Above the library are the three rooms of the gallery, probably intended as an enclosed loggia for dining or exercise, their distinct geometries and interconnecting plan recalling the sequence of spaces in a Roman baths. Below the heavily gilded ceilings are relatively plain walls ornamented with a frieze of festoons of flowers and leaves emerging from woven baskets supported on female heads – perhaps an allegory of the creation of the Corinthian capital (described by Vitruvius as a female order derived from a basket placed inadvertently on top of an acanthus plant that unexpectedly breaks into leaf). The main room to the west is the red velvet room, in which Burlington displayed the major paintings in his collection, its ceiling (by William Kent, whom Burlington met in Rome on his second grand tour) an allegory of the arts. The adjacent square blue-velvet room on the entrance front, used as a study and hung in Burlington's day with Dutch landscapes, has an exotically rich ceiling supported on heavy brackets with a central allegory of architecture (also by Kent). The wealth of decoration involved in the gilded ceiling, deep-blue walls, ruched silk blinds and ornate gilded overmantel, squeezed into a tiny space, borders on camp. Opening off it was the red closet – in a sequence reminiscent of Russian dolls, the smallest of the three rooms in the west range and the one that held the most, and most precious, paintings. Opposite the red velvet room in the eastern flank is the green velvet room, also primarily for the display of pictures. The bedchamber to the south was originally hung with tapestries; the closet beyond it probably functioned as Lady Burlington's study.

To the north-east is the link building, built in 1732–33 to connect the new annexe to the old house, perhaps as a result of Burlington's decision to make Chiswick his main home. No one knows whether this was regarded as a permanent arrangement or whether he intended eventually to extend the annexe and pull down the old house as his ancestors were to do half a century later. Originally the link building consisted of a hall connected to a loggia at right-angles to it (now destroyed). The first-floor hall is subdivided by two Corinthian colonnades; the ground-floor room (now containing a sphinx and statues purloined from Hadrian's Villa outside Rome) has screens of Tuscan columns. The once lavishly furnished summer parlour beyond was described by Horace Walpole (see Strawberry Hill, page 195) as 'Lady Burlington's Dressing Room, built at her own Expence'. Today it has information about the subsequent history of the house.

After Burlington's death Chiswick was inherited by the 5th Duke of Devonshire (his grandson by his daughter Charlotte) who in 1788 pulled down the old house and added heavy flanking wings to his grandfather's delicate design. The 5th Duke's wife Georgiana (daughter of the 1st Earl of Spencer; see Spencer House, page 66) was a leading political hostess for the Whig party and Whig leader Charles Fox died at Chiswick in 1806. The 6th ('bachelor') Duke entertained Tsars Alexander 1 and Nicholas 1 and Queen Victoria and Prince Albert here; prime minister George Canning died at Chiswick in 1827. From 1858 the house was let to tenants including the Duchess of Sutherland – who received both Gladstone and Garibaldi here – the Prince of Wales (in the 1870s) and from 1892 to 1929 T S and C M Tuke, Quaker pioneers in the treatment of mental health. The Devonshires sold the house to the council in 1929 and the wings were demolished in 1956–57 under the auspices of the ministry of works to re-expose the purity of Burlington's concept. At the time his reputation was riding high: he had recently been rehabilitated by Rudolf Wittkower and others and was revered as an important precursor to the modern movement (as Richard Hewlings points out in his excellent guidebook, at the progressive Bartlett School of Architecture in London, under the guidance of Reyner Banham, English neo-Palladianism and post-1920 modernism were the only two history courses available). The house has been run by English Heritage since 1984.

In addition to his own pioneering work, Burlington fulfilled an important role as a patron, housing William Kent, musician George Frideric Handel (see page 45), poet John Gay and sculptor Guelfi in his

Piccadilly home. Even after his resignation from politics he had enough connections to obtain positions of importance for his protégés (Kent, for instance, worked on Kensington Palace, see page 90, and was made deputy surveyor of the king's works in 1735). And behind Burlington House in Piccadilly he laid out an estate of fashionable houses, two designed by himself, one by Kent, four by Campbell and two by Leoni, in streets whose names reflect the sources of his vast wealth: Cork Street for his paternal ancestors, Clifford Street for his maternal ancestors and Savile Row for his wife's family.

ADDRESS Burlington Lane, London W4 2RP (020 8995 0508) **OPEN** April to September: daily, 10.00–18.00; 1 October to 31 October: daily, 10.00–17.00; closed from 1 November to April 2003, then open Wednesday to Sunday, 10.00–18.00 **ADMISSION** £3.30/£2.50/£1.70 **ACCESS** call first to check staff availability **GETTING THERE** rail Chiswick/ Underground Turnham Green

GUNNERSBURY PARK MUSEUM

The core of the ugly neoclassical stuccoed Large Mansion that houses Gunnersbury Park Museum was built early in the 19th century by developer Alexander Copland, possibly with the involvement of Sydney Smirke, whose brother was one of Copland's executors. Though it's no longer possible to be certain which rooms were added at which point, it seems that the house as it stands today – in particular the over-extended south façade, 11 bays long with a central three-storey section with arched first-floor windows over a Doric loggia – is very much Smirke's creation, whether from before or after he was engaged as architect by financier Nathan Mayer Rothschild (1777–1836) who bought the house in 1835.

Rothschild, whose clients included the British government to whom he'd loaned money to fund the Napoleonic wars, had been advised to avoid ostentation because of the secret nature of the deals by which he had amassed his fortune. Following his death his wife Hannah set aside such concerns, holding a house-warming 'breakfast' two years later at which she entertained 500 guests at a cost of £2000 – around one-seventh of the price Nathan paid for the house and its grounds. Following Hannah's death the property passed to her son Lionel (1808–79), a friend of Disraeli who in 1858 became Britain's first practising Jewish MP after an 11-year fight for his right to be admitted to parliament without having to swear a Christian oath. (In 1875 the Rothschilds loaned Disraeli's government the funds to secure the Suez Canal, earning themselves £100,000.) Lionel's third son Leopold was a race-horse enthusiast and established a stud at Gunnersbury. All three generations were known for their philanthropy, in particular their funding of education and healthcare. The house remained in the family until it was sold to the council in 1925.

Nathan hired Smirke to make improvements as soon as he bought the house, enlarging the kitchens and servants' quarters and building an

orangery, but it was probably Hannah who commissioned the imposing French-inspired neoclassical interiors that can be glimpsed behind the museum's changing displays. The rooms to the east and west of the entrance hall were originally the parlour and library respectively. Behind the library, in the heart of the house, is a further hall or 'corridor', top lit with an oval gallery at first-floor level. Along the south elevation is a run of three grand rooms accessed via an anteroom. The central drawing room, flanked by the loggia, is an elegant space divided into three by two sets of Ionic marble columns, its prettily decorated ceiling featuring a trellis pattern and oval painting of the four seasons. The dining room to the west and drawing room to the east are higher with more heavily moulded ceilings, richer door surrounds and sturdier columns; the drawing room has a conservatory that echoes the curve of its eastern bay.

The council has laudably tried to increase the property's relevance to local people by concentrating resources on the servants' quarters – usually neglected in house restorations but here the only part set up as it was occupied. The size of this wing brings home the amount of labour involved in catering to the whims of a wealthy family and its guests before modern services arrived. The 1881 census lists Lionel's widow Charlotte in residence along with 13 female and seven male servants – two cooks, a butler, three servants and a footman – plus 13 coachmen. Here you can see the cosy chef's room, a laundry, a butchery with a cold cupboard constantly replenished with ice from the ice house in the garden, and two kitchens. The photograph of the 25 staff employed by Leopold in 1915 illustrates the last gasp of a social structure mercifully largely defeated by the end of World War 1.

ADDRESS Popes Lane, London W3 8LQ (020 8992 1612)
OPEN April to October: Monday to Friday, 13.00–17.00; Saturday and Sunday, 13.00–18.00; November to March: daily, 13.00–16.00; kitchens: April to October, weekends and bank holidays only
ADMISSION free
UNDERGROUND Acton Town

HAMPTON COURT PALACE

Hampton Court Palace makes it into this book by the skin of its teeth, its eastern end apparent on the fringes of just some editions of the London *A–Z*. That this eastern third can clearly be seen to be composed of ranges of buildings grouped around two courtyards – the larger one Fountain Court – and that these courtyards are in fact modest in comparison with the grand scale of Base Court behind the main entrance are indications of the scope of the enterprise. Hampton Court is simply vast. This, coupled with its marginal geographical status, means the level of detail in this entry is necessarily curtailed.

The palace at the core of Hampton Court was built by Thomas Wolsey from 1515, the year he became a cardinal and was appointed lord chancellor to Henry VIII. The son of an Ipswich butcher, he had a meteoric rise to power, and by this stage was in receipt of a healthy income from his roles as archbishop of York and administrator of the sees of Bath and Wells and the abbey of St Albans. His parvenu displays of wealth – including not only the creation of the palatial Hampton Court but also lavish entertainments (his household numbered 429) at the Westminster townhouse Henry later converted into Whitehall Palace – irked the 23-year-old king. His failure to procure papal consent for Henry's divorce from his first wife Catherine of Aragon eventually led to the forfeiture of all his property to the crown and his arrest for high treason. He died in 1530 on his way from York to London.

Wolsey's palace was unprecedented in scale and grandeur, but this didn't prevent Henry from spending a further £62,000 (about £18 million in today's terms) on rebuilding and refurbishing it. Designed to impress visiting dignitaries (in August 1546 the French ambassador and his retinue of 200 gentlemen together with 1300 members of Henry's court were entertained for six days), it also functioned as a vast holiday camp, with tennis courts, bowling alleys, pleasure gardens and hunting freely available. In the course of his reign Henry was to spend only 811 days here (on average three weeks a year), though his queens were more frequent visitors and it was the venue for three of his six honeymoons.

Wolsey's house began as a relatively modest affair surrounding Clock Court (still the centrepiece of the complex), with a great hall to the north, a range of royal suites to the east and private and service spaces to the south and west. It was later extended westwards by the creation of the considerably larger Base Court, surrounded by 40 guest suites each consisting of two rooms and a garderobe. Base Court today is still largely as Wolsey intended, though the wings flanking the entrance gate were added by Henry VIII to house communal lavatories – grandly titled the Great House of Easement and seating up to 28 people at a time – and kitchens.

The palace has been divided into six separate trails to facilitate visitor orientation. The recommended route begins with Henry VIII's state apartments, which extend north from Clock Court. The magnificent great hall, built on the site of Wolsey's smaller hall and breathtaking in scale with one of the finest existing hammerbeam roofs, gives the clearest impression of the king's ambitions. The adjacent horn room – lined with antlers dating back to the 17th century and a gory testament to the park's attractions as a hunting ground – was originally a waiting room for the servants attending the 600-strong banquets next door. The vast great watching chamber, originally the entrance to Henry's state apartments, housed his yeoman of the guard. The chapel royal still retains its elaborately modelled star-spangled Tudor ceiling; the delicately carved screen by Grinling Gibbons was installed by Queen Anne in the early 18th century.

The second visitor trail through the vast complex of the Tudor kitchens is prefaced by a model of the palace at 11.00 on midsummer's day in 1542 with a commentary that details the logistics of feeding and clearing up after the hundreds of guests. The Wolsey Rooms & Renaissance Picture Gallery route passes first through a series of small rooms

thought to have been part of the cardinal's private lodgings, two of them lined with superb original linenfold panelling.

Little was done to Hampton Court between Henry's death and 1689, when William III and Mary II hired Christopher Wren to transform the palace into a Versailles that would provide an alternative to the disliked Whitehall Palace and at the same time reinforce their status as legitimate rulers ushering in a new Protestant age. Though Wren's original plan to demolish the entire complex except the great hall was dismissed, much of the Tudor royal apartments (accessed via the great watching chamber) were pulled down, to be replaced by state apartments planned around the new Fountain Court. Cost-cutting and hasty construction led to the collapse of the south range in December, killing two workmen, and only the shell of the new buildings was complete when Mary died in 1694. Work stopped, but four years later, after Whitehall Palace had burned down, William began the decoration of the interiors. Only the king's apartments, in whose design he was intimately involved, were completed by his death in 1702.

These make up the fourth visitor route, accessed via Wren's operatic colonnade on the south elevation of Clock Court, which makes this a fittingly transitional space linking literally and stylistically the imposing Tudor Base Court to the west and the fussy William and Mary Fountain Court to the east. The change of style is immediately apparent in the spectacular king's staircase, its walls and ceilings painted by Antonio Verrio. The mural features an allegory that glorifies William as Alexander the Great, triumphing over the Stuarts as his predecessor did over the Caesars, and shows him being commended to the gods by Hercules. It is intended to leave the visitor in no doubt as to William's divine and politically sanctioned right to take the throne from his Catholic uncle James II. This is backed by a display of military might in the stark guard chamber beyond in the form of some 3000 weapons arranged in grand geometric designs. The procession along the *piano nobile* of the new south front overlooking the privy garden continues through the presence chamber, eating room, privy chamber, withdrawing room, great bedchamber, little bedchamber and closet. Each has a more or less grand red throne which courtiers were supposed to bow to even when empty.

The presence chamber is dominated by a painting by Godfrey Kneller of William's arrival in England to claim the throne. The eating room, where the king would occasionally dine in public, has picture frames and doorcases exquisitely carved with fruit and flower motifs by Gibbons, who was responsible for most of the woodwork in these rooms. The culmination of William's grand design comes in the great bedchamber – in which he was dressed in the morning in front of privileged courtiers – where the baroque ceiling decorations by Verrio, tapestries, gilded furniture and red-draped bed, topped with ridiculous plumes, conspire to give the impression of no expense spared. The little bedroom is where William actually slept and the adjacent king's closet was his private study, from which two jib doors lead to the back staircase and the stoolroom, equipped with a lavatory probably made for Charles II.

On the ground floor are the king's more intimate private apartments beginning with three simple oak-panelled rooms with overmantels carved by Gibbons, the walls hung with paintings from the king's collection including one of him as King Solomon. The scale of the orangery, which stretches almost the full length of the state apartments above, reflects the new fashion for orange trees following the accession of the House of Orange, and is a further symbolic marker of William's status. The private drawing room, closet and dining room beyond were first opened to the public in 1992 following an ambitious restoration programme to repair the damage wrought by a fire of 1986.

Despite William and Mary's equal status as rulers, the queen's state apartments, left unfinished at Mary's death, are a much less grand affair. The fifth route on the visitor itinerary, they run along the north side of Fountain Court and make up the palace's new east front facing Long Water, created by Charles II, and the home park, where William's horse famously made a mountain of a molehill, fatally injuring its rider. Queen Anne commissioned Verrio to decorate the drawing room, but most of the refurbishment was the work of George II who fitted out several rooms while still Prince of Wales and lived here with his wife Caroline from 1714 until he quarrelled with his father in 1717. He completed the work after he acceded to the throne in 1727 and Queen Caroline used the apartments extensively.

The modest queen's staircase was redecorated in 1734 with reliefs by William Kent, whom George and his father had employed at Kensington Palace (see page 90). The guard chamber and presence chamber to the north of Fountain Court, the former with a coved ceiling supported by bold brackets and a marble chimneypiece featuring life-size sculptures of the yeomen of the guard, were designed by John Vanburgh in 1717–18. Their stark austerity is a thoroughly modern contrast with the baroque richness of the king's apartments. The public dining room, originally intended as a music room, is the entry point to the suite of state apartments along the palace's east front. The queen's audience chamber – still with its original red throne-canopy – leads to the central drawing room where Verrio's paintings for Queen Anne constitute an allegory of British naval power that includes images of Cupid drawn by seahorses and a camp portrait of her feckless husband George before the fleet. The paintings were disliked by George II, who had them covered in wallpaper.

The queen's state bedchamber is decorated in red with a baroque ceiling by James Thornhill, royal serjeant painter to George I who had preceded Kent at Kensington. The impressive queen's gallery was hung by William III with Andrea Mantegna's *Triumph of Caesar*, now in the lower orangery but lit at such low levels its beauty is hard to decipher. George II installed the tapestries that line the walls today. The queen's closet was interconnected by a door to William III's closet; beyond it is the room of the ladies of the bedchamber who in George and Caroline's time included his mistress Henrietta Howard (see Marble Hill House, page 189). According to the vice-chamberlain Lord Hervey, Caroline delighted in assigning Henrietta the most menial duties.

George II was the last king to occupy Hampton Court, making his final visit in 1737, shortly before Caroline's death. Under George III much of the palace was divided into rent-free grace-and-favour apartments, a system that lasted until the 1970s. It was first opened to the public by Queen Victoria in 1838.

The final trail is through the Georgian rooms which form part of the eastern range of Clock Court and surround three sides of Fountain Court. The Cumberland Suite in the Tudor range on the eastern side of Clock Court was designed in 1731 by Kent for George II's second son the Duke of Cumberland. The presence chamber has a neo-Tudor ceiling with pendants but the bedchamber boasts sumptuous classical cornices and a bed recess screened with paired Ionic columns. The oak-panelled communication gallery running the length of the western range of Fountain Court is hung with portraits by Peter Lely commemorating the unlovely ladies of the court of Charles II. The cartoon gallery along the court's southern flank was designed by Wren for William III to house Raphael's *Acts of the Apostles*.

The queen's private apartments, which run parallel to the state apartments along the east side of Fountain Court, were also built by Wren for Mary II but lay empty until 1716 when they were refurbished for the Prince and Princess of Wales. The sequence runs from the drawing room, set up for a game of quadrille, through the bedchamber, which has locks on the door so its occupants could spend the night undisturbed, the dressing room and bathroom, closet (and garderobe) to the dining room. The private oratory boasts a fine octagonal dome and skylight.

A walk round the exterior of Hampton Court – built almost entirely of red brick with stone dressings – clearly reveals the two main stages of its creation. The symmetrical west (entrance) front with its turrets and battlements is largely as it was in Tudor times (some of it thanks to Victorian restoration), though the two-storey entrance gate was originally higher. The north front housing the service areas makes no pretence at unifying its collection of Tudor buildings behind a regular façade. Wren's 23-bay east front facing Long Water, by contrast, is a model of symmetry: three storeys high with a row of small round windows above those of

the *piano nobile* and topped by a balustrade, it has a seven-bay ashlar-faced projection at the centre, with the middle three bays projecting further and crowned by a pediment supported by elaborate fluted columns. Though it attempts the grandeur of Versailles, it lacks the necessary scale. The south front is made up of a similar regular Wren façade flanked by the exterior of Wolsey's Base Court, which is largely hidden by Wren's lower orangery.

For an architectural gem on a smaller scale it's worth visiting William III's banqueting house, where the lushly erotic paintings by Verrio compete with the fine river views.

ADDRESS Hampton Court Road, East Molesey, Surrey KT8 9AU (020 8781 9500)
OPEN March to October: daily, 9.30–18.00 (Monday from 10.15); November to February: daily, 9.30–16.30
ADMISSION £10/£8.25/£7.25/family ticket £33
ACCESS limited
RAIL Hampton Court

HOGARTH HOUSE

> He swerved between elation and anxiety, becoming more prone to anger or melancholy in times of stress… He won favours and commissions, then mocked himself and his patrons. He worked with his fellow artists, then turned on them again, feeling isolated and misunderstood. All the time he nervously assessed his achievement, judging it sometimes confidently by his own standards, sometimes miserably by the response of critics, sometimes resignedly, simply by the money he made.
>
> Jenny Uglow on Hogarth at 60, from *Hogarth A Life and a World* (1997)

William Hogarth bought the Chiswick house that now bears his name in 1749 and used it as his summer retreat for the remaining 15 years of his life. Then aged 53, he was a household name thanks to the popular success of such print series as *A Harlot's Progress* (1732), *A Rake's Progress* (1735) and *Marriage A-la-Mode* (1745). The Engravers' Act of 1735, for which he had lobbied vigorously, protected him from pirate copyists, so assuring him a substantial income. He was co-proprietor of the academy in St Martin's Lane – the leading school for painting and the graphic arts – and was a governor of St Bartholomew's Hospital, the Foundling Hospital and Bedlam. He had an apparently affectionate relationship with his wife Jane – daughter of James Thornhill, serjeant painter to George I and II (responsible for decorations at Hampton Court and Kensington Palace, see pages 224 and 92) – with whom he had eloped in 1729. And he had a wide circle of acquaintances within the London club and drinking scenes as well as several close and loyal friends. Yet these were not happy years.

The Chiswick house, described by its new owner as 'the little country box by the Thames', was reached via a small track from Chiswick Lane and was surrounded by high walls similar to those that shield it from the heavy traffic today. Probably built in the first decade of the 18th century and first appearing in public records in 1718, it was a simple two-storey brick cottage, two rooms wide and one room deep. Hogarth doubled its size, adding a kitchen extension to the western end with a room above and raising the roof to create a third storey. It's likely he also installed the grand bay with arched windows above the entrance, which dominates the front of the house. Though Hogarth must often have been unhappy, bitter and angry, the house feels as if it might have worked as a comfortable and comforting escape from the pretensions and pressures of the London art world – a modest retreat where you could put up your feet, relax and be soothed by the simple and intimate pleasures of family life.

Chiswick at the time was little more than a village, though in the first half of the century a few grand houses had sprung up including the Palladian villa built by Lord Burlington (see page 209) and William Kent, who in 1722 had ousted Hogarth's future father-in-law from the commission for decorating Kensington Palace. Hogarth despised and derided both men. While most of Hogarth's life – in terms both of time and intellectual and emotional energy – still centred on London, where he retained a house in the fashionable Leicester Fields (now Leicester Square), he did find like-minded neighbours at Chiswick including Thomas Morell, one of Handel's librettists (see page 49). His house was often full of women – his wife Jane, her mother Lady Thornhill, Jane's young cousin and companion Mary Lewis and Hogarth's sister Anne. Though Jane and William were childless, they supervised Chiswick wet-nurses for children left at the Foundling Hospital and invited foundlings and village children to their home.

The 1750s began well for Hogarth with the publication in 1751 of his prints *Beer Street* and *Gin Lane* (on display in the dining room here). 'Beer Street' is a traditional scene of comic revelry whereas the disturbing 'Gin Lane' depicts a city of wrecked humanity. (Gin had arrived from Holland with William and Mary and by the 1750s almost one in five houses in Holborn was licensed for its sale.) *The Four Stages of Cruelty* (displayed in the same room) was published six days later. Hogarth

declared his aim to be 'preventing in some degree that cruel treatment of poor Animals... the very describing of which gives pain'. But the moral of the series – whose anti-hero Tom Nero moves from torturing a dog and whipping a nag to the murder of a maidservant that results in his hanging – obviously goes further. Hogarth was determined his prints should be cheap enough to be bought by the poor for whom he claimed they were chiefly intended and so eschewed the fine detail that would make engraving too expensive.

Hogarth's other successful print series from his time in Chiswick was *Four Prints of an Election* (displayed in the library), a satire on the antics leading up to the election of 1754, many of its details based on the corrupt practices in Oxfordshire revolving around local squire Sir James Dashwood. Not completed until 1758, the series shows the country teetering on the brink of anarchy. The paintings from which the prints were derived were eventually bought by John Soane in 1823 and hang in the picture room of his museum (see page 62).

Whatever his success with the public, Hogarth found himself increasingly isolated within the art world. The son of a schoolteacher who had unwisely sunk his funds into a Latin-speaking coffeehouse and ended up in prison for debt, he had served his apprenticeship with a silver-plate engraver rather than on a grand tour. Pragmatically as well as idealistically he championed the notion of a British school of art of equal value to the French and Italian traditions imitated by many of his fellow artists and lauded by such cognoscenti as Burlington. He had long been embroiled in a battle with his colleagues at St Martin's Lane about whether the school should be run on democratic principles as he wished or as a more formal, elite-led academy along the lines of those in Paris and Rome. It was a battle Hogarth was to lose with the establishment of the Royal Academy, with his arch-rival Joshua Reynolds as its first president, just four years after his death.

Despite the success of his satirical prints and moral dramas, Hogarth felt the need to prove himself a painter of the stature of his father-in-law and the equal of French and Italian old masters. In 1751 he advertised the sale of the paintings for his popular 1745 *Marriage A-la-Mode* print series (displayed in the bedroom here) by auction at his London home. But just two bids were received and the paintings were sold for only 120 guineas rather than the £500 Hogarth had been expecting. The public humiliation was a bitter blow. The following year he began the laborious task of writing and rewriting *The Analysis of Beauty* (on display in the library here), a treatise setting out his theories on art and painting with which Morell helped in the latter stages. The work was remarkably well received, though criticisms of Hogarth's pretension, dogmatism and lack of learning sent him into a fury. For much of 1755–56 he worked on a vast altarpiece for St Mary Redcliffe church in Bristol, but it led to no further commissions. Then in February 1757 he announced in the *London Evening Post* that he would thenceforth devote his time to portrait painting. Though he received a few commissions, he seemed more comfortable painting friends and family whose portraits he was often loath to part with. (His 1757 portrait of his close friend actor David Garrick and his wife Violette was not handed to its subjects until after Hogarth's death.)

In spring 1757 Hogarth was appointed serjeant painter to King George II following the resignation of his brother-in-law John Thornhill. It was a highly lucrative post which he had coveted since the death of his father-in-law, but he almost immediately began to belittle it, seeing it as a less illustrious role than Reynolds' job of painting the court beauties, not least because payment was made by the Board of Works, which also dealt with plumbers, bricklayers and masons. From now on Hogarth was responsible for all commissions for painting and gilding including such high-profile commands as the decoration of the Chapel Royal for young George III's wedding in 1761 and of Westminster Hall for his coronation two weeks later.

Despite such public recognition, Hogarth remained determined to demonstrate his worth as a painter of serious subjects. His greatest folly was *Sigismunda*, undertaken in 1758 at the request of Richard Grosvenor, who commissioned a painting on a subject of Hogarth's choice at a price named by the artist. Grosvenor was expecting a comedy of manners like *The Lady's Last Stake*, commissioned by his friend the Earl of Charlemont and using a young Hester Thrale (a friend of Dr Johnson's, see page 37) as its model. Instead, Hogarth chose as his subject Boccaccio's story of a young woman who against the will of her father married his lower-class protégé, only for the father to kill his son-in-law and send his heart to his daughter in a jewelled cup which she fills with poison and drinks. The story had obvious resonances with Hogarth's past and he used sketches of Jane grieving at the recent death of her mother as his model for the stricken heroine. Hogarth named his price as 400 guineas – nearly the same as had been paid recently at auction for an Italian-school painting of the same subject. But Grosvenor wriggled out of the agreement and once more Hogarth was subject to public humiliation.

In the early 1760s Hogarth became close to a group of young satirists that included Charles Churchill, who from 1762 was deputy editor of *The North Briton*, an audacious opposition paper that derided prime minister John Bute (owner of Kenwood, see page 138) and supported the populist cause of opposition leader William Pitt, in particular his desire to continue the Seven Years War with France. In his 1762 print *The Times*, Plate 1 Hogarth suggested the damage Pitt had done Britain and showed *The North Briton* as the fuel feeding the fire. The paper's editor John Wilkes retaliated by devoting an entire issue to a scabrous attack on Hogarth, mocking him as 'house-painter' to the court, doubting his authorship of the *Analysis*, deriding *Sigismunda* and criticising his vanity, envy and malevolence. Hogarth's response – a caricature of Wilkes (displayed in the library) – drew an even more vehement denunciation from Churchill.

Hogarth had been ill for almost a year after the rejection of *Sigismunda* and now his health deteriorated further. For some time he had been becoming increasingly vague (a story has him returning home via a hackney coach from Mansion House when his own carriage was parked outside) and the last two years of his life were largely devoted to making rambling notes for an autobiography and revising his prints, working much of the time in his studio in Chiswick. After his death in 1764 Jane lived on at Chiswick for a further 25 years with Mary Lewis and until 1771 with Hogarth's sister Anne. Lewis continued to live here until her death in 1808 when the house was let to various tenants. It was bought by Lt Col Robert Shipway in 1901 and opened to the public in 1904. Five years later it was gifted to the council.

The house today is panelled and painted turquoise throughout (no traces of Hogarth's decorative schemes remained when restoration was undertaken) with furniture made at the turn of the 20th century by the Chiswick Artworkers Guild based on pieces from Hogarth's paintings. On the left of the present front door is the unprepossessing three-bay dining room, originally divided into two tiny rooms by a central staircase when the room's central window would have been the original front door. It is here that the Hogarths received visitors. To the right, site of the current reception desk, would have been the small servants' hall, with a trapdoor to the cellar below. Beyond was the kitchen, destroyed in World War II and now rebuilt as an exhibition space.

The narrow curved staircase leads to a landing from which a further staircase gave access to the second-floor bedrooms for relatives and dormer rooms for servants. Above the dining room in the only other self-contained room was Hogarth's small bedroom where a 1745 self-portrait with his beloved pug (one of many he owned in the course of his life) reveals the short stature and round face with its full mouth and snub nose that seems a refined version of the features of many of his characters. The parlour on the other side of the landing is a charming room that extends into the large bay. The room beyond, above the kitchen extension, was a library. Hogarth's studio was above the stable block in the garden. It collapsed in 1868.

ADDRESS Hogarth Lane, Great West Road, London W4 2QN (020 8994 6757) **OPEN** Tuesday to Saturday, 13.00–18.00; Sunday, 13.00–18.00 (17.00 in winter) **ADMISSION** free **ACCESS** ground floor only **GETTING THERE** rail Chiswick/ Underground Turnham Green

OSTERLEY PARK

Osterley has for most of its history been associated with bankers. It was built in the late 1570s by Sir Thomas Gresham, founder of the Royal Exchange; in 1683 Nicholas Barbon, an unscrupulous financier, building speculator and pioneer of fire insurance, bought it with the idea of emulating the 'mercantile magnificence' of his honourable predecessor. Barbon raised a mortgage of £12,000 on the property (which he had acquired for only £9500); one of the guarantors was Sir Francis Child, the son of a Wiltshire clothier, who had been sent to London, Dick Whittington-style, to serve an apprenticeship as a goldsmith. Like Whittington, he married the boss' daughter, in this case his sole heir; like Whittington, he became alderman, lord mayor and an MP and amassed a considerable fortune. By the end of the century Child's banking and jewellery business was one of the largest in London; he was knighted in 1689 and appointed jeweller in ordinary to William III in 1698. But it wasn't until 1713, a few months before his death, that he was able to claim Osterley, which had been empty and the subject of legal wrangling since Barbon's debt-ridden death in 1698. Francis was succeeded by three of his sons: Robert, who survived his father by only seven years; Francis, who as head of the bank and director of the East India Company for 17 years built on his father's prestige and fortune; and Samuel, the only one of the 11 brothers to have married. All three lived at Osterley.

Gresham's red-brick two-storey house was approximately square, built around a central courtyard surrounded by a loggia off which opened a single range of rooms. Four stair turrets were positioned in the internal angles. (When Queen Elizabeth visited she complained that the courtyard would be better divided by a wall, which Gresham built overnight to please her.) It's likely that Barbon took down the stair turrets and replaced them with towers, topped by gothic ogee cupolas, at the corners

of what for clarity will be called the west (actually south-west) front, as part of alterations which he claimed made the house uninhabitable to put off his creditors from moving in. It's probable the second Francis Child raised the height of the house to create a proper third storey and then raised the entrance and inner courtyard to first-floor level, as now, so this floor could become a *piano nobile* and the ground level a semi-basement for services. The entrance hall was placed in the east front with a library above. All the fronts had pediments and Samuel added two turrets to the entrance side to match Barbon's west front.

Samuel's son Francis was the first of the family to have been educated along with the nobility at Westminster and Oxford and among his first acts on coming into his inheritance in 1756 were the purchase of a fittingly grand collection of books and embarkation on a series of improvements at Osterley. He refurbished the library above the entrance hall and inserted Venetian windows at both ends of the gallery that runs along the west front. But like his predecessors, Francis made his alterations piecemeal, working from the inside out with little concern for the overall composition. It was left to Robert Adam to transform the house into what Horace Walpole described as 'the palace of palaces... so improved and enriched, that all the Percies and Seymours of Sion must die of envy.'

Adam may have been recommended to Francis by the 1st Duke of Northumberland, his neighbour at Syon (see page 249), but another possible candidate is Sir Francis Dashwood, whose brother-in-law and nephew John and Charles Walcot were in debt to Child's Bank to the tune of £16,500. The Walcots had arranged Francis' uncontested return as MP for Bishop's Castle in March 1761; Dashwood commissioned Adam to produce designs for his own houses at Hanover Square and West Wycombe Park. Francis wanted to give Osterley a modern image and to reduce its size, but Adam's first plan – which involved the demolition of the entire east front and part of the north and south wings and refacing the exterior in stone or stucco – was dismissed as too ambitious. Francis then died, on the eve of his wedding, and work on the scheme as built began in 1764 under the eye of his brother Robert, who spared no expense in having Adam remodel his family home which his wife Sarah then filled with porcelain, pictures and drawings.

If Osterley today is very much as Adam left it, it's perhaps thanks to Robert and Sarah's only daughter Sarah Anne, who at the age of 17 eloped with John Fane, 10th Earl of Westmorland. Robert, who died two months later, left his fortune to his daughter's second child to prevent it from going to the main line of the Westmorland family; when his widow Sarah died in 1793 her heir Sarah Sophia Fane was only eight years old. Sarah Sophia married George Villiers, 5th Earl of Jersey, and the couple made their home at Middleton Park in Oxfordshire. (A society wit, she inspired the character of Zenobia in Disraeli's novel *Endymion*.) The house was let until 1883 after which it became the venue for a series of Saturday-to-Monday parties, attended by politicians, princes and writers and organised by George's grandson Victor and his wife Margaret. (Visitor Henry James made Osterley the backdrop for his novella *The Lesson of the Master*.) Victor and Margaret's son George died in 1923, only eight years after his father, to be succeeded by the present earl George Francis, who opened the house to the public in 1939 and gave it to the National Trust a decade later. Much of the Adam-period furniture, which was purchased by the nation and placed in the care of the V&A, is still in situ.

Though Adam transformed the exterior of the Childs' messy Elizabethan mansion by regularising the fenestration (which entailed the removal of the Venetian windows inserted only two years earlier), removing the floating pediments on the north and south fronts, and so on, Francis' refusal to have the red-brick walls refaced adds immeasurably to Osterley's charm: it's the combination of the turrets topped by gothic ogee cupolas, the warm brick and Adam's frozen neoclassical formality that makes such a romantic impression. Adam's masterstroke, however, came with his second response to his client's request that he reduce the house's size: by demolishing the centre of the east wing and bridging the gap with a massive transparent double-height portico, he provided an entrance whose drama could hardly be bettered.

The visitor to Osterley goes through the portico and across the court-

yard to the entrance hall. Sadly, the proportions of this long, low space deprive it of impact, despite Adam's trademark apses at each end and mix of Cipriani reliefs of Bacchus and Ceres (reflecting the room's doubling as a dining room, as at Kenwood, see page 143) and trophy panels like those made for Syon. Vestibules at each inner corner lead to the north and south passages which run along the courtyard sides of these flanks with rooms opening off them; the west front beyond the entrance hall is taken up entirely by a long gallery.

The library – which opens off the north passage – has pedimented bookcases designed around the collection Francis had bought some ten years earlier. Painted all white to allow the books to dominate and decorated with a wealth of delicate small-scale low-relief, its restraint and elegance echo the entrance hall at Syon. The breakfast room beyond (adjoining the portico) was largely untouched by Adam.

The eating room at the other end of the north passage, flanking the entrance hall, is decorated in pink and turquoise with an appropriate array of vines, wine jugs and panels depicting eating and drinking. The largely unadorned long gallery beyond, off which opens a turret room fitted with a wooden commode, had been refurbished in the mid 1760s and Adam's intervention was limited mainly to the replacement of the Venetian windows, the choice of wallpaper and the design of the mirrors. The rather dingy drawing room at the south side of the entrance hall has a ceiling modelled on the Temple of the Sun in Palmyra, a motif also used for the hall at West Wycombe Park.

The tapestry room – next in line along the south passage and the first space in Adam's state apartment – is a stunning contrast. Described by Walpole as 'the most superb and beautiful [room] that can be imagined', its walls are completely lined – probably at Adam's suggestion – by tapestries from the Gobelins factory in Paris made up of medallions depicting the loves of the gods set against a red backdrop of stylised flowers dotted with darting, surprisingly lifelike birds. The chimneyboard, firescreen and furniture are covered in matching fabric.

The state bedchamber next door has a delicate green-painted ceiling on the theme of love, its central medallion inspired by Angelica Kauff-mann's painting of one of the three graces being enslaved by love with smaller surrounding medallions by her future husband Antonio Zucchi. It pales into insignificance in comparison with the monstrous state bed that dominates the room – a temple to love decorated with nymphs, garlands, dolphins, sphinxes and *putti* topped by a dome garlanded with silk flowers that was too much even for Walpole. ('What would Vitru-vius think of a dome decorated by a milliner?') The adjoining Etruscan dressing room has roundels depicting joyful nymphs and *putti* making music and dancing set within a stylised geometric framework.

The great stair off the north passage is screened by two sets of columns (Corinthian below, Ionic above) that echo the portico. The baluster is identical to that at Kenwood. The simple decorative scheme allows the central ceiling painting by Rubens to dominate. In an uncanny echo of Barbon's fire-insurance experience, the original, along with several other paintings from the house, was mysteriously destroyed in a fire soon after it was moved to Jersey following Osterley's acquistion by the National Trust.

On the upper floor are the yellow taffeta bedroom and the Childs' pri-vate apartment: Mr Child's dressing room, Mr Child's bedroom and Mrs Child's dressing room. Refreshingly simple, spacious and light, they are largely as refurbished for Francis Child by Matthew Hillyard in 1759. Below stairs are a substantial kitchen, operational until the 1930s, and, as befits a banking dynasty, a strongroom installed by the 9th Earl of Jersey in 1929 to display the family silver.

ADDRESS Jersey Road, Isleworth, Middlesex (020 8560 3918)
OPEN April to October: Wednesday to Sunday, 13.00–16.30

ADMISSION £4.40/£2.20/family ticket £11.00
ACCESS ground and principal floors
UNDERGROUND Osterley

PITSHANGER MANOR

My object in purchasing these premises was to have a residence for myself
and family, and afterward for my eldest son, who… had also shown a decided
passion for… Architecture, which he wished to pursue as a profession.
I wished to make Pitzhanger Manor-house as complete as possible for the
future residence of the young Architect.
John Soane

Pitshanger Manor is the house bought by John Soane (1753–1837) in 1800
as a weekend retreat, a place for entertaining friends and clients that
would reflect and enhance his status as an architect and a future residence for his elder son John, then aged 14, whom he hoped would follow
him in his beloved profession. Ten years later the house was on the market: Soane's roles as surveyor to the Bank of England (he succeeded
Robert Taylor, architect of Asgill House, see page 178, in 1788), professor
of architecture at the Royal Academy (from 1806) and clerk of works at
the Royal Hospital in Chelsea (from 1807) were becoming increasingly
demanding and his son's debt-ridden behaviour at Cambridge (where
much of the money was used to buy medical treatment) was seen by his
self-made and self-educated father as feckless and extravagant. In fair-
ness to Soane, he regarded his own impoverished upbringing and lack of
connections as his greatest professional disadvantage and wanted to give
his children a better start. But his overweening attempts to dominate
them led to a lifelong feud with the younger son, George, while he never
overcame his disappointment with John; a diary entry following a visit to
Pitshanger in 1820 reads: 'Walked round poor Ealing. O John, John:
what has idleness cost you.'

Soane was attracted to Pitshanger in part because its southern extension had been the first job he worked on after he left the Oxfordshire

home of his bricklayer father to become an apprentice to George Dance the Younger in London in 1768. Dance got the commission from Thomas Gurnell, whose daughter Mary he was to marry four years later. The Gurnell family's association with the house – which was probably built in the mid 17th century – goes back to the start of the 18th century. In 1685 John Wilmer, a wealthy silk merchant closely linked with the nonconformist movement, bought Pitshanger from nonconformist clergyman Dr John Owen. In 1711 Wilmer's eldest daughter Grizell married Quaker Johnathan Gurnell, also a merchant who later established a bank (in a fitting link with Soane, three of their descendants were governors of the Bank of England). Johnathan and Grizell lived at Pitshanger from 1721 until it passed to Thomas on his mother's death in 1756.

Faced at last with no client to please, an unconfined site and a substantial budget (Soane's income for 1800 was the equivalent of about £350,000 in modern terms; Pitshanger cost the equivalent of about £150,000 to buy), Soane took his time in deciding what to do. In a scheme for which more than 100 drawings survive in the Sir John Soane's Museum (see page 58), he eventually knocked down the whole of the Gurnells' house – 'an incongruous mass of buildings deficient in symmetry and character' – except the Dance extension. The three-bay entrance (east) front of the building he created in its place, immeasurably grander than the adjacent Dance wing, records how far he had come. (The extension on the other side, which replaces a colonnade leading to the servants' wing, is a Victorian addition and a building designed as a lending library in 1940.)

The three bays of Soane's façade, with windows on the ground floor only and medallions above, are framed by four Ionic columns supporting a projecting entablature surmounted by statues of female figures in a variation on the entrance to the Bullion Court in the Bank of England's Lothbury Court, itself an adaptation of the Triumphal Arch of Constantine at Rome. (The statues were taken from the Temple of Pandrosus at Athens and bought by Soane for £62 in 1801 as part of a job lot that included the 73 balusters and six vases that make up the Pitshanger parapet.) Soane's aspirations embraced the notion of himself as the founder of an architectural dynasty along the lines of the Dances and Wyatts and the various classical motifs of his new façade placed its creator firmly in a line of great architects stretching back to antiquity. Inside, as a precursor to the museum he was to establish in Lincoln's Inn Fields, he displayed his collection of paintings and transformed a room in the basement into a mock-gothic 'monks' dining room' to accommodate the antique architectural fragments he was gradually amassing.

Pitshanger was thus a calling card as much as was Soane's London house. In addition to using it as a showcase for his ideas, he spent a fortune furnishing and equipping it, with his wife Eliza busily engaged in buying suitable items at auction. The family moved in first in 1804 and the house became the location for a series of summer parties guaranteed to make it a talking point among the potential clients Soane was concerned to impress. But the organisation and constant entertaining took its toll on Eliza, who felt isolated during her husband's frequent absences to oversee his work commitments. John and George were at school in Margate from 1802 and went up to Cambridge in 1805 and 1806 respectively and she and the boys much preferred to spend holidays in London, Margate or with Soane's family in Chertsey. Pitshanger succeeded as a salon but never became a family home.

The visitor enters into a narrow vestibule, its lofty ceiling and upper walls decorated with low-reliefs. To the left is a dressing room probably intended for Soane's own use and now containing information about the house. The small space with its neat fireplace and curved wall is extravagantly lit by one of the two large arched windows of the entrance front. Behind it is the small drawing room, whose full-length arched windows originally opened on to a conservatory that ran the length of the rear of the house. Hogarth's *A Rake's Progress* – which Eliza bought at auction at Christie's for 570 guineas in 1802 – once hung here (now replaced by copies). Double doorways lead to the library, a beautiful, typically Soanean space with a big central French window that would also have opened on to the conservatory. The trellis-pattern decoration of the

groin-vaulted ceiling echoes the breakfast parlour of 12 Lincoln's Inn Fields; the walls on either side of the window, the overmantel and the niches that flank the fireplace are typically furnished with mirrors to enhance the sense of space. The breakfast room opposite the dressing room has a more sombre colour scheme, its Greek-key patterns and linear tracery chosen to complement the funerary urns, vases and sculptures on display. The shallow dome of the ceiling – its centre painted with cloud effects – is supported by four attenuated Egyptian caryatids painted to resemble bronze.

The vast eating room in the ground floor of the Dance extension is where Soane would entertain such friends as J M W Turner and John Flaxman, his colleagues at the Royal Academy and influential figures within the government and Bank of England, attracted presumably as much by Eliza's intelligent and pleasant company as by that of her hypersensitive, irascible husband. In the centre of the north wall is a semi-circular niche designed for a serving table; Dance's compartmentalised ceiling decoration with its lacy arabesques and rosettes survives. The room's drama is enhanced by a mirroring extension to the rear added in 1901 at the same time as the entrance-front porch. The monks' dining room in the basement has a typically Soanean plethora of arches and pedimented niches for the display of objects purloined from Greek, Roman and Egyptian sites. The tearoom next door was formerly a laundry.

The balusters of the elegant stone staircase, toplit by an oval lantern, are similarly recycled, this time more prosaically from the Gurnells' original house. The present dispiriting municipal grey replaces a rich colour scheme that included 'black Marble & gold veins' for the basement, 'Porphyr' for the ground level and 'French rouge' for the first floor. The bust of Minerva was installed by Soane.

The first-floor drawing room above the eating room was also intended for use on formal occasions. The large, pleasant space has an elaborate plaster ceiling designed by Dance and much admired by Soane. The east wall originally had three windows (the central one was bricked up c. 1832 and the single window opposite enlarged); the pilasters that

frame them are echoed on the west wall. The rest of the first floor consisted of four modestly sized bedrooms, one of which (above the small
drawing room) is open to the public. The combination of a cross- and
barrel-vaulted ceiling echoes the arrangement in the library.

Some 30 years after the Soanes left Ealing the house was bought by
Spencer Walpole and became the home of his four unmarried sisters-in-
law, Frances, Maria, Louisa and Frederika Perceval, whose father was
assassinated while he was prime minister in 1812. (His bust can be seen in
the stairwell.) Frederika lived in Pitshanger until 1900. Her nephew sold
the house to the council which turned it into a library. The present Martinware room to the north, devoted to a display of Martinware pottery
including an over-the-top 1891 fireplace, was added during the Percevals'
residency. The extension beyond it, now an art gallery, was built in 1940.
The library moved out in 1984 and the house was restored as a museum
and arts venue.

ADDRESS Mattock Lane, London
W5 5EQ (020 8567 1227)
OPEN Tuesday to Saturday,
11.00–17.00
ADMISSION free
UNDERGROUND Ealing Broadway

SYON HOUSE

Syon House is the only major London mansion still in private hands, and though the sycophantic guidebook is coy about its present owner's finances, the *Sunday Times* 'rich list' of 1999 places the 12th Duke of Northumberland at number 87 in the UK, a rank he shares with the Queen. Notable recent predecessors in a family line that has been traced back to Charlemagne include the 10th Duke Hugh (title-bearer from 1940 to 1988), who led the 1968 government investigation into bovine foot-and-mouth disease; Helen, 8th Duchess and mistress of the robes to the late Queen Mother; the 6th Duke Algernon (1867-99), who with his wife Louisa was a prominent member of the Catholic apostolic movement; and the 3rd Duke (another Hugh, 1817-47), whose receipts from coal and rent made him the richest commoner in Britain and whose wife was governess to the future Queen Victoria. The 3rd Duke used some of his wealth to face the house in Bath stone, install the battlemented porch on the west front, remodel the north wing and build a magnificent free-standing conservatory in the grounds.

Syon was originally an annexe to an abbey for the Order of St Bridget established at Twickenham in 1415 by Henry V as part-fulfilment of his father Henry IV's penance for his role in the death of Richard II. Following the reformation it became crown property and was eventually secured by Edward Seymour, Duke of Somerset, protector to the young Edward VI, who began to build the house that forms the shell of the present building. After Seymour's execution in 1552 for plotting against the crown Syon had various owners until in 1597 it was granted to Henry Percy, 9th Earl of Northumberland, who added the battlements and corner towers. During the previous 60 years it had housed Catherine Howard as she awaited execution and the coffin of Henry VIII on its way from Westminster to Windsor and was the place where the ill-fated Lady Jane Grey reluctantly accepted the offer of the crown made by her father-in-law John Dudley, who owned the house until he in turn was executed.

Henry Percy was a favourite of James i until his cousin Thomas was suspected of involvement in the gunpowder plot, at which point he was imprisoned in the Tower of London for 17 years. His son Algernon rose to the rank of lord high admiral and following Charles i's imprisonment was appointed governor to the royal children, who from 1646 to 1649 were housed at Syon. Algernon's son, the 11th Earl, died only two years after his father, leaving an infant daughter, Elizabeth, as his sole heir. She eventually married Charles Seymour, Duke of Somerset, and the couple were mistress of the stole and master of the horse to Queen Anne. (After Elizabeth's death in 1722 Charles married Charlotte Finch, whose younger sister Elizabeth was the wife of the Earl of Mansfield at Kenwood, see page 145.) Charles' son Algernon also outlived his father by only two years and was succeeded by his daughter Elizabeth, wife of Sir Hugh Smithson, who in 1766 was created 1st Duke of Northumberland. An associate of the 3rd Earl of Bute (the previous owner of Kenwood) and at one time considered a likely successor to him as prime minister under George iii, Smithson engaged Bute's protégé Robert Adam to work on his homes of Northumberland House in London, Alnwick Castle and Syon (1762–73).

The exterior of Syon is plain to the point of austerity, its unadorned stone façades relieved only by battlements. The house is approximately square, built around a courtyard, with square turrets at the outer corners. Each flank is two storeys high with a sub-basement. On the ground floor (here the *piano nobile*) the west and south flanks are one room deep, the east wing has a long gallery (transformed by Adam into a library) on the outside and a suite of smaller rooms on the courtyard side and the north wing was extended by the 3rd Duke, who added the oak passage (which functions as a long gallery) to the outside. The east front (best appreciated from Kew Gardens) is topped dramatically by a statue of the straight-tailed Percy lion.

Adam's plans for Syon proposed a grand suite of rooms taking up the

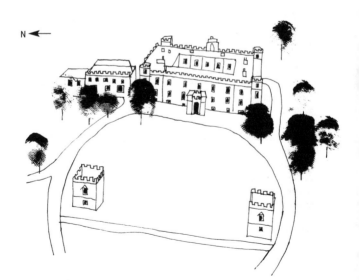
N

whole of the *piano nobile* connected via four ovals to a circular saloon that almost filled the courtyard. In the event only five main rooms on the west, south and east sides were realised, though among these are some of his finest. The plain west front gives way to a stunning entrance hall that fully realises the architect's brief 'to create a palace of Graeco-Roman splendour'. A double cube just over 20 metres long, it cleverly accommodates the uneven levels of the Jacobean house by placing the stairs up to the adjacent rooms in a coffered apse at one end and a vaulted recess at the other, screened by Doric columns. The original decorative scheme was pure white, relieved only by the black and white chequerboard floor. (Sadly, the hall was repainted in 1974 to a colour scheme devised by John Fowler which picks out the wonderfully delicate plasterwork in muted greys and creams.) Among the imposing copies of antique sculpture is a bust of the 1st Duke, a balding Englishman got up in a toga.

The richly decorated anteroom in the south-west corner provides a startling contrast. Again Adam manipulates the space, here positioning the 12 Ionic columns – 'obtained' by his brother James in Rome and venereed in verd-antique scagliola – to create the impression of a square space further defined by the brightly coloured scagliola floor. The heavy ceiling is gilded, as are the statues in various states of undress that top the columns and the trophy panels that flank the entrance, which to modern eyes appear almost cubist in their deconstructed effect. Though Syon's grounds were transformed by 'Capability' Brown into a wonderfully informal landscape at the same time as Adam was introducing neoclassical formality to the house's interiors, the woodland and lake are barely visible through the windows, and Adam's rooms are decidedly inward-looking, never attaining the harmony of nature and architecture he achieved at Kenwood.

The dining room in the south wing is almost a triple cube with the doorways at each end positioned in apses screened by Corinthian columns. The colour scheme is refreshingly subtle after the excesses of the anteroom, though for the ceiling decoration Adam eschewed the delicacy of the entrance hall in favour of a vigorous pattern of fans and palmettes. The adjacent red drawing room – hung with crimson silk and with a remarkable coved ceiling inset with 239 medallions painted by Cipriani with lifelike figures in classical poses – is again a colourful and more sumptuous contrast. One of the Adam-designed pier tables has a top formed of mosaic 'found' in the baths of Titus in Rome. Apparently the 1st Duke, whose careful accounting led him to query Cipriani's demand to be paid more for medallions containing two figures, was caught trying to avoid import duty on the large French mirrors by smuggling them into the country in a diplomatic bag. Peter Lely's portrait of Charles 1 and his son James, Duke of York, is thought to have been painted at Syon when the 10th Earl had charge of the royal children. A jib door allows a glimpse into a 'private' study on the courtyard side of the building, left as furnished by the 10th Duke with a worn leather chair, a desk stacked with family photographs and a prominent crucifix.

The stunning long gallery/library – its length almost ten times its width – takes up the whole of the east front. Unlike at nearby Osterley (see page 240), where the library is plainly decorated to allow the books to dominate, here Adam transformed a traditional panelled Jacobean gallery into a room 'finished in a style to afford variety and amusement' to the ladies of the house. Virtually every surface is covered in a palette of pink, blue and gold that echoes the glittering tooling on the many books. A false bookcase conceals a door that allowed the ladies to walk out on to the lawn. Above the books are portrait medallions tracing the lineage of the Percys via Harry Hotspur back to Charlemagne – a bald statement by the 1st Duke of the credentials of the family into which he had married. The tables below have informal snapshots of the family today. One of the two turret rooms is decorated with oriental wallpaper; the other is a richly stuccoed pink, blue and gold boudoir.

The print room in north-east corner, hung with family portraits, was enlarged by the 3rd Duke at the same time as he provided Syon with a traditional-style long gallery in the form of the oak passage that runs the length of the north front, half-panelled with timber rescued from the Jacobean house. From the print room visitors can look into the duchess'

sitting room on the courtyard side of the east wing and the green drawing room on the courtyard side of the north wing, both 'still regularly used'. The small sitting room – more like a display of family life than a room that's lived in – contains furniture of various styles including two armchairs with covers embroidered by the 8th Duchess Helen and her sister in the 1930s. The much larger drawing room has a preponderance of roomy sofas and some sweet snapshots of little girls practising flamenco dancing that soften the gloom cast by the grim family portraits. The only modern item is the telephone – none of the Northumberlands' wealth, it seems, is squandered on contemporary design. Next to the drawing room are the private dining room – available for corporate functions – and a remarkably functional kitchen adjoining the entrance hall.

Visitors to Syon should be aware that the house is only one element in a family-friendly tourist park that includes an aquarium, a butterfly house, an adventure playground and the beautiful gardens, through which runs a model train.

ADDRESS Syon Park, Brentford, Middlesex TW8 8JF
(020 8560 0882)
OPEN March to October: Wednesday, Thursday, Sunday, 11.00–17.00

ADMISSION £6.95/£6.50/family ticket £15
ACCESS none
GETTING THERE Gunnersbury Underground, then bus 237 or 267

[charlton/eltham/
greenwich]

Charlton House **258**
Eltham Palace **261**
Flamsteed House **267**
Queen's House **270**
Ranger's House **273**
Woodlands **277**

CHARLTON HOUSE

Charlton House looks built to impress. Designed in 1607, less than ten years before Inigo Jones' radical neo-Palladian Queen's House (see page 270), it is one of London's most significant and last Jacobean mansions. Sturdy and unwieldy in comparison with Jones' beautifully proportioned gem, it was built for Sir Adam Newton, tutor to Henry Prince of Wales, son of James I, and is attributed to John Thorpe, architect of Audley End in Essex and probably of the core of Kensington Palace (see page 90). Following the Civil War it was sold to Sir William Ducie, a tradesman who spent his considerable fortune on repairing and redecorating his home and lavish entertaining. On his death it was bought by East India merchant Sir William Longhorne, who passed it to the Maryon Wilson family in whose hands it remained until World War 1, when it was offered to the Red Cross. The side extension was added in the late 19th century by Norman Shaw for Sir Spencer Maryon Wilson. The house was bought by Greenwich Borough Council in 1925 and is now run as a community centre.

Built on an H plan, Charlton House has a massive three-storey, seven-bay red-brick façade with stone dressings, its elaborate central bay reminiscent of a solid brown fruit cake decorated with white icing. The twin towers at the sides of the two wings are topped by ogee roofs. You enter into an impressive double-height hall that stretches the depth of the central section of the house – an impractical arrangement since until the minstrels' gallery was added by moderniser Sir Thomas Maryon Wilson in the 1830s (along with bathrooms, and wolves and bears for the park) there was no connection between the two sides of the first floor, which was therefore given over to small-scale bedrooms. The grand suites were installed on the second floor, and very grand they are too.

Most imposing is the wood-panelled long gallery, which runs the full

23-metre depth of one of the wings, with a bay at the side extending into the tower. Used by the Maryon Wilsons as a museum, it has stained-glass windows featuring the Ducie coat of arms which were installed to celebrate his marriage. The gallery leads into the squarish white room whose elaborate stone fireplace sports two tiers of caryatids and relief scenes from biblical and classical mythology. The Dutch room above the entrance hall – originally the salon – has a magnificent original plaster frieze and ceiling hung with pendentives. The walls were formerly panelled to full height all the way round and the fluted pilasters repeated at intervals. The richly carved black marble fireplace is flanked by striking statues of Vulcan and Venus. Ducie is said to have seen the reflection of a highway robbery in the marble and sent his servants to apprehend the thieves.

Charlton House is now a community centre, so public access depends on what events are planned that day. However, even if you only see the entrance hall and the magnificent oak staircase, its balustrades carved in the shape of plants with strings of plaster fruit and leaves decorating the walls behind, becoming more and more elaborate as it reaches the grand upper storey, it's worth a visit.

ADDRESS Hornfair Road, London SE7 8RE (020 8856 3951)
OPEN Monday to Friday, 9.00–22.00; Saturday, 10.00–17.00
ADMISSION free
RAIL Charlton

ELTHAM PALACE

Eltham Palace is one of the ugliest stately homes I've seen. Tacked on to a 15th-century great hall surviving from the royal palace that formerly occupied the site, this 1930s playhouse built for millionaire socialites Stephen and Ginie Courtauld is a triumph of surface over substance and decoration over architecture.

Eltham manor first fell into royal hands in 1305 when Anthony Bek, Bishop of Durham, presented it to the future Edward II. For a quarter of a millennium, until the death of Henry VIII, it was one of the most used royal residences and one of only six palaces large enough to accommodate the 800-strong court. Edward III spent much of his youth here; Henry IV occupied Eltham for ten of his 13 Christmases as king; Henry VI and Henry VIII lived here for a large part of their boyhoods (in 1499 the palace was the site of a meeting between the latter, a nine-year-old prince, and Erasmus). However, Elizabeth I preferred the more convenient Greenwich, and Eltham was let out to tenants connected with the court. During the 17th century the buildings fell into decay; by the 19th – with the exception of a few structures such as the delightfully simple Tudor house, once occupied by Elizabeth I's chancellor, still standing beside the 1470s stone entrance bridge – the palace had deteriorated into a picturesque ruin.

The choice of Eltham as the site for a thoroughly modern country house was a romantic and visionary one; the Courtaulds' mistake was to hire relatively inexperienced architects distinguished by their social connections rather than their portfolio. John Seely, the creative arm of Seely and Paget, professed himself inspired by Christopher Wren's work at Hampton Court (see pages 222 and 225), which he mistakenly read as an attempt to restore the medieval palace rather than to create a Renaissance masterpiece. And you only have to look at Seely's entrance façade – the

elegantly curved neoclassical arcaded stone porch; the squat red-brick blocks of the wings with their windows painted municipal British racing green; the twin towers (over the stairwells) with pagoda-style roofs; and a roofscape that marries a concrete and glass-brick dome with three Tudor gables rescued from the ruins – to realise that eclecticism has its limits and rationality its place. It's a shame so much money didn't stretch to generous proportions or ceiling heights and that the courageous championing of modernity visible in the ocean-liner sleekness and technological innovation of the interior didn't translate into a modernist exterior.

The most striking space is the entrance hall, which seems to have functioned like a hotel lobby (male and female toilets and a pay-phone are positioned just off it; cigarettes and cocktail glasses are set out ready and waiting). Designed by Rolf Engströmer, this was reportedly the first Swedish-style interior in Britain, inspired by Stockholm Town Hall which the Courtaulds had visited in 1928. But the initial sense of splendour crumbles on closer inspection – the circularity of the dome and the Marion Dorn carpet belies the triangular plan (give or take a few curved edges); the entrance wall is decorated with bizarrely vulgar marquetry scenes of Italy (with the Courtaulds' yacht moored in Venice's lagoon) and Sweden, guarded by a larger-than-life Roman soldier and Viking respectively. However, the high room is well lit by a clerestory as well as the dome and Engströmer's furniture has an elegant simplicity.

The drawing room, designed by Italian playboy aristocrat Peter Malacrida, is a mish-mash of styles: a monumental marble fireplace; false beams on the low ceiling painted to imitate Hungarian folk art (Ginie was of Hungarian and Italian parentage); art nouveau-style wrought-iron grilles over the French windows; plain black gothic-arched cupboard doors protecting Stephen's collection of Italian porcelain. Malacrida also designed the boudoir and library – surprisingly small rooms lined with wood, making the concealed lighting in the ceilings necessary even on a bright day. Ginie's boudoir is dominated by a six-seater sofa surrounded by shelving for books, lamps and telephones (the house was fitted with a state-of-the-art private exchange). In this 1930s semi writ large, Stephen's library has the feel of the office of a provincial bank manager. The books take up less wall space than the many pictures, for whose protection he designed an ingenious system of wood panels that could be pulled down from above and were themselves hung with woodcuts and engravings in an arrangement perhaps inspired by the picture room in Sir John Soane's Museum (see page 62). The art includes 14 Turner watercolours and a grim bronze of a sentry, a reduced version of a Manchester war memorial designed by his World War 1 comrade-in-arms Charles Sergeant Jagger; the literature books about the empire, the slave trade, mountaineering and collecting as well as a section on English schools which he presumably used to argue the toss with Board of Education president Rab Butler, who drafted the reforming 1944 Education Act at Eltham.

The dramatic light and scale of the great hall – built by Edward IV from 1475 to 1480 – drive home the paucity of the previous rooms. Comparable in size with the great hall at Hampton Court, which it predates by half a century, it was 'restored' by the Courtaulds in a manner influenced by the contemporary film industry's visions of medieval England (from 1931 Stephen was on the board of Ealing Studios). Among the additions were the minstrels' gallery (the hall was to be used as a music room), a quantity of 17th-century furniture, some lanterns on angular art-deco poles and hangings made of the 'art silk' (rayon) on which the family fortune was based – presumably the hefty budget didn't run to tapestries. Tacked on to the far end is an orangery and squash court (Ginie was a keen player) which is pleasant enough from the inside if you ignore the overscaled Ionic pilasters but from the outside couldn't have shown less sensitivity to the grandeur of its neighbour.

The twin stairwells accessed from the entrance hall rise to a ridiculous height, presumably in a bid to enliven the exterior with a couple of towers. On the landing hangs a picture of the Courtaulds upstaged by the glorious, stripy-tailed lemur Mah-Jongg, bought at Harrods in 1923. The big surprise in Stephen's bedroom (designed by Seely) is not the pictures of his heroes Beethoven and Julius Ceasar above the chaste-looking three-quarter bed but the blue-tinged wallpaper (from Sandersons) depicting Kew Gardens that forms a panorama covering the upper part of the two side walls, including the door leading to the blue-tiled bathroom which strives for a *hamam* effect. Ginie's room – circular in plan and thus the cause of more awkward leftover spaces – is more generous and better lit, though I'd hardly describe it as sensual. Her en-suite bathroom gives the impression that the designer (Malacrida again) has unravelled the art-deco style into its parts – onyx walls; a gold mosaic-clad niche containing a statue of Psyche above a curved bath; an aggressively angular mirrored dressing table with a shiny black top – and failed to stitch them together again.

Along the corridor faced by the Tudor gables is Mah-Jongg's cage, originally decorated with tropical murals and furnished with a bamboo ladder leading to the flower room off the entrance hall. The guest rooms have numbered doors as in a hotel, except for the one labelled 'Batmen'. The Venetian suite, one of only two double guest bedrooms, was designed by Malacrida perhaps with Ginie's Italian mother in mind. It includes such nonsense as a 17th-century model tabernacle utilised as a cupboard and a door faced with false books to match the real bookshelves opposite. The en-suite bathroom (probably by Seely) is simple and modern in contrast, lined in plain yellow Vitrolite (a new easy-to-clean surface) and with a bidet, the height of European chic.

The most successfully decorated room is the dining room. It has a dramatic art-deco fireplace in ribbed aluminium and black marble inlaid with a mother-of-pearl Greek-key pattern; black doors with the same pattern in silver and applied lacquer animals, perhaps inspired by the delicate 18th- or early-19th-century Chinese screen at the entrance to the great hall; an aluminium-leaf ceiling; pale wood walls and furniture including an elegant dining suite with chairs upholstered in salmon-pink leather. The moderne style was underwritten by state-of-the-art technology – central-heating coils concealed in the ceiling; a centralised vacuum-cleaning system; synchronous clocks; a network of loudspeakers throughout the ground floor.

The Courtaulds left Eltham Palace in 1944, leaving their home to the

Army Educational Corps until 1995, when English Heritage took over the site. Eight years is not long to occupy a house you've commissioned and to some extent designed yourself – perhaps its fundamental failings became all too apparent once wartime austerity put paid to the glamorous showmanship its interiors project so well.

ADDRESS Court Yard, London SE9 5QE (020 8294 2548; www.english-heritage.org.uk) **OPEN** Wednesday to Friday, Sunday and bank holiday Mondays: April to September, 10.00–18.00; October, 10.00–17.00; November to March, 10.00–16.00 **ADMISSION** £6.20/£4.70/£3.10 **RAIL** Eltham

FLAMSTEED HOUSE

For all the turn-of-the-millennium fuss made of Greenwich as the place by which the world sets its clocks, the first astronomer royal John Flamsteed (1646–1719) lived in modest style. And his house, built by Christopher Wren for a mere £520 19s 1d from materials recycled from the Tower of London and Tilbury Fort, is a simple, elegant piece of architecture by contrast with Wren's ornate Royal Naval College down the hill completed some 30 years later. The idea of an observatory was suggested to Charles II by a French protégée of his mistress Louise de Kéroualle. Wren proposed Greenwich as a site and in 1675 the clergyman and mathematician Flamsteed was appointed at a salary of £100 per annum from which he was expected to buy his own instruments. In 1692 he married Margaret Cooke, who helped him with his observations alongside two assistants.

Wren's original house-cum-observatory was a square, two-storey red-brick building with elaborate wood dressings made to look like stone and two high square turrets at the ends of the three-bay front. The small pavilions to the sides were added in 1772–73 and the extension at the back that now functions as a museum was built between 1790 and 1835 to give more space to subsequent astronomer royals. A portrait of the bewigged Flamsteed, with his generous nose and heavy brows, has him looking suitably serious; engravings of the house soon after completion show how little the shell has changed.

Flamsteed's living quarters on the ground floor – a series of modest wood-panelled rooms – have been recreated with furniture loaned by the V&A. There is no ostentation here, whether in the dining room set with a simple meal, the bedroom with its narrow bed (presumably he and Margaret, busily stargazing, didn't spend much time there) and dressing table on which sit a curly grey wig and gilt mirror, the study with its floor piled with books or the sparsely furnished rectangular hall.

The breathtaking moment comes with the light-filled double-height octagonal observatory that takes up the whole of the first floor. The tall narrow windows were designed to accommodate long telescopes and the view from the balcony of the Queen's House, Royal Naval College and river beyond is one of London's finest. The lofty ceiling has a delicate plasterwork frieze of flowers and berries; patrons Charles II and James II, toes pointed as if to curtsey, stand above painted wood panelling inset with copies of the ornate Thomas Tompion wall clocks whose accuracy allowed Flamsteed to determine whether the earth rotated at a constant speed (Margaret sold the originals after her husband's death). On the stairs is an etching of the room in use soon after it was built.

The ultimate purpose of Flamsteed's work was to produce a map of the stars that would aid navigation by enabling sailors to calculate longitude at sea. The problem was so acute that in 1714, stunned by such accidents as the drowning of almost 2000 men off the Scilly Isles, parliament offered £20,000 for a solution. Though this was eventually claimed by clockmaker John Harrison in the 1770s after 20 years of wrangling to have his chronometer – the forerunner of all precision watches – validated, Flamsteed's 45 years at the Royal Observatory and 30,000 observations produced *Historia Coelestis Britannica*, a catalogue of some 3000 fixed stars. Flamsteed was obsessive and perfectionist, and when Isaac Newton, president of the Royal Society, who had used Flamsteed's observations to verify his theories of planetary and lunar motion, forced him to publish a work he considered incomplete in 1712 he bought and burned the 300 (out of 400) copies he could lay his hands on. The *Historia Coelestis Britannica* was republished posthumously in 1725 – another example of a great British achievement built on low pay and miserable working conditions.

ADDRESS Royal Observatory, Greenwich, London SE10 (020 8858 4422; www.nmm.ac.uk) **OPEN** daily, 10.00–17.00

ADMISSION free **GETTING THERE** rail Maze Hill/DLR Island Gardens

QUEEN'S HOUSE

Now a venue for special exhibitions organised by the National Maritime Museum, the Queen's House is a hit-and-miss affair depending on how it's being used. The first Palladian villa in Britain, based on the Medici villa at Poggio a Caiano outside Florence, it was designed by Inigo Jones in 1616 for James I's wife Queen Anne of Denmark. After her death in 1619 the king lost enthusiasm for the project and work was abandoned. In 1629 Charles I decided to have the building completed for his French queen Henrietta Maria, who lived here until 1644 when she was exiled during the Civil War (she returned to the house as queen mother from the restoration until her death in 1669). The house later became the official residence of the ranger of Greenwich Park and from 1806 was a school for seamen's children. It was restored in 1935 as part of the National Maritime Museum.

Elizabethan and Jacobean mansions were basically medieval buildings with Renaissance ornament tacked on; Jones, who at the point when he planned the Queen's House had just returned from a visit to Italy armed with Palladio's *Quattro Libri dell'architettura*, reinterpreted the master's works to design integral Renaissance buildings whose characteristics were restraint and fine proportions. The extent of the revolution he introduced can be gauged by comparing the strikingly simple Queen's House – essentially a square white box – with the unwieldy plan and fussy detail of Charlton House (see page 258) designed less than ten years earlier.

The two-storey Queen's House was originally two rectangular blocks – each seven bays by two, built of brick and faced in plaster with rustication on the lower floor – linked by a central covered bridge over the main Woolwich to Greenwich road to give the first floor an H plan. Stone was used for the window architraves, cornices and the slender Ionic columns of the recessed first-floor loggia on the south front; entrance was via a

curved double staircase to the north. In 1662 Charles II commissioned Jones' son-in-law and pupil John Webb to build two more connecting bridges at the sides to give the first floor the square profile it has today. The Doric colonnades that line the former road were introduced in 1807.

The domestic scale and unadorned exterior of the Queen's House are a welcome contrast with the attention-seeking baroque of the Royal Hospital for Seamen (now the Royal Naval College), which Christopher Wren completed for William and Mary in 1705. (Wren's initial design obscured the view of the Queen's House from the river; when Mary objected he was forced to slice his plan in two.) The house's most impressive space – and one no exhibition designer could destroy – is the entrance hall, a perfect, light-filled cube with a gallery at first-floor level and a black and white marble floor radiating from a central circle. Its pattern echoes the arrangement of the panels of the painted ceiling above (a copy of the original, now in Marlborough House, by Orazio Gentileschi and his daughter Artemisia, one of the first professional female artists and the subject of a recent controversial film by Agnès Merlet). The original staircase to the east – a spiral with an open well and no inner supports, its wrought-iron balustrades a pattern of tulips – looks incongruously modern and was indeed the first of its kind in Britain. The first-floor state apartments to the east and west of the entrance hall – the Queen's drawing room and bedroom – both have remarkable painted ceilings.

The Queen's House was restored in 1990 – money wasted unless it's used for exhibitions that retain the integrity of its spaces and allow its architectural beauty to be appreciated. Perhaps the curators could take a leaf from the Renaissance and seek a respectful fusion of art and science.

ADDRESS National Maritime Museum, Greenwich, London SE10 9NF (020 8858 4422; www.nmm.ac.uk)

OPEN daily, 10.00–17.00
ADMISSION free
GETTING THERE rail Maze Hill/ DLR Island Gardens

RANGER'S HOUSE

Crooms Hill, the western border of the Royal Park of Greenwich, was a popular site for courtiers' houses while Greenwich was in royal occupation until the early 1680s. Captain Francis Hosier, who had made huge sums of money from selling his share of ships' cargoes, probably chose it as the location for his new home in about 1700 because of the social contacts the area afforded (his patron the Earl of Berkeley had family nearby and he knew the astronomer royal John Flamsteed, see page 267), its easy access to the sea and its proximity to the newly established Royal Hospital for Seamen (now the Royal Naval College). His charming two-storey house, its seven-bay red-brick façade enlivened by a Portland stone balustrade at roof level, string course at first-floor level and elaborate centrepiece (with a mask of Neptune above the door), was built to a standard early-18th-century villa design. Unfortunately Hosier had little opportunity to enjoy it; for much of the time of his occupancy he was away at sea, and in 1727 he died of yellow fever on duty in the Caribbean.

In 1740 the house was bought by John Stanhope, who on his death eight years later left it to his elder brother, the diplomat and politician Philip, 4th Earl of Chesterfield (1694–1773). Chesterfield added a single-storey bow-fronted gallery in contrasting yellow brick (designed by Isaac Ware) to the south side to accommodate his growing collection of old masters. He had at first been reluctant to take the house on, preferring the more fashionable Twickenham where his friend the Countess of Suffolk had built Marble Hill House (see page 189), but shortly after his acquistion of the property he resigned from government, ending his public career, and as his age and deafness increased Greenwich's tranquillity and relative isolation became welcome. In the 1780s lawyer and collector Richard Hulse added a north wing which mirrors Chesterfield's gallery at the front of the house but runs only half its depth.

From 1807 to 1813 the house was leased by Augusta, Dowager Duchess of Brunswick, the sister of George III, whose daughter Princess Caroline, the estranged wife of the future George IV, lived in Montagu House next door. Their presence made Greenwich newly fashionable. In 1815 the house was nominated as the residence of the ranger of Greenwich Park, an honorary position whose previous incumbents had occupied the Queen's House (see page 270). Subsequent residents were George III's niece Princess Sophia Matilda (from 1815 to 1844), who divided the gallery into three and replaced much of the panelling; the statesman, antiquarian and prime minister Lord Aberdeen (1845–60); Lord Canning (1861–62); Queen Victoria's third son Arthur (1862–73); the Countess of Mayo (1877–88); and Field-Marshal Lord Wolseley (1888–96). The house was acquired by London County Council in 1902 and restored in the 1960s. It now holds the Suffolk Collection of 17th-century paintings and hosts exhibitions of contemporary art on the first floor.

From the simple entrance hall turn right into the crimson camblet parlour, a small but well-proportioned panelled room that in Hosier's and Chesterfield's day served as the everyday dining and living room. Chesterfield's gallery beyond is a remarkable contrast in scale and atmosphere, an unashamedly grand space with three curved bays, each furnished with three windows from which he claimed to enjoy 'three different, and the finest, prospects in the world'. The decorative compartmentalised ceiling is original; the elaborate fireplace was probably installed from another room in the house. Chesterfield's Tintorettos, van Dycks, Claudes and Poussins have been replaced by a gallery of beruffed Cecils, Howards and Sackvilles.

The green silk damask parlour, restored to match its appearance in Hosier's day, was his principal parlour and in Chesterfield's time was an antechamber linking the more imposing gallery and dining room, which Ware substantially remodelled. The dining room's present red colour scheme was used by both Hosier and Chesterfield. On the south wall is a portrait of Chesterfield's distant cousin Philip Stanhope (1755–1815) who inherited the house but visited it only occasionally. As with his natural son, Chesterfield bombarded 'Sturdy' with letters of advice about his education and behaviour, and in the portrait we see him squashed uncomfortably into a pink satin suit, with learned books on the table. The advice didn't stick – by the time Chesterfield died Sturdy was heavily in debt and the only story of his life in the house involves a drunken dinner, whose guests included the Prince of Wales, which ended with Sturdy falling down the front steps and seriously injuring his head.

The small panelled room off the dining room functioned as an anteroom in Hosier's day and as a still room for preparing tea and coffee and storing cakes, jams and liqueurs in Chesterfield's. Today it's furnished as a study with a 1749 letter in Chesterfield's mechanically neat hand inviting friends to relieve the isolation of his country retreat.

Chesterfield's 200 letters of advice to his natural son were published posthumously and became a guide for a generation of young gentleman to such subjects as table manners, deportment, food and wine, art and politics. But they had their critics: Samuel Johnson, who had found Chesterfield woefully inadequate as a patron for his *Dictionary* (see page 32), criticised them as teaching 'the morals of a whore and the manners of a dancing-master'. The Victorians too deplored them, their attitude summarised in a picture of c. 1880 which shows the solid Johnson and a number of other poor (read deserving) subjects awaiting an audience with Chesterfield, who ignores them in favour of a train of decorated fops. It's an image that makes you question the veracity of the portrait after Gainsborough that hangs opposite showing the master at the age of 76 as a kind and wise personification of old age.

ADDRESS Chesterfield Walk, Blackheath, London SE10 9QS (020 8853 0035)
OPEN daily, 10.00–13.00, 14.00–18.00; winter 10.00–16.00
ADMISSION £4.50/£3.40/£2.30
ACCESS limited
RAIL Greenwich, Blackheath

WOODLANDS

This elegant house was built in 1774 by G Gibson, who also designed Lewisham parish church, for John Julius Angerstein (1735–1823), the founding father of Lloyds of London and a collector whose paintings formed the nucleus of the National Gallery. His son and grandson served as local MPs and the family occupied the house until 1870. From 1923 to 1967 it was used as a convent (Mycenae House next door was built as an annexe in the 1930s); the London Borough of Greenwich bought it in 1972 and today it serves, appropriately enough, as an art gallery and local-history museum.

Engravings and pictures in a glass case upstairs show Woodlands at the time of its construction as a delightful five-bay stuccoed country villa; today it has a rather forlorn air. The exterior has been spoiled by the addition of an ugly bay window at the front and an overscaled portico in comparison with the delicate original; the porch on the side has been blocked up; an extension at the rear, while successfully aping the distinctive curved bay windows with their delicate swagged decoration, detracts from the original's symmetry and simplicity.

Inside you can still get some sense of the elegant ground-floor rooms and a few original features such as the doors, doorcases and decorative ceilings remain.

ADDRESS 90 Mycenae Road, London SE3 7SE (020 858 4631; www.greenwich.gov.uk) **OPEN** Monday and Tuesday, 9.00–17.30; Thursday, 9.00–20.00; Saturday, 9.00–17.00

ADMISSION free **ACCESS** very limited **GETTING THERE** rail Westcombe Park/Underground North Greenwich, then bus 422 or 108

[east london]

Eastbury Manor House **280**
Hall Place **283**
Red House **286**
Valence House **294**

EASTBURY MANOR HOUSE

A great house, ancient, and now almost fallen down, where tradition says the
Gunpowder Treason Plot was at first contriv'd, and that all the first
consultations about it were held there.
Daniel Defoe, *A Tour throughout the Whole Island of Great Britain*, 1772

Eastbury Manor House – a red-brick Tudor mansion with chimneystacks designed to impress – sits incongruously in the middle of a
crescent of council houses. Owned by the National Trust since 1918,
when it was saved from demolition as the area was developed, and leased
to the local council as the headquarters of its arts unit, it opens nine Sat-
urdays a year with all guns blazing: on the day I visited, displays of Elizabethan music and dance, spinning and basket-weaving, Tudor games,
pot and t-shirt painting, a model-railway exhibition, astrology readings
and guided tours were all included in the admission price. Unsurprisingly, it was difficult to get a sense of Eastbury as a house.

Eastbury was built in 1557–58 as a country residence for wealthy merchant Clement Sysley on land that until the reformation had belonged
to Barking Abbey. In 1592 Clement's son Thomas leased it to his step-
brother Augustine Steward to pay off his debts to his stepfather. It's
possible the house was occupied by Lord Monteagle, a Catholic peer
and brother of one of the conspirators in the 1605 gunpowder plot.
Monteagle was warned not to go to parliament that day and tipped off
the king. One of the rooms also contains the coat-of-arms of John
Moore, whose stepdaughter married conspirator Francis Tresham. During the early 18th century the house was occupied by a succession of tenant farmers and fell into increasing disrepair; from 1834 it was used as
farm buildings and to accommodate farm labourers.

Like its predecessor Sutton House (see page 170), Eastbury is built on

an H plan, with a three-bay great hall in the bar of the H connecting two seven-bay ranges to the east and west that flank a walled courtyard to the south. The evocatively worn entrance porch on the north front would originally have led via a screen into the great hall; now the visitor enters a corridor containing the 19th-century stairwell. The east wing was made up of the family's summer and winter parlours (the former, its brickwork exposed, now functions as a café); in the west wing were the steward's room (now lined with 17th-century panelling) with a raised floor to accommodate the cellars below, the kitchen (partially restored) and the buttery and pantry (now toilets).

Vertical circulation was via two circular stairtowers, one for servants and one for the family (the eastern family tower was partially demolished c. 1814, though the moulded brick handrail can still be seen from the courtyard). The servants' staircase, a spiral of solid oak, is one of the few remaining evocative spaces. The bedroom in the south-west corner, with a closet and garde-robe (toilet) opening off it, the latter in the same position as today's ladies loo, was probably Clement Sysley's. Above the great hall is the painted room with 17th-century wall paintings depicting landscapes and seascapes, probably done by artists from the Netherlands. The long gallery above the parlours was originally divided into several smaller rooms. Both spaces have their original beams and in the mercifully peaceful attic you can still see much of the roof's original timberwork.

ADDRESS Eastbury Square, Barking, Essex ID11 9SN (020 8507 0119)
OPEN first Saturday of the month, 10.00–16.00

ADMISSION £1.50/50p/family ticket £4
ACCESS limited until completion of renovations in November 2002
UNDERGROUND Upney

HALL PLACE

Hall Place doesn't need the annoying piped Tudor music to evoke atmosphere. Despite its chequered history of occupation, this dramatically schizophrenic house has survived remarkably intact and is well able to hold its own against the range of money-making and community roles it currently plays. The house began life as a relatively modest manor built by city merchant Sir John Champneis in about 1537. Unusually, it was constructed of rubble masonry with flint infill – perhaps because as a recent lord mayor of London Champneis had access to large quantities of medieval stone made available by Henry VIII's destruction of religious buildings. His house consisted of a central great hall flanked by two wings in a U plan: the west wing included a small chapel, parlour and bedrooms; to the east was a service wing. Following Sir John's death in 1556 his son Justinian enlarged and altered this part of the house to its present form.

Justinian's son sold the property to London merchant Robert Austen, who more than doubled its size by dramatically mirroring Champneis' black and white horseshoe with a red-brick extension tacked on to the back of the great hall, its ten-bay south wing fully enclosing a new court-yard. Though Austen extended his house during the interregnum of the 1650s, he flourished equally during the restoration of the monarchy and the house was to remain in his family until 1772 when it was inherited by distant relative-by-marriage Sir Francis Dashwood. It was rented out as a school until 1849; in 1870 it was restored and let to tenants including early-20th-century music-hall star Denise Orme and the Countess of Limerick from 1917 to 1943. From 1935, when it was sold to Bexley Council, it was one of Britain's grandest council houses. It was used again as a school from 1957 until its restoration in 1968.

Though the ground-floor corridor containing the information desk

[east london]

looks pleasingly Tudor, it is in fact the northern wing of Austen's 1650 extension (the only part of the later house usually open to the public) given beams and half-timbering over a quarter of a millennium later by Lady Limerick. The great hall is more authentic. Unlike earlier examples at Croydon Old Palace, Eltham Palace or Carew Manor, its coved ceiling consists of a lattice of beams, their intersections marked by hand-carved bosses, with plaster between. It was originally two rooms: an almost square, double-height hall with a single large bay window in the central flank of the house and at the eastern end a food store or buttery, possibly doubling as a dining hall for the servants, with a gallery above. It was probably Justinian who amalgamated the two and reduced the size of the gallery to create a grander, though still relatively domestically scaled space and allow the addition of another window (made of wood, not stone) to give the central façade of the house, if not the interior of the hall, its present somewhat cramped symmetry. The kitchen in the eastern wing beyond the buttery is currently being restored. Mirroring the buttery in the western wing is a parlour lined from floor to ceiling with square wood panels punctuated by wooden pilasters.

The upper floor of the east wing, beyond the gallery, is an unatmospheric display space. The western wing contains two rooms: the first, originally the master bedroom, was transformed between 1660 and 1680 by the addition of an elaborate ornamental plasterwork ceiling decorated with animals and grotesque figures; the second, added by Justinian, is a long gallery with a plasterwork ceiling installed in the 18th century. Both are accessed by off-centre large double doors fitted when cumbersome hooped dresses became fashionable. It's worth peering out of the windows in the upper corridor for the view of Austen's courtyard, its ground floor originally open cloisters.

ADDRESS Bourne Road, Bexley, Kent DA5 1PQ (01322 526574) **OPEN** Monday to Saturday, 10.00–17.00; summer only: Sunday and bank holiday Mondays, 11.00–17.00 **ADMISSION** free **RAIL** Bexley

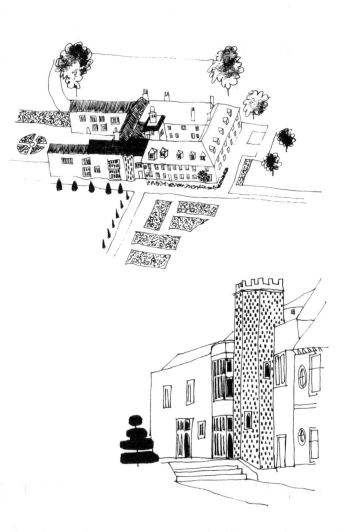

RED HOUSE

She haunts me still… an apparition of fearful and wonderful intensity… this dark silent medieval woman with her medieval toothache. Morris himself is extremely pleasant and quite different from his wife.
Henry James, 1868

The idea of Red House was hatched by three men in a boat during a rowing trip down the Seine in summer 1858 – William Morris (1834–96), architect Philip Webb, whom Morris had met two years earlier during his year-long apprenticeship with gothic-revivalist architect G E Street, and Charles Faulkner, a Birmingham mathematician whom Morris had met at Oxford through his friend Edward Burne-Jones. At the time Morris had abandoned architecture to pursue the pure art of painting at the passionate behest of pre-Raphaelite artist Dante Gabriel Rossetti, with whom Burne-Jones was a pupil. In February 1858 Morris had become engaged to Jane Burden, a groom's daughter he and Rossetti had spotted at an Oxford theatre. Rossetti asked Jane to model for the frescoes he was planning for the new debating hall of the Oxford Union. Though the project proved disastrous – the paint began to rub off before the job was finished and Morris' contribution was so amateurish it made his mentor laugh – through it Morris not only met his future wife but discovered the talent for which he is best remembered when he was allocated the job of decorating the ceiling.

Red House was conceived by Morris as a home for his future wife and family and a 'small Palace of Art of my own' which would satisfy his dreams of communal living and purpose first given shape in an abandoned idea for a monastery he and his friends planned to found after their days at Oxford (see Water House, page 308). It seems that the five years he and Jane lived there – from the summer of 1860 to November 1865 –

were the happiest of their life: their two daughters Jenny and May were born in 1861 and 1862 respectively and the house was filled each weekend with such friends as Webb, Faulkner, poet Algernon Charles Swinburne, the Burne-Joneses (Edward had married Georgina, the vivacious daughter of a Methodist minister, in June 1860), Rossetti and his wife Elizabeth Siddal (who committed suicide in 1862), and Rossetti's mentor Ford Madox Brown. As well as producing furnishings, hangings and murals for the house, the friends spent time playing bowls, touring the countryside in the medieval-style coach Morris had built, eating, drinking and talking. 'It was the most beautiful sight in the world', wrote a visitor, 'to see Morris coming up from the cellar before dinner, beaming with joy, with his hands full of bottles of wine and others tucked under his arms.'

The solitary occupation of painting had made the gregarious Morris irritable and miserable; in the collaborative nature of the decorative arts he found a vocation more suited to his temperament. In 1861 Brown had the idea of formalising the friends' ad hoc crafts activities and the commissions he, Burne-Jones and Webb were receiving for furniture and stained-glass by founding with Rossetti, Faulkner and P P Marshall, a surveyor friend, the firm of Morris, Marshall, Faulkner & Co. It was hoped that by taking part in the production and sale of their designs, the artists would avoid the division of manual and intellectual labour that according to Ruskin produced a society of 'morbid thinkers, and miserable workers'. The firm – established in 1861 using the £900 per annum Morris received from the shares in a Devonshire copper mine he had inherited from his father plus a loan of £100 from his mother – was to revolutionise 19th- and 20th-century design, but its development proved the death knell for Morris' dream. In the early years it ate steadily into his inheritance and though by 1865 its prospects were improving, its success required new London premises, while the effort of managing the enterprise from Red House was becoming increasingly taxing. At first Morris suggested adding another wing to the house for the Burne-Joneses and buying land for workshops nearby. But his friends' ill health made the north-facing, isolated Red House impractical and Morris –

whose own prolonged attack of rheumatic fever had made the daily journey to London impossible – was forced to choose between home and
business. His grief was so great he never saw Red House again.

Morris had married Jane because of her beauty rather than her personality; Swinburne stated frankly that he should have been content to
have 'that wonderful and most perfect stunner of his to look at or speak
to. The idea of marrying her is insane.' And it seems that while he was
very much in love with her, she found his wildly oscillating enthusiasms
and irascible personality difficult to deal with and retreated into defensive, enigmatic silence, aggravated by nervous rheumatism (that
'medieval toothache'). Just two years after the couple left Red House
Rossetti asked Jane to model for him again and fell passionately in love
with her. Morris was generous to a fault, taking out a joint tenancy with
his rival of the Manor House in Kelmscott, where Jane and their daughters spent much of their time, and retreating through journeys to Iceland
– his latest passion – and his friendship with Georgina Burne-Jones
(whose husband was having an affair). It seems that Jane and Rossetti
continued their liaison for about a decade, after which she terminated it
for the sake of the children. The marriage survived: according to a
description of the Morris and Jane in the 1890s by George Bernard
Shaw, with whom May Morris had a 'mystic betrothal': 'He could not sit
in the same room without his arm round her waist. His voice changed
when he spoke to her as it changed to no one else. His wife was beautiful, and knew that to be so was part of her household business. His was
to do all the talking. Their harmony seemed to me to be perfect.'

Red House was a three-dimensional statement of Morris' principles:
a challenge to the dominance of the machine and a call for a return to
human values and traditional craftsmanship embodied in a rosy vision of
the medieval age. Drawing on the forms and materials of vernacular
English country architecture – a massive barn-like tiled roof, red brick
and irregular fenestration that expresses what lies within rather than
conforming to the demands of the façade – it was a marked contrast to
the neoclassical regularity and painted stucco then fashionable. May

Morris wrote of her father that 'when he came to the furnishing of Red House, nothing could be found that would satisfy him'. So the weekend visits of the couple's friends turned into working parties in which Burne-Jones and Rossetti painted glass, tiles and furniture – most of which was designed by Webb – Morris drew flower patterns for hangings that Jane and her sister embroidered and Faulkner painted the geometrical ceiling patterns laboriously picked out in the wet plaster. The walls were distempered in pale colours as a backdrop for a grand series of wall paintings – though Morris' most lasting legacy is the wallpaper that lines the house today, originally all the walls were to be covered with murals or hangings. The aim was to recreate the atmosphere of a miniature medieval castle; rather than being a rejection of Victorian gloom and clutter, the principal rooms were dark and elaborately furnished.

The exterior is that of a fairytale cottage writ large: the asymmetrical façades, the heavy overhanging roofs punctuated by projections and recesses, the turrets, towering chimneystacks and porches with gothic arches contribute to the appearance of a house that has grown up organically. Despite the many, seemingly randomly placed windows, Red House seems to enclose a private world rather than presenting a series of façades for public display. The lawn at the inner angle of the L plan – its main feature a well surmounted by a conical roof – was originally an outdoor room enclosed by the trellis that inspired Morris' first wallpaper.

The main entrance is near the middle of the north wing; the entrance hall cuts through this wing to the staircase at the inner angle of the L. To the east of the hall, beyond two rooms closed to the public (a bedroom and waiting room in Webb's plan), is a gallery leading to the house's other entrance, a porch Morris romantically referred to as the Pilgrim's Rest in reference to the house's location on the old London-to-Canterbury road. To the west of the entrance hall is the drawing room (formerly the dining room); the other wing of the L beyond it contains service space: a bathroom (formerly a storeroom), utility room (formerly a pantry), dining room (formerly a kitchen and the only ground-floor room in this wing open to the public) and kitchen (formerly a scullery).

Like the exterior, the entrance hall eschews symmetry and grandeur, its differently scaled doors arranged in accordance with the demands of the rooms around it. The built-in settle-cum-bureau designed by Webb is a typical reinvention and amalgamation of traditional forms; much of Morris' unfinished painting of medieval knights and ladies was unsurprisingly covered over. The oak staircase, with its tapered newel posts and minimal carving, is a triumph of simplicity while the bold blue and white geometrical pattern that adorns the ceiling, which follows the form of the roof of the tower, has a surprising drama lacking in Morris' more delicate designs. The walls were to be completely covered with paintings by Burne-Jones of Trojan War scenes re-enacted in medieval costume.

The gallery leading to the Pilgrim's Rest – lit by windows with panes patterned by Morris and Burne-Jones – is accessed through incongruous leaded-glass double doors, some of whose panels are scratched with the names of friends (including Arthur Lasenby Liberty) May Morris brought back to view the house after her father's death. The former dining room is dominated by an ungainly Webb dresser stained and lacquered in Morris' favourite dragon's-blood red, its relatively conventional bottom half surmounted by a shelf divided into narrow compartments by barley-twist balustrading in turn surmounted by small cupboards topped by three pointless 'gables' that almost touch the ceiling. In a concession to his desire to banish the division between art and craft, Morris allowed his bricklayers to design the fireplace, here and elsewhere.

Morris' workroom in the north-eastern wing is above the ground-floor bedroom and study, extending over the Pilgrim's Rest and part of the gallery to form an L. Like the entrance hall, it gives the impression of using up leftover space with no concern for proportion or symmetry – the door and fireplace are both off centre and there is an extraordinary range of windows on two levels – an effect both disquieting and satisfying in that it improvises so successfully. Like most of the first-floor rooms it penetrates the roof to give a dramatic ceilingscape. A corridor lit by circular leaded windows leads past a small dressing room to William and Jane's bedroom above the hall – a long, thin, north-facing room originally hung with embroidered blue serge with a mural on the theme of the Garden of Eden begun by Elizabeth Siddal.

The drawing room above the former dining room – the largest and loftiest room in the house and intended by Morris to be 'the most beautiful room in England' – is lit by three tall casement windows in the north elevation and the dramatic oriel in the west elevation. The settle designed by Morris was brought from his previous home in Red Lion Square; Webb added a canopy that replicates a minstrels' gallery but in fact isn't high enough to stand in and simply gives access to the loft. The settle is flanked by three of the seven planned wallpaintings by Burne-Jones, one of which depicts William and Jane crowned at a wedding feast, standing in for the medieval subjects of Froissart's romance 'The Tale of Sire Degrevaunt'. Above the ground-floor service rooms are two guest bedrooms and the servants' room, whose careless design reveals the limitations of Morris' champagne socialism. Though divided into three – giving each occupant barely room for a bed – the room is lit by a single window so only one occupant benefits from natural light.

From 1952 until his death in 1999 Red House was lived in by architect Edward Hollamby, who undertook its painstaking restoration. It's still inhabited by his widow, and a pleasingly minimal effort to tidy up is made before visits, to judge by the clothes scattered around the guest bedrooms. Morris' dream of a purpose-designed home and studio may not have materialised for him, but seems to have worked well for another family who spent almost half a century appreciating the home in which he spent only five years.

ADDRESS 13 Red House Lane, Bexleyheath, Kent DA6
OPEN closed until autumn 2003; call 020 8331 8138 day for details
ACCESS limited
ADMISSION £4
RAIL Bexleyheath

VALENCE HOUSE

The only surviving manor house in Dagenham, Valence House is located in the middle of the vast Becontree estate, part of an ambitious suburban housing project begun by the London County Council after World War 1 to reward the families of veterans and rehouse some 100,000 slum-dwellers. The largest council-housing estate in the world, its 25,000 homes were completed between 1921 and 1934. Valence House takes its name from Agnès de Valence, granddaughter of the French wife of King John (1167–1216), who spent 19 years of widowhood here following the death of her third husband. Its last occupants were the May family – three generations of formidable women and a shadowy farmer patriarch – who lived here from 1879 until the house was acquired by the council in 1921.

Valence House is accessed via a grim path past factory buildings, after which its charmingly irregular white-painted elevations, arranged in an L, come as a welcome surprise. The history of the house's development is apparently as long and complicated as that of its ownership, but despite its present role as a local-history museum, little effort is made to make either accessible to the visitor. The earliest part of the present timber-framed structure dates from the 1400s; one wall of the corridor outside the Valence and period rooms was the original façade, and the remains of the jetty can be seen at ceiling level. A survey of 1649 – at which point Valence was confiscated by Cromwell from the Dean and Chapter of Windsor – reveals a much larger building boasting 15 hearths.

As Valence House is configured at present, the entrance wing contains a modern activities room, the Fanshawe Room and the reception area. The Fanshawe room is lined with wooden panels dating from the late 16th century and hung with a collection of portraits of the Fanshawe family, who lived in neighbouring Parsloes Manor. (Among them are

Peter Lely's picture of the foppish Sir Thomas and his wife.) The other wing houses a recreation of a chemist's shop, a Victorian servants' parlour with eerie waxwork figures and a café. Up the 17th-century oak staircase with its elegant twisted balusters are the O'Leary gallery, named after the librarian who instigated the idea of a local-history museum, a room with displays about Dagenham, a 17th-century room and a recreation of a Becontree-estate kitchen and living room in 1945.

ADDRESS Becontree Avenue, Dagenham, Essex RM8 3HT (020 8227 5293; www.barking-dagenham.gov.uk) **OPEN** Tuesday to Friday, 9.30–13.00, 14.00–16.30; Saturday, 10.00–16.00 **ADMISSION** free **GETTING THERE** rail to Chadwell House, then bus 62/Underground to Becontree, then bus 62

[north-east london]

Bruce Castle **298**

Forty Hall **300**

Millfield House **303**

Queen Elizabeth's Hunting Lodge **304**

Vestry House **306**

Water House **308**

BRUCE CASTLE

Bruce Castle takes its name from the family of spider-watcher Robert de Bruce, who owned the land on which it sits before it was confiscated when he joined the war for Scottish independence at the end of the 13th century. The house as it stands today – a seven-bay, three-storey red-brick manor with two full-height polygonal end bays and an elaborate central porch – comes across as a feeble, small-scale imitation of Charlton House (see page 258) that eloquently makes the point that when it comes to architecture, 'Try, try, and try again' may not be the best motto. Inside, the demands of generations of schoolboys and a century of public ownership have destroyed any grandeur the interior may once have possessed.

We know that in 1514 the site was occupied by a simple courtyard house owned by William Compton, groom of the bedchamber to Henry VIII; a tower in the grounds, possibly built as a falconry, dates from about this time as does some of the brickwork in the west bay. The house was radically remodelled between 1682 and 1684 by Henry Hare, the 2nd Lord Coleraine, following his second marriage to the rich and powerful Lady Sarah, Duchess of Somerset (his first wife is said to have been so ill-treated she killed herself and her son by jumping off the balcony). One room deep and nine bays long, with wings at each end extending to the rear, Henry's new house had the E-plan south front we see today. His grandson – another Henry – extended his home to the east at the beginning of the 18th century and added a range of rooms along the north front to give the present heavily pedimented rear façade, its ground-floor windows set within arches, perhaps intended as a loggia. James Townsend, an MP married to the second Henry's illegitimate daughter, remodelled the uppermost storey to its current profile, replacing the pitched roof and gables of the south front with a flat roof and parapet to give the house a more Georgian look.

Subsequent owners have included John Eardley Wilmot, who helped refugees fleeing first the American War of Independence and then the French Revolution, and the Hill family, who extended the house to the rear in 1860 to accommodate a boys' progressive boarding school run without corporal punishment according to a system of self-discipline developed by co-founder Rowland Hill. Hill left teaching in 1833 and was subsequently the originator of the penny postage system. Soon after the school's closure in 1891 the house was sold to the council; it opened as a museum in 1906.

The large entrance hall ran the full depth of the first Henry's house; the room beyond, which has information about the development of the building, was the centrepiece of the north range added by his grandson. The two rooms that make up the east wing are now an inventor's centre and postal museum; the polygonal east bay houses 1930s office equipment. The bay and room to the west are a kitchen and café. A large, impressive room above the entrance hall is an exhibition space.

ADDRESS Lordship Lane, London NI7 8NU (020 8808 8772)
OPEN Wednesday to Sunday, 13.00–17.00

ADMISSION free
GETTING THERE rail Bruce Grove/ Underground Wood Green, then bus 243

FORTY HALL

Forty Hall was built in 1629–32 for City merchant Nicholas Rainton, a fabric importer and a puritan (see the cheerless portrait in the Rainton room) who had refused to lend money to Charles I and was imprisoned briefly in 1640 for failing to supply accounts to the crown. The architect was Edward Carter, who had worked with Inigo Jones, whom he succeeded as surveyor to the king's works. Rainton retired to Forty Hall at the outbreak of the Civil War in 1642 and since his children and grandchildren had all predeceased him by the time of his death four years later, the property was inherited by a great-nephew. Purchased by what was to become the Parker-Bowles family in 1895, it was sold to the council in 1951.

Forty Hall is a well-proportioned three-storey red-brick Jacobean mansion that compresses the features of grander residences into a compact square plan. Three of its elegantly simple five-bay façades have been compromised by the addition of elaborate porches at the turn of the 18th century. The house was extended to the west in 1636 with further additions in c. 1800, 1898 and 1928 to augment the kitchens and service quarters. Though it was once thought the roof of Forty Hall was initially supported on gables as at Boston Manor (see page 207) it is now believed to have been one of the first hipped roofs in the country.

The passage between the front and garden entrances divides the house into the grand rooms to the east – surprisingly small, though perfectly formed – and the more cramped service quarters to the west. The great hall in the north-east corner – a medieval concept writ tiny – would have been used for formal receptions and was originally divided from the passage only by a screen until the central arch was filled in by a door to transform the room into a parlour in c. 1788. The plain panelling (originally unpainted), bold strapwork ceiling – prefabricated and laid out on

the floor before being lifted and plastered into place – and dominant asymmetrically positioned fireplace, its cherub heads and obelisks signifying prestige and power, fade into insignificance beside the elaboration of the 17th-century screen wall with its arcades, scallop shells and semi-grotesque busts. In the drawing room to the south is more panelling, a delicate plasterwork ceiling and an original fireplace and overmantel incorporating a series of paired Doric half-columns.

The Rainton room in the south-west corner was transformed in the mid 18th century by replacing the party wall with the adjacent corridor by a screen with a ceiling-high central arch supported on fluted Ionic columns. The cupboard to the right of the fireplace was probably once a privy with a chute down to the cesspit. The rooms between the Rainton room and the present reception area would originally have been the kitchen and pantry; the reception area was the steward's room (before the Civil War stewards were often the younger sons of gentlemen), conveniently located to supervise the running of the house, its plasterwork decoration of musical instruments and scores probably done c. 1750 when such motifs became popular. The staircase, last remodelled in 1897, has beautiful twisted balusters which may date from a rebuilding in c. 1700. Several of the upstairs rooms – which house an eclectic range of exhibits – have 17th-century ceilings and early-18th-century panelling.

As at Gunnersbury Park (see page 216), the elegance of the family rooms at Forty Hall was maintained by a horde of servants living both in the house and in various outbuildings. At Forty Hall the latter have an elegance of their own, and it's certainly worth peeping through the flamboyantly mannerist brick gateway at the west of the house to the colonnaded inner courtyard that once housed the stables, a brewhouse, millhouse, laundry and the servants' hall.

ADDRESS Forty Hill, Enfield EN2 9HA (020 8363 8196) **OPEN** Saturday, Sunday, 13.00–16.30

ADMISSION free **ACCESS** ground floor only **GETTING THERE** rail Enfield Town, then bus and short walk

MILLFIELD HOUSE

Little of Millfield House's chequered history is apparent from its genteel exterior. It's an attractive nine-bay, two-storey late-18th-century brick mansion, its central three bays slightly recessed and fronted by a shallow curved porch, the outer flanks with pretty tented verandahs probably dating from the early 19th century. Internally, the finest features are the circular entrance hall and sinuous cantilevered staircase topped by an oval lantern. To the right of the entrance is the ground-floor gallery, with a neoclassical frieze of urns and husk garlands and fine door surrounds; to the left are the plainer bar and committee room.

The house first appears in the minutes of the Edmonton vestry in 1796 where it's mentioned that it had lately been let to the ambassador of the German empire. Robert Mushet of the Royal Mint died here in 1828; in 1849 the building was sold to the Strand Union Guardians as a school for workhouse children from crowded inner London. In 1915 the building was converted into a hospital for epileptics; when this closed in 1971 the house was acquired by the council and converted to its present role as an arts centre and venue for council training days. Visiting is a hit-and-miss affair depending on which rooms are in use.

ADDRESS Silver Street, London
N18 1PJ (020 8803 5283)
OPEN daily, 9.00–22.00

ADMISSION free
ACCESS very limited
RAIL Silver Street

QUEEN ELIZABETH'S HUNTING LODGE

Well I remember as a boy my first acquaintance with a room hung with faded
greenery at Queen Elizabeth's Lodge by Chingford Hatch in Epping Forest
(I wonder what has become of it now?), and the impression of romance that it
made upon me!... yes, that was more than upholstery, believe me.
William Morris, *The Lesser Arts of Life*, 1882

Sited at what feels like the start of the countryside and looked after by an
enthusiastic team huddled around a single fan heater in order not to dis-
turb its venerable timbers with 21st-century-standard central heating,
Queen Elizabeth's Hunting Lodge retains something of the original
magic that inspired William Morris, along with much of its original
woodwork. The building was commissioned by Henry VIII, though it's
unlikely he visited it as by the time of its completion in 1543, four years
before his death, he was already in poor health.

Based on an L plan with an integral stair tower, the three-storey structure – made up of massive oak timbers which challenged the skills of
Tudor carpenters – was originally a form of grandstand for viewing the
hunt, its sides open to the elements. Elizabeth I may have used the lodge
as she is known to have hunted in the forest on a number of occasions; in
1589 she ordered a survey as the structure was in a state of disrepair. Hunting in Elizabethan times was very much a staged affair, popular as an
entertainment for visiting dignitaries, with the deer driven by dogs via a
series of corrals and ambushes towards the hunting party in the lodge and
then slaughtered with a showy display of riding and archery. The queen
would first approve the droppings presented to her by the head huntsman
to determine whether the chosen stag was a suitable quarry and would
slice through the dead animal at the end to assess the quality of the meat.

The lodge's most dramatic space is the top-floor room with its far-reaching views over the forest. From the 17th century, when the timber frame was covered in plaster and windows inserted, this was used for sessions of the manor court where complaints about rent and land distribution would be brought before the lord of the manor. The middle floor – laid out with a feast – would have been draped and highly decorated. The unplastered ground floor was for servants.

Though not strictly speaking a house, the lodge was lived in by a keeper from the 17th century and for several generations was the home of the Watkins family. It was acquired by the Corporation of London in 1878 and while the top floor was used as a tea room and then to house the collection of Epping Forest Museum, the lower floors were lived in by the Butt family until 1926.

ADDRESS Ranger's Road, London
E4 7QH (020 8529 6681)
OPEN Wednesday to Sunday,
13.00–16.00 or dusk

ACCESS ground floor only
ADMISSION free
RAIL Chingford

VESTRY HOUSE

Though little different in plan or appearance from a contemporary five-bay double-fronted family home, Vestry House was in fact a purpose-built workhouse expected to accommodate 30 to 40 'paupers' in six of its eight smallish rooms. It was built in 1730 by the vestry – an assembly of all the ratepayers of the parish which was responsible for many aspects of local government including providing for the poor – just eight years after an act of parliament first permitted the construction of workhouses. A workroom was added to the rear in 1756 and the vestry meeting room to the left of the entrance was almost doubled in size in 1779 by extending it into the front yard (it was also given its own separate entrance). The rear extension was used as a police station for 30 years from 1840, when the paupers were moved to the new Union Workhouse (now Langthorne Hospital) in Leyton, and subsequently as an armoury for the Walthamstow Volunteers and as a builder's yard. From 1882 the front part of the building was the headquarters of the Walthamstow Literary and Scientific Institute and from 1892 it was a private house, occupied first by the Maynard family and then by Constance Demain Saunders, who gave it to the council in 1930.

The ground-floor rooms to the left of the entrance (now a gallery) were originally the vestry meeting room with the workhouse-master's room – in which he and his wife would cook and eat – at the rear. The paupers cooked and ate in the two kitchen areas to the right (now offices and a shop). The bedrooms above the gallery are now one long space with displays of Victorian household objects. Those above the paupers' kitchens house toys and games and a reconstructed Victorian parlour, its polished furniture and multitude of homely ornaments a reminder of the middle-class norms enjoyed by those who kept the poor in such miserable conditions. By the 1820s Vestry House accommodated more than 80 poor, issued with clothes with the badge 'w.p.' (Waltham-stow Poor) sewn on the shoulder, three primitive meals a day washed down with beer brewed on the premises, medical care and basic education for their children. Both adults and children had to work for their keep (the plaque above the entrance bore the legend 'if any would not work neither should he eat').

The transition between the original building and the rear extension, roofed over in the early 19th century, has a chilling display of truncheons. The extension, panelled in wood taken from the 1596 Essex Hall, demolished in 1933, now houses cases of clothing and uniforms, though an original police cell, complete with graffiti, has been preserved. The area to the left, roofed over in 1934, was formerly an exercise yard surrounded by a 4-metre wall. The space above the panelled room – originally a paupers' dormitory accessed only by a ladder – is now a local-history archive.

ADDRESS Vestry Road, London E17 9NH (020 8509 1917) **OPEN** Monday to Friday, 10.00–13.00, 14.00–17.30; Saturday, 10.00–13.00, 14.00–17.00

ADMISSION free **ACCESS** ground floor after September 2002 **UNDERGROUND/RAIL** Walthamstow Central

WATER HOUSE
(THE WILLIAM MORRIS GALLERY)

William Morris' family – his mother Emma, plus two older and two younger sisters and four younger brothers – lived at Water House for only eight years, during most of which time William (1834–96) was away from home, first at school at Marlborough and then at Oxford. But the house provided the backdrop for two dramatic announcements to his long-suffering mother which were to transform the course of his life and arguably of late-19th- and early-20th-century design: his decision to turn his back on the church – a vocation he had chosen at Marlborough, perhaps inspired by the romance of singing Elizabethan church music in the neo-gothic chapel newly designed by Edward Blore – in favour of a career as an architect and then to quit architecture for the pure art of painting.

The Morris family had moved to Walthamstow from their huge Woodford mansion in 1848 following the death of Morris' bill-broker father. It was a step back from heady affluence to respectable prosperity thanks to the fluctuating value of the family's shares in a Devonshire copper mine. Morris junior was sent to Marlborough – a 'progressive' school with little organisation, no prefects and no uniform where the boys were allowed to ramble and birdnest at will – at the age of 14; his first stay at Water House was for the Christmas vacation of 1848–49. Three years later, following a rebellion at the school, he was brought back to Walthamstow to prepare for Oxford under the guidance of the Reverend F B Guy, with whom he spent some of the following year in Devon. In 1853 he went up to Exeter where on his first day he encountered Birmingham grammar-school boy Edward Burne-Jones. Through Burne-Jones he was to meet the group of friends – mathematician Charles Faulkner, also from Birmingham, and later painters Dante Gabriel Rossetti, Ford Madox Brown and William Holman Hunt – who through the pre-

Raphaelite brotherhood and the arts-and-crafts movement were to stamp their mark on 19th-century art and design. By the time his family left Water House in 1856 Morris had attained his majority, giving him access to an annual income of £900, and was articled to gothic-revivalist architect G E Street, in whose office he met Philip Webb, designer of his arts-and-crafts manifesto Red House (see page 286).

Morris' time at Oxford – where he became known as much for his explosive rages as for his purple trousers, swaggering bow ties and the rampant curly hair and beard that framed his pale, sensitive face – shaped many of his ideas. Through the Birmingham contingent he met people who had first-hand experience of the inhuman conditions in which workers lived following the industrial revolution – this tempered his romanticism and inspired his future socialism as well as fuelling a common desire for a return to a pre-industrial age. The friends would spend long evenings reading aloud (poetry, particularly Tennyson, was seen as a relevant and revolutionary activity) and it was probably here that Morris established his preference for the writers who from 1890 he would publish using typefaces of his own design through his Kelmscott Press. In 1855 the brotherhood set aside some of Morris' inheritance to found a magazine (the scheme superseded a previous notion of establishing a monastery and living together in chastity) in which William published the first examples of the poetry that was to reach its critical peak in *The Earthly Paradise* (1868–70). And on holidays to France with Burne-Jones the friends discovered the Italian pre-Raphaelite art and gothic-cathedral architecture that were to influence their painting and stained-glass design.

Though Water House and Walthamstow lacked some of the romantic appeal of Epping Forest, which Morris had explored avidly in his early childhood, the moat at the back of the house (which gave it its name) provided opportunities for swimming, sailing, skating and fishing, its central island a fantasy fairyland on which the children spent most of their days. The handsome, three-storey nine-bay brick mansion with symmetrical three-bay bows at either end was probably built in the late

1740s; an early reference describes a 'new built capital brick messuage or tenement' valued at £200 and owned by Catherine Woolball on her marriage to Sir Hanson Berney in 1756.

Through the elaborate porch supported on Corinthian columns on the southern entrance front is a spacious square hall that runs the full depth of the house, paved in Morris' day with marble flags. Water House is very much a museum of Morris' life and work with no attempt at an evocation of the way his family inhabited it, and the darkened rooms to the west trace the course of his eventful career. Room one, with the large bow at the front, deals with his childhood, his days at Oxford, the early days of his design company Morris, Marshall, Faulkner & Co. and his relationship with his wife Jane Burden up to the crisis in their marriage in the early 1870s. Room two, in the single-storey extension beyond, is devoted largely the wallpapers, fabrics and tapestries of the 1870s and 1880s. Room three, behind room two in the extension, has examples of books printed by the Kelmscott Press and pamphlets from Morris' time at the head of the Socialist League (1884-89), plus the satchel from which he distributed them. Room four, behind room one, has furniture, pottery and stained-glass. On the other side of the hall is a gallery with works by Alma-Tadema, Madox Brown, Burne-Jones and Rossetti.

At the top of the fine Spanish chestnut staircase is a huge landing that also runs the full depth of the house; Morris apparently used to like to read at the window seats here. The rooms to the west house a collection of paintings and objects donated by painter Frank Brangwyn, who worked for Morris & Co from the early 1880s. Opposite is a collection of furniture manufactured by Arthur Heygate Mackmurdo's Century Guild, a co-operative established in 1882 along the lines of MMF&Co.

The year after the Morris family left, Water House was bought by Edward Lloyd, whose *Lloyd's Illustrated London Newspaper* (later *Lloyd's Weekly News*), founded in 1842, had by 1863 reached a circulation of 350,000. In 1876 he bought the *Daily Chronicle*, which he transformed into a paper of national importance. The father of 24 children, he left Water House in 1885 because the new houses being built in the area 'did

not provide the right kind of companions for the social life of his growing children', according to the daughter of a former employee. It was a
sentiment echoed by Morris, who in later life described Walthamstow as
'once a pleasant place enough but now terribly cocknified and choked up
by the jerry builder'.

The house was given to the council by Edward Lloyd's son Frank in
1899, at which point it was almost derelict. In 1911 it became a school
clinic and dental surgery and in 1950 opened as a museum.

ADDRESS Forest Road, London
E17 4PP (020 8527 3782;
www.lbwf.gov.uk/wmg)
OPEN Tuesday to Saturday, first
Sunday every month,
10.00–13.00, 14.00–17 .00

ADMISSION free
ACCESS ground floor only
GETTING THERE Underground
Walthamstow Central, then
15-minute walk or bus from
station

[north-west london]

Avenue House **314**

Church Farmhouse Museum **315**

Grange Museum of Community History **317**

Headstone Manor **318**

AVENUE HOUSE

This eclectic house – its façade an ugly asymmetrical stuccoed mish-mash, its rear a sprawling if picturesque mix of rustic Italianate tower, romanesque arches and gothic windows – was built in 1859 by the Reverend Edward Philip Cooper. He inherited the land from the Allen family, owners of the Bibbesworth estate, whose manor house was what is now the Sternberg Centre on East End Road. In 1874 the house was bought by Henry Charles 'Inky' Stephens, son of Dr Henry Stephens, inventor of the famous ink. Stephens became MP for Finchley in 1887 and bequeathed his house to his constituents on his death in 1918. It was opened to the public in 1928, suffered a major fire in 1989 and since its restoration in 1993 has operated as a venue for meetings and functions.

Stephens extended the house in 1884, adding the drawing room at the east end. Presided over by a portrait of the man and his horse, this space is dominated by its fussy windows and kitsch mock-medieval ceiling. The elegance of the original drawing room (the salon) – part of which is now hived off into a corridor leading to a conservatory housing a small collection of Stephens memorabilia – is still suggested by the fine proportions, semi-circular bay to the garden, original panelling and fireplace. The original condition of Stephens' laboratory, above the drawing room, can be glimpsed from photographs showing an arts-and-crafts wood-panelled room with a built-in inglenook. Don't miss his more successful addition, a charming stableblock to the east of the house with a fairytale French gothic tower topped by a dovecote.

ADDRESS East End Road, London N3 3QE (020 8346 7812) **OPEN** Monday to Friday, 8.00–22.00 **ADMISSION** free **UNDERGROUND** Finchley Central

CHURCH FARMHOUSE MUSEUM

Built in c. 1660, only 15 years before Christopher Wren's Flamsteed House (see page 267), this charming red-brick farmhouse gives an insight into the lives of the rural middle-classes away from the elegance of the court and its acolytes. The house was the tenanted property of the Powis family – lords of Hendon manor – until 1756 when actor David Garrick bought the manor and the farm was sold to a Mr Bingley. Some ten years later ownership passed to Theodore Henry Broadhead, whose descendants owned the farmhouse until 1918 – mostly letting it to tenants – at which date the freehold was sold to George Dunlop, whose father Andrew had been the lessee from 1870. The property was acquired by Hendon Council in 1944 and from 1951–55 it was restored as a local-history museum. The space is now divided between reconstructions of 19th-century life and galleries for temporary exhibitions.

Though surrounded today by leafy Hendon suburbia, at the peak of its productivity Church Farm boasted more than 80 hectares of land, mostly devoted to making hay for the London market in fields fertilised symbiotically by dung swept up from the city's streets. Hendon produce was in high demand – according to John Middleton's *View of the Agriculture of Middlesex* (1798) the area turned out the best hay in the county – but by the mid 19th century suburban housing was beginning to replace the fields (Hendon station was built in 1868 and the Underground reached Golders Green in 1907). Within half a century factory work had superseded a millennium of agriculture as the main form of employment.

The original three-bay house, two-and-a-half storeys high and one room deep, had two rooms on each floor with a central chimney stack in the large room to the east. The attic was used to store grain and the cellar as a dairy. The original front door was probably at the back, facing the farmyard. Most of the two-room rear extension was added before 1754;

the staircase was installed in the late 18th or early 19th century; the front porch and west bay date from the late 19th century. The 35-centimetre-thick walls are of Flemish-bond red brick and most of the rooftiles are original. The most striking architectural feature is the dramatic chimney stack with its six grouped shafts.

Though the upper floor is used as an exhibition space, the integrity of the rooms has been retained and it's not difficult to imagine these as light-filled (if cramped) bedrooms. The sagging wooden beams and bowed floors (with notices warning that no more than 15 people should occupy the room at any one time) add atmosphere; the fireplaces are Victorian. The ground-floor extension has a display of 19th-century laundry equipment including washing dollies, mangles and flat irons. The kitchen is set up as it might have been in the 1820s, its huge walk-in fireplace sporting an array of implements that resemble medieval instruments of torture. The small central oak-panelled dining room is furnished with an oval table and Windsor chairs dating from the 1850s.

Hendon Council bought Church Farm in 1944 intending to demolish it for redevelopment. More enlightened views prevailed, and today's affluent suburbanites have at least a glimpse into the village life of an alien past. Some things, however, are depressingly familiar. According to Middleton: 'Women are frequently employed [in hay-making]… Their hours of labour are the same with those of the men. But the price of their labour is only one half of what is paid for the same work to their fellow-labourers of the other sex.'

ADDRESS Greyhound Hill, London NW4 4JR (020 8203 0130) **OPEN** Monday to Thursday, 10.00–12.30, 13.30–17.00; Saturday, 10.00–13.00, 14.00–17.30; Sunday, 14.00–17.30 **ADMISSION** free **UNDERGROUND** Hendon Central

GRANGE MUSEUM OF COMMUNITY HISTORY

This rambling two-storey L-shaped brick cottage, all that's left of a once thriving farm complex, stands forlornly in the centre of a four-lane roundabout just off the North Circular Road. It was originally one of the outbuildings of The Grove – a substantial house built just after 1700 by Thomas Wingfield and from 1886 the home of the Royal Canine Hospital. The Grange was converted into a house by solicitor James Hall, who bought The Grove and its outbuildings at the beginning of the 19th century. He installed the gothic sash windows and divided the interior into rooms; a sale catalogue of the 1870s describes it as having 'drawing, dining and breakfast rooms, 8 bedrooms, bathroom, butler's pantry, kitchen, larder and other domestic offices'. The house was bought by the council in 1962 and renovated as a museum in the 1970s.

Though little of the interior can be appreciated today, the museum has a late-Victorian parlour room-set and an Edwardian draper's shop. A photographic exhibition with taped reminiscences traces the history of Brent from the 1920s. The snapshots of local life are many and varied – queuing for the opening of B B Evans' sale in 1958; a West Indian service led by a visiting Jamaican preacher; a Gaelic dance competition. They tell the story of an area which has moved from the time when minority cultures had to be largely self-sufficient to the genuine multiculturalism of the 21st century. Not much of a house, perhaps, but a good museum.

ADDRESS Neasden Lane, London NW10 1QB (020 8452 8311) **OPEN** January to July: Monday to Friday, 11.00–17.00; August to December: Tuesday to Friday, 11.00–17.00, Sunday 14.00–17.00 **ACCESS** very limited **ADMISSION** free **UNDERGROUND** Neasden

HEADSTONE MANOR

Approached via a bridge over Middlesex's only water-filled moat, Headstone Manor looks like nothing more than an old farmhouse in the middle of a field. Yet behind this unremarkable exterior lies the oldest timber-framed house known to have survived in the county while the remains of the aisled hall and two small rooms to the right of the house viewed from the bridge constitute the oldest surviving structure in this book.

Headstone takes its name from a corruption of de la Hegge, the name of a family who from 1233 owned the land on which it stands. The oldest part of the present house has recently been dated to 1310; excavations indicate that the moated enclosure may have been full of buildings in medieval times. The manor was acquired as a local residence for the archbishops of Canterbury by John Stratford in 1344 and was leased to tenants from 1382 – including the Redynge family who lived here for more than 100 years from 1397. Tenants were bound by an agreement that specified the proportion of produce and the accommodation due the archbishops on their visits. In 1545 the house was surrendered to Henry VIII, who sold it to one of his court favourites, Sir Edward North. In 1631 it passed to the Rewse family (Simon Rewse was receiver-general to Lord North), who added a tower, porch and small room at the rear. In 1649, the Rewses having incurred debts during their support for the king in the Civil War, it was sold to William Williams. He added a substantial new wing, including a cellar, pantry, kitchen and bedroom, that almost doubled the house's size. The massive chimney stack with its diamond-shaped shafts dates from this time. The wing at the rear was added in the 1770s when the front of the house was given a fashionable brick façade. In 1925 the house was sold to Hendon Rural District Council and in 1986 it became part of the Harrow Museum & Heritage Centre.

Headstone is currently the subject of an ambitious restoration programme and until recently the only parts open to the public were two of the mid-18th-century rooms – low ceilinged and of rough construction – fitted out as a 1930s kitchen and parlour. The elegant late-18th-century granary, three storeys high with a surprising number of windows on its upper floors, was moved to the site from nearby Pinner Park in 1991. Even more impressive is the 1506 tithe barn – an uninterrupted space 45 metres long and 8 wide. Despite containing a café and a series of 19th-century room set-ups, its magnificence is undiminished.

[north-west london]

ADDRESS Harrow, Middlesex HA2 6PX (020 8861 2626)
OPEN closed until spring 2004; then Thursday to Saturday, 12.30–17.00; Sunday, bank holidays, 10.30–17.00
ADMISSION free
GETTING THERE Harrow-on-the-Hill Underground, then bus

[carshalton/cheam/croydon]

Addington Palace **322**
Carew Manor **324**
Honeywood **326**
Little Holland House **327**
Old Palace, Croydon **332**
Whitehall **335**

ADDINGTON PALACE

Built by Robert Mylne for alderman Barlow Trecothick, lord mayor of
London in 1770–71, this Palladian villa was completed in 1778 by which
time both its owner and the Palladian movement were dead. A painting
used in a promotional leaflet for the current owners' country club shows
a seven-bay two-storey mansion, with a central porch and pediment and
mansard roof, flanked by two four-bay wings fronted by single-storey
pavilions with single-storey extensions at each end, the whole built of
Portland stone. The reality today is somewhat different.

In 1807 Addington was acquired by means of an act of parliament for
the use of the archbishops of Canterbury following the sale of the nearby
Old Palace (see page 332). Archbishop Howley (1828–48), fresh from a
stint of rebuilding at Fulham (see page 87), enlarged the house to the scale
visible in the painting by building up the original single-storey four-bay
wings to match the height of the main building and extending them at
ground level to create a chapel and library. In 1898 Archbishop Temple
sold the palace to South African diamond merchant Frederick Alexander
English who engaged Richard Norman Shaw to restructure it, effectively
destroying its proportions and elegance by raising the main block by a
storey to allow for a double-height mock-medieval great hall and step-
ping it forward, presumably to create an imposing entrance space. In 1914
the house was taken over by the Red Cross for use as a hospital and in
1928 it was made into an hotel by Addiscombe Garden Estates. It was
purchased by Croydon Corporation in 1951 and from 1953 was leased to
the Royal School of Church Music. Its current owners acquired it in 1996.

The brief guided tour leads from Shaw's misconceived great hall,
complete with minstrels' gallery, to the more modest music room created
by Shaw from Howley's chapel. The well-proportioned lecture room
behind the great hall, its delicate plasterwork ceiling inset with Wedg-

wood-style medallions, leads to the library. The central staircase with its glazed cupola and wrought-iron balustrade is Shaw's most successful space. The robing room in the other pavilion was converted into a games room with a central skylight surrounded by moulded fruit and flowers; beyond it is a vaulted conservatory used by the school as a chapel in which you can get married if you can fix on a date a year in advance. Tea and coffee are served in the common room, which mirrors the lecture room. In the basement gym the building's occupants strive to retain the grace the palace itself has lost.

ADDRESS Gravel Hill, Croydon, CRO 5BB (020 8662 5000)
OPEN guided tours on 8 September, 17 November,

9 December 2002
ADMISSION free
ACCESS limited
RAIL Gravel Hill

CAREW MANOR

More than most stately homes, Carew Manor has been successively rebuilt in line with contemporary fashion – a point made most clearly at the end of the guided tour which takes visitors (wearing hard hats) to the cellar where you can see walls layered like an onion. Originally a moated fortified house built by Sir Nicholas Carew in the mid 14th century, in 1520 it was inherited by another Sir Nicholas Carew. A one-time favourite of Henry VIII, he fell from grace in 1537 and was executed; his house and estate were forfeit to the king. The house was restored to the family by Mary I and in the 1570s Nicholas' son Francis engaged in a substantial bout of rebuilding and landscaping. Rebuilt again with a classical façade by another Nicholas in the early 18th century, the house was occupied by the Carews until gambler Charles Hallowell Carew was forced to sell in 1859 to pay off his debts. The Lambeth Female Orphan Asylum gave it its final facelift, adding the present Victorian-gothic red-brick façades, the clocktower and the cross passage at the front that closes off the courtyard. The building has been a school since 1954.

The great hall, the only part of the house open to the public, was probably built by Sir Richard Carew between 1493 and 1520. Though looking like similar ceilings elsewhere, the roof is in fact a fake – made of small pieces of wood covered with mouldings to give a false impression of thickness, perhaps as a cost-cutting exercise.

ADDRESS Church Road, Beddington, Surrey (020 8770 4781; www.sutton.gov.uk) **OPEN** occasional tours at 14.00 and 15.30; advance booking necessary **ADMISSION** £3 **ACCESS** limited **RAIL** Sutton

HONEYWOOD

Honeywood was originally Wandle Cottage, a modest dwelling two rooms wide and one room deep in an attractive position overlooking one of Carshalton's many ponds. It is one of the few remaining examples of chalk and flint chequerwork construction, and the expanses of original exterior wall exposed in the two 19th-century extensions alone make Honeywood worth a visit.

The 17th-century cottage comprised what are now the shop and tea-rooms on the ground floor and two rooms on the first floor, the smaller fitted out as an Edwardian dining room and the larger as an exhibition space for displays about the area's history. Both feel extremely old with their irregular shapes and alarmingly sagging low ceilings. The front room of the boxy north extension of 1896 is set up as a nursery; more elegant is the two-room mid-19th-century extension at the rear.

Around 1903 a top-lit billiards room and garden room were added to the south and the house took the name Honeywood after a house on the site of the extension. The billiards room has remained intact. The wood-panelled space contains the original table, placed under a skylight, surrounded by purpose-made leather sofas and fittings. The garden room is a light-filled, delicately detailed space with a mullioned bay and stained-glass side windows with a pattern of hearts and stylised leaves. Don't miss the Edwardian bathroom behind the dining room which has the 'mayor's loo' from Sutton municipal offices – a fine affair decorated inside and out with blue flowers.

ADDRESS Honeywood Walk, Carshalton (020 8770 4297)
OPEN Wednesday to Friday and bank holidays, 11.00–17.00; Saturday and Sunday, 10.00–17.00
ADMISSION £1
ACCESS ground floor only
RAIL Carshalton

LITTLE HOLLAND HOUSE

> I built my Ideal House and all it contained… with only a small weekly wage
> of forty-five shillings;… with no practical experience of building, and without
> the aid of either a builder or an architect; which undertaking appeared to
> my friends to be a very ill-advised business indeed.
> Frank R Dickinson, *A Novice Builds His Own Ideal House*

When Frank Reginald Dickinson (1874–1961) began in October 1902 to build the home he was to occupy for 57 years, his aim was to create a house that 'stood up by itself, without the help of its neighbour; a house with beautiful things inside… a house and home that its like does not exist anywhere in these isles'. Inspired by the ideals and aesthetics championed by William Morris' arts-and-crafts movement and John Ruskin, who knew and liked the area, he bought a plot of land and subscribed to a mutual building society which awarded each £300 collected to one of its members selected by ballot. Frank had previously lived in a London basement, and while the money would have bought him a ready-built home, he was determined to go it alone. Unfortunately the cheapest builder's quote came in at £600, so he took his annual leave from his job at the Doulton factory in Lambeth and with the help of a brother on leave from the navy and another unemployed brother to act as foreman, plus a hired labourer, he began to lay the foundations ('I found… digging trenches was a much more strenuous labour than drawing plans on paper').

Within three months a shell was constructed to the plans he and his fiancée had been poring over (his attitude to Florence is a mix of reverence and condescension: 'I do not know if she understood a plan', he remarks in his memoir). They had been working together on the basic essentials of furniture in his parents' cellar for the previous year or so. Then came just over a year of weekends and holidays spent fitting the

kitchen and bedroom before he and his bride moved in on 28 March 1904, their wedding night. Florence, meanwhile, had paid for the coveted green Cumbrian roof slates with the money saved for her trousseau: 'Could any woman make greater sacrifice?' asks Frank.

The house as built is charming and refreshingly free of pattern-book preconceptions, though layered with all that self-sufficiency are streaks of sentimentality and moralising. Frank anthropomorphises his creation shamelessly – 'there is also just another shy little window which has slipped round the front corner...' – while a quote accompanying a portrait of his 'good Master' Ruskin inset into the pine panelling in the dining room strikes terror in the heart: 'We will try to make some small piece of English ground beautiful peaceful & fruitful. We will have... none idle but the dead. We will have no liberty upon it; but instant obedience to known law & appointed person; no equality upon it; but recognition of every betterness that we can find & reprobation of every worseness.'

The simple pebbledash exterior with its ribbon windows – 'no fanciful sham Tudor work, but just plain brick' – gives way to a small lobby with doors to the comfortable kitchen in which the family would breakfast and a roomy living/dining space that runs from front to back of the house. In the front is the dining area; the rear is a sitting room with built-in settles on either side of the fireplace. All the furniture was designed and made by Frank in a mix of arts-and-crafts aesthetics – the attenuation of Mackintosh here, the tapering legs and square profiles favoured by Liberty and Mackmurdo there (he was an avid reader of *The Studio*). There are few non-essentials – a gramophone, an Italian walnut cakestand, some decorative pottery – yet the space is far from austere and the atmosphere bespeaks a confident sensuality, the hand of someone who has been prepared to rethink his family's needs from scratch and cater to them using the materials and forms of his choice rather than bowing to fashion and convention. In short, it is very modern, both in its conception and the stripped-down minimalism that has resulted – especially in comparison with the Victorian/Edwardian clutter of a home such as Linley Sambourne's (see page 101).

The beams between the two living areas are carved with crude stylised representations of plants and animals, but the major decoration is centred on the two fireplaces. The one in the dining room is topped by watercolour copies by Frank of paintings by two of his favourite artists: a Turner flanked by Victorian artist G F Watts' buxom *Eve Triumphant* and *Eve Repentant*. (Frank named his home Little Holland House in homage to Watts, who had lived in a house of that name for more than 20 years.) The sitting-room fireplace has dancing nymphs and Pans above which Frank's oil triptych *Give to us each our daily bread* expresses his world view: in the middle is the working man, earning his wage by the sweat of his brow, while in the side panels science and industry, the monarchy, the church and the law wait with their hands outstretched for his money. Despite Frank's description of the house as 'a centre for gatherings and festivities, country dancing, play acting, musical evenings and discussion groups' along the lines of Morris' Red House (see page 286), the family portraits inset in the dado panelling are joyless: daughter Isabel is depicted as a severe and modern young woman while son Gerard looks positively cross; only Florence is softened by a smile.

The staircase that leads up from the dining room is itself a thing of beauty. The decoration in the master bedroom – accessed like the other rooms by unusually large, roughly finished doors with simple fittings ('a narrow door suggests meanness') – is in blues and greens: a dreamlike frieze of stylised trees and lakes and a blue-tiled fireplace above which is a copy of part of Burne-Jones' *The Sleeping Beauty* given the couple as a wedding present by an art-student friend. The theme, unsurprisingly, is sleep not sex. Gerard's room contains a carved wedding chest made by father and son and a dressing table in which the son successfully translates his father's principles into a 1930s aesthetic.

ADDRESS 40 Beeches Avenue, Carshalton SM5 3LW
(020 8770 5000)
OPEN March to October: first Sunday of the month, 13.30–17.30
ADMISSION free
ACCESS limited
RAIL Carshalton Beeches

OLD PALACE, CROYDON

The Old Palace, Croydon is certainly impressive, but anyone whose schooldays were the bane of their lives should go prepared to sit at classroom desks and chairs, listen with attention to the verbose guided tour and participate in the compulsory break for tea and Kit-Kats.

The palace was the last in a series of staging posts set up on the road to London by the archbishops of Canterbury after their acquisition of Lambeth Palace towards the end of the 12th century. In 1780 it was sold by the church because of its 'low and unwholesome situation'. A century later they were reluctantly given it back, on condition it was made into a place of education. It has been a school since 1889.

The palace today consists of irregular ranges of buildings, mostly from the 14th and 15th centuries, grouped around two small courtyards. The tour begins in the great or banqueting hall – the most impressive room of the palace as it stands today – built in its present form in about 1450 by Archbishop John Stafford. Though considerably less dramatic in scale than its near-contemporary at Eltham Palace (see page 263), the lofty space, its original oak arch-braced hammerbeam ceiling supported by Spanish chestnut tie beams installed in 1748, has a magic the school stage and chairs have not destroyed. It was here that Archbishop Thomas Cranmer reluctantly condemned to death Protestant martyr John Frith for denying transubstantiation in 1533; Cranmer was a frequent visitor to Croydon, where he installed the woman to whom he was secretly married and accommodated Catherine of Aragon between her divorce and her death three years later – a poignant period no doubt since Catherine and Henry VIII had spent a lot of time here before their marriage.

The adjacent guardroom, used as a withdrawing room after banquets in the hall, was built by Archbishop Thomas Arundel around 1400 and is one of the earliest uses of brick in Britain. The name probably dates from

1412, when the young James I of Scotland was a prisoner here. The dramatic barrel vault was Arundel's attempt to create the impression of the upturned hull of a ship (a popular metaphor for the church). The room next door, with a fine low-moulded Tudor ceiling, was built as a private dining room by Archbishop John Morton at the end of the 15th century.

Morton also built the passageway linking this wing of the palace with the chapel at the other side of the north courtyard. Here you can see a haunted Jacobean staircase and a windowpane etched with placement instructions to the Elizabethan glazier: 'next ye chapel'. Probably built by Archbishop Bourchier (1460–80), the chapel has a fine carved screen installed by Morton and a raised pew built for Elizabeth I by her mentor Archbishop Matthew Parker in the 1560s. The west pews and altar rail date from the time of Archbishop Laud, who embellished the chapel, moved the altar from the centre (as decreed by Reformation lore) to the end and repaired the stained-glass and crucifix, all of which was used as evidence against him leading to his execution for endeavouring to 'overthrow the Protestant religion' in 1645. Note the four negroid heads that form part of the coat of arms of Archbishop Juxon (1660–63) on the east pews, suggesting a shameful family connection with the slave trade.

After tea in the Norman undercroft, the oldest surviving part of the palace, now distinguished by a mass of exposed heating pipes, the tour continues through the bedroom used by Elizabeth I, which retains its original Tudor ceiling but not much else, to the long gallery. Used for dancing, exercise and entertainment, this dates from the late 15th or early 16th century and is thought to be one of the oldest of its kind. It was here in 1587 that Elizabeth made Sir Christopher Hatton lord chancellor (he was said to be a fine dancer).

ADDRESS Old Palace Road, Croydon, Surrey CRO 1AX
OPEN call 020 8253 1009 for dates
ADMISSION £4/£3/family ticket £10, all including tea; guided tour only, approximately 2¼ hours
ACCESS limited
RAIL East Croydon or West Croydon

WHITEHALL

Built probably for a yeoman farmer around 1500, a decade before the birth of Henry VIII, Whitehall's sparsely furnished, rickety rooms strongly evoke times gone by while the core of the building, helpfully exposed and elucidated for the visitor, gives an insight into Tudor construction techniques. The original house was two storeys high, three rooms long and one room deep. The foundations are chalk blocks (exposed below one of the original exterior walls in the Victorian kitchen extension); the timber frame – of unseasoned and untreated local elm and oak, probably felled only months before – was made up in the carpenter's yard, marked to facilitate reassembly (some marks are visible in one of the attic rooms), dismantled and re-erected on site. (The ease with which this could be achieved was proved as late as 1922 when a similarly constructed house just south of Whitehall was dismantled and moved to allow the road to be widened.) The slightly larger, overhanging frame for the upper storey is supported on the upper-floor joists, which were cut to project beyond the lower-floor frame – a method called continuous jettying. The frames were then infilled with wattle covered with daub or rye dough (a mix of straw and clay) which was in turn coated with lime plaster. The roof is a crown-post construction originally covered in thatch or tiles (the post, beam and rafters are exposed in the attic). The windows – wooden mullions set in the gaps between the timbers – would have been unglazed and shuttered.

Visitors enter through the porch, added c. 1550, to the hall, which takes up about half the ground area of the original house. To the right is the service room, probably used to store food (open on request); to the left is the parlour, a pleasant square space furnished as a kitchen/dining room with a large inglenook fireplace (the fussy leaded windows here and in the hall are Georgian). Behind the hall and service room is the refreshment room, added along with the rooms above in about 1650. The new kitchen behind the parlour and the mezzanine bathroom were added around 1840, soon after the frame was weatherboarded. The exhibition room – a lean-to flanking the parlour – was probably built as a wash-house in the mid 19th century.

The staircase tower was added at about the same time as the porch, giving access not only to the first floor, formerly reached by ladder, but also to the newly created attic rooms. The mezzanine room allows a clear view of the original exterior wall and the external jettying of the upper storey. The bedroom above the parlour has a 17th-century door, found in one of the attic rooms, carved with Charles I's last word – 'Remember' – and 'D.O.M.' (*Deo optimo maximo*, 'To God most high'). This royalist graffiti suggests Whitehall may have been the home of the Reverend George Aldrich, in 1645 the founder of Cheam School. In the dramatically sloping room above the porch is a display of material about the school – which boasted Prince Philip among its pupils just before it moved to Headley in 1934 – and its famous 18th-century headmaster William Gilpin. The bare attic rooms give the strongest sense of having gone back in time to the extent that it's a shock to see and hear the traffic outside.

About a century after Aldrich's alleged residency Whitehall was leased by John Killick. In 1785 it was purchased by his son James, remaining in the family until it was sold to the council in 1963. From 1853 – the start of more than a century of female ownership and occupancy – it was the home of James' grand-daughters Harriet and Charlotte (their parents, William and Lucy, had lived with 11 children at Whitehall, one of whom became a respected sea captain in the China tea trade and founded a ship-broking firm still trading today). Harriet was a governess to the rector's children, Charlotte a governess to the headmaster's daughters and a music teacher at the school. We know that in 1881 three schoolmasters lodged in Whitehall with the sisters and their servant Ann Baker, and the spacious attic above the refreshment room recreates the homely living quarters of a late-19th-century teacher complete with a table set for tea, books and magazines, pictures and prints. The first of the attic rooms contains a display about the Killick family including photographs of the formidable-looking Susan Mary and Harriet Maud Muller – Charlotte and Harriet's great-nieces who lived in the house from Harriet's death in 1914 until Harriet Maud's in 1959 – in the garden with their women friends.

ADDRESS 1 Malden Road, Cheam, Surrey SM3 8QD (020 8643 1236) **OPEN** Wednesday to Friday, Sunday, bank holiday Mondays, 14.00–17.00; Saturday, 10.00–17.00 **ADMISSION** £1.20/60p **ACCESS** ground floor only **RAIL** Cheam

[carshalton/cheam/croydon]

WHITEHALL

Built probably for a yeoman farmer around 1500, a decade before the birth of Henry VIII, Whitehall's sparsely furnished, rickety rooms strongly evoke times gone by while the core of the building, helpfully exposed and elucidated for the visitor, gives an insight into Tudor construction techniques. The original house was two storeys high, three rooms long and one room deep. The foundations are chalk blocks (exposed below one of the original exterior walls in the Victorian kitchen extension); the timber frame – of unseasoned and untreated local elm and oak, probably felled only months before – was made up in the carpenter's yard, marked to facilitate reassembly (some marks are visible in one of the attic rooms), dismantled and re-erected on site. (The ease with which this could be achieved was proved as late as 1922 when a similarly constructed house just south of Whitehall was dismantled and moved to allow the road to be widened.) The slightly larger, overhanging frame for the upper storey is supported on the upper-floor joists, which were cut to project beyond the lower-floor frame – a method called continuous jettying. The frames were then infilled with wattle covered with daub or rye dough (a mix of straw and clay) which was in turn coated with lime plaster. The roof is a crown-post construction originally covered in thatch or tiles (the post, beam and rafters are exposed in the attic). The windows – wooden mullions set in the gaps between the timbers – would have been unglazed and shuttered.

Visitors enter through the porch, added c. 1550, to the hall, which takes up about half the ground area of the original house. To the right is the service room, probably used to store food (open on request); to the left is the parlour, a pleasant square space furnished as a kitchen/dining room with a large inglenook fireplace (the fussy leaded windows here and in the hall are Georgian). Behind the hall and service room is the refreshment room, added along with the rooms above in about 1650. The new kitchen behind the parlour and the mezzanine bathroom were added around 1840, soon after the frame was weatherboarded. The exhibition room – a lean-to flanking the parlour – was probably built as a wash-house in the mid 19th century.

The staircase tower was added at about the same time as the porch, giving access not only to the first floor, formerly reached by ladder, but also to the newly created attic rooms. The mezzanine room allows a clear view of the original exterior wall and the external jettying of the upper storey. The bedroom above the parlour has a 17th-century door, found in one of the attic rooms, carved with Charles I's last word – 'Remember' – and 'D.O.M.' (*Deo optimo maximo*, 'To God most high'). This royalist graffiti suggests Whitehall may have been the home of the Reverend George Aldrich, in 1645 the founder of Cheam School. In the dramatically sloping room above the porch is a display of material about the school – which boasted Prince Philip among its pupils just before it moved to Headley in 1934 – and its famous 18th-century headmaster William Gilpin. The bare attic rooms give the strongest sense of having gone back in time to the extent that it's a shock to see and hear the traffic outside.

About a century after Aldrich's alleged residency Whitehall was leased by John Killick. In 1785 it was purchased by his son James, remaining in the family until it was sold to the council in 1963. From 1853 – the start of more than a century of female ownership and occupancy – it was the home of James' grand-daughters Harriet and Charlotte (their parents, William and Lucy, had lived with 11 children at Whitehall, one of whom became a respected sea captain in the China tea trade and founded a ship-broking firm still trading today). Harriet was a governess to the rector's children, Charlotte a governess to the headmaster's daughters and a music teacher at the school. We know that in 1881 three schoolmasters lodged in Whitehall with the sisters and their servant Ann Baker, and the spacious attic above the refreshment room recreates the homely living quarters of a late-19th-century teacher complete with a table set for tea, books and magazines, pictures and prints. The first of

the attic rooms contains a display about the Killick family inc[...] photographs of the formidable-looking Susan Mary and Harriet [...] Muller – Charlotte and Harriet's great-nieces who lived in the [...] from Harriet's death in 1914 until Harriet Maud's in 1959 – in the g[...] with their women friends.

ADDRESS 1 Malden Road, Cheam, Surrey SM3 8QD (020 8643 1236) **OPEN** Wednesday to Friday, Sunday, bank holiday Mondays, 14.00–17.00; Saturday, 10.00–17.00 **ADMISSION** £1.20/60p **ACCESS** ground floor only **RAIL** Cheam

[index]

[london houses]

Abercrombie, Patrick 116
Adam, James 145, 252
Adam, Robert 12, 14, 138, 139, 141, 142,
   143, 145, 146, 202, 237, 238–241, 250,
   253
Addington Palace 87, **322–324**
Adelaide, Queen, wife of William IV
   24, 207
Aitchison, George 94, 95, 98
Aitken, Mary 83–85
Anne of Denmark, Queen, wife of
   James I 270
Anne, Queen 89, 223, 224
Apsley House **12–17**
Arbuthnot, Harriet 15
Argyll, John Campbell, 2nd Duke of
   138
Arundel, Archbishop Thomas 332
Arup, Ove 157
Asgill House 7, 9, **178–180**
Asgill, Sir Charles 178
Ashbee, Charles Robert 80
Atkinson, William 141
Augusta, Duchess of Brunswick 23,
   275
Austen, Robert 283
Avenue House **314**

Baker Street 54, 57
Banham, Reyner 214
Barber, Francis 33
Barbon, Nicholas 235
Barking 282
Barking Abbey 280
Barnes, George 46
Beadnell, Maria 30
Beckford, Richard 52
Beckford, William 52
Becontree Avenue 295

Beddington 325
Beerbohm, Max 36
Bek, Anthony, Bishop of Durham 260
Bentley, Richard 196, 201
Bexley 284
Bexleyheath 293
Binning, Lady Katherine 123
Bishop's Avenue 88
Blackheath 276
Blackwell, Ursula 155, 156, 159
Blomfield, Charles James, Bishop 86
Blore, William 20, 21, 23, 25
Boehm, Edgar 95
Bonaparte, Joseph 14
Bonaparte, Josephine 14, 117
Bonaparte, Napoleon 14
Bordoni, Faustina 51
Boston Manor **207–208**
Boston Manor Road 208
Boswell, James 34, 37
Bourchier, Archbishop 334
Bourne Road 284
Brangwyn, Frank 310
Brawne, Fanny 132, 136, 137
Brentford 255
Breuer, Marcel 122
Bridges, William 138
Broadhead, Theodore Henry 315
Brook Street 46
Brown, Lancelot 'Capability' 252
Brown, Abraham 45
Brown, Charles 132–137
Brown, Ford Madox 288
Bruce Castle **298–299**
Bruce, William 182
Brunel, Isambard Kingdom 100
Bryant, Julius 142
Buckingham Gate 25
Buckingham Palace 7, **18–25**

Buckingham, John Sheffield, Duke of
18, 21
Burgh House **121–122**
Burgh, Reverend Allatson 121
Burlingham, Dorothy 126, 131
Burlington House 210, 213
Burlington Lane 215
Burlington, Richard Boyle, 3rd Earl of
48, 209–215, 229
Burne-Jones, Edward 286–293, 308, 309
Burne-Jones, Georgina 288, 289
Burnet, Bishop Gilbert 184, 185
Burton, Richard 97
Bute, John Stuart, 3rd Earl of 138
Butterfield, William 87

Caldecott, Randolph 95
Campbell, Colen 90, 189, 190, 192, 209
Carew Manor **325**
Carew, Francis 325
Carew, Sir Nicholas 325
Carew, Sir Richard 325
Carlton House 18, 20, 23, 66
Carlyle's House **79–85**
Carlyle, Jane Welsh 7, 79–85
Carlyle, Thomas 6, 79–85
Caroline of Brunswick, Princess 89
Caroline, Princess of Brunswick, wife
of George IV 18, 23
Caroline, Queen, wife of George II 224
Carshalton 326, 331
Carter, Edward 300
Carter, Elizabeth 37
Catherine of Aragon 332
Century Guild 310
Chambers, William 18
Champneis, Sir John 283
Chandos, Lord 48
Charles I, King 270

Charles II, King 223, 272
Charlotte, Princess, daughter of
George IV 24
Charlton House **258–259**
Cheam 337
Chester, Eliza 134
Chesterfield Walk 276
Chesterfield, Philip Dormer Stanhope,
4th Earl of 32, 34, 273, 275, 276
Chevalier d'Eon de Beaumont 115
Cheyne Row 79, 85
Cheyne Walk 100
Child, Sarah Anne 238
Child, Sir Francis and family 235, 237
Chiswick 229
Chiswick Artworkers Guild 234
Chiswick House **209–215**
Chorley, John 85
Church Farmhouse Museum **315–316**
Churchill, Charles 233
Chute, John 196, 198, 201, 202
City Road 75
Clarke, Joseph 53
Cleyn, Franz 185
Clitherow family 207
Clitherow, General John 208
Coates, Wells 122, 156
Cockerell, Samuel Pepys 87
Coleraine, Henry Hare, 2nd Lord
298–299
Coleridge, Samuel Taylor 64
Compton, William 298
Cooke, Margaret 267, 268
Cooper, Edward Philip 314
Copland, Alexander 216
Coppin, Sir George 90
Court Yard 265
Courtauld, Stephen and Ginie
260–265

[london houses]

Cox, John 172, 173, 175
Crane, Lionel 175
Crane, Walter 95, 105
Cranmer, Archbishop Thomas 332
Crooms Hill 273
Croydon 324, 332–334
Cuzzoni, Francesca 51

Dali, Salvador 129
Dance, George, the Younger 58, 60, 71, 244, 247
Danson House 9
Darwin, Erasmus 84
Dashwood, Sir Francis 237, 283
Dashwood, Sir James 231
De Morgan, Evelyn 107–111
De Morgan, William 98, 107–111
Defoe, Daniel 280
Dene, Dorothy 98
Desmoulins, Elizabeth 33
Devonshire Terrace 29
Diana, Princess of Wales 90
Dickens House Museum **27–31**
Dickens, Catherine 27, 29
Dickens, Charles 6, 27–31, 79
Dickinson, Florence 327, 329, 331
Dickinson, Frank R 327–331
Dilke, Charles Wentworth 134
Dr Johnson's House **32–38**
Dorn, Marion 262
Doughty Street 27, 31
Ducie, Sir William 258, 259
Dudley, John 250
Dysart, Elizabeth, Countess of 150, 182–188
Dysart, Lionel, 3rd Earl of 184

Eades, William 123
East Molesey 227

Eastbury Manor House **280–282**
Eastbury Square 282
Edward II, King 260
Edward III, King 260
Edward IV, King 263
Edward VII, King 21, 116, 117
Edward, Duke of Kent 89
Elizabeth I, Queen 304, 334
Elizabeth II, Queen 7, 18, 24
Eltham Palace 8, **260–265**
Enfield 302
English Heritage 214, 265
English, Frederick Alexander 322
Engströmer, Rolf 262
Epping Forest 304, 309
Epping Forest Museum 305
Erasmus 260
Essex Hall 307
Essex, James 198

Fane, Sarah Sophia 238
Faulkner, Charles 286, 288, 291
Fenton family 123
Fenton House **123–125**
Fenton, James 124, 125
Fichtl, Paula 129
Finchley 314
Fitzherbert, Mrs Maria Anne 18, 192
Flamsteed House **267–268**
Flamsteed, John 267, 268, 273
Flaxman, John 64, 247
Fleming, Ian 157
18 Folgate Street **39–43**
Forbes, Malcolm 109
Forest Road 311
Forty Hall **300–302**
Forty Hill 302
Foundling Hospital 46, 229

Franklin, Benjamin 9
Frederick, Prince of Wales 116
The Freud Museum **126–131**
Freud, Anna 126, 128, 131
Freud, Ernst 126, 129
Freud, Sigmund 6, 126–131
Fulham Palace **86–88**

Gad's Hill Place 28, 29, 30, 31
Gandy, J M 64, 65
Gardiner, Canon Evelyn 172
Garrick, David 32, 34, 37, 232, 315
Gay, John 48, 51
Gee, Joshua 123, 125
Gentileschi, Artemisia 272
Gentileschi, Orazio 272
George I, King 89
George II, King 89, 224
George III, King 18, 89, 225
George IV, King 20, 23, 24
George v, King 21, 23
Gibbons, Dr William 121
Gibbons, Grinling 220, 223
Gibson, G 277
Gilpin, William 336
Gladstone, William 53
Goethe, Johann Wolfgang von 84
Goldfinger, Ernö 155–161
Gough Square 32, 38
Grange Museum of Community
    History **317**
Greek Street 52, 53
Greenwich 267, 268, 272
Gresham, Sir Thomas 235
Greyhound Hill 316
Gropius, Walter 122
Grosvenor, Richard 232, 233
The Grove, *see* Grange Museum of
    Community History

Grylls, Thomas 121
Gunnersbury Park Museum
    216–218
Gurnell, Johnathan 244
Gurnell, Thomas 244
Gwynn, Nell 150

Hall Place **283–284**
Ham House **181–188**
Hampstead Lane 147
Hampstead Wells 121
Hampton Court Palace 7, **219–227**
Hampton Court Road 227
Handel House Museum **45–51**
Handel, George Frideric 6, 45–51
Harmsworth, Cecil 32
Harrow-on-the-Hill 319
Hauptfuhrer, Fred 7, 178
Hawksmoor, Nicholas 90
Headstone Manor 6, **318–319**
Heidegger, John James 48
Hendon 315
Hendrix, Jimi 45
Henrietta Maria, Queen, wife of
    Charles I 270
Henry VI, King 260
Henry VIII, King 219, 220, 260, 298,
    304, 335
Herbert, Lord 190
Hewlings, Richard 214
Hill, Rowland 299
Hillyard, Matthew 241
Hinde, John 151
Hobart, Dorothy and John 193
Hogarth House **228–234**
Hogarth Lane 234
Hogarth, Catherine 27
Hogarth, Jane 228, 229, 233
Hogarth, Mary 27

[london houses]

Hogarth, William 6, 41, 46, 48, 62, 92, 228–234
Hollamby, Doris 7
Hollamby, Edward 293
Holland Park Road 99
Holland, Henry 66
Holme, Thea 7, 79
Holmes, Sherlock 54–57
Home, Lady 153
Homerton High Street 175
Honeywood **326**
Hornfair Road 259
Hosier, Captain Francis 273
House of St Barnabas-in-Soho **52–53**
Howard, Catherine 249
Howley, Michael Francis, Bishop, *then* Archbishop 86, 322
Hulse, Richard 273

Ibbetson, Julius 147
Isleworth 241
Isokon 8, 122, 156
Iveagh bequest 146
Iveagh, Edward Cecil Guinness, 1st Earl of 141

Jagger, Charles Sergeant 263
James 1, King 270
James 1, King, of Scotland 334
James, Henry 238, 286
Jennens, Charles 51
Jersey Road 241
Jersey, George Villiers, 5th Earl of 238
John Wesley's House **71–75**
Johnson, Elizabeth (Tetty) 33, 34, 36
Johnson, Samuel 7, 32–38, 276
Jones, Ernest 128
Jones, Inigo 270, 300
Jordan, Mrs Dora 24

Juxon, William, Archbishop 334

Kauffmann, Angelica 23, 145, 241
Keats Grove 137
Keats House **132–137**
Keats, John 7, 132–137
Kensington Gardens 93
Kensington Palace 7, **89–93**
Kent, William 66, 90, 92, 93, 192, 213, 224, 225
Kenwood **138–147**
Keppel, Alice 116
Kew Palace 9
Killick family 336, 337
Kingsley, Charles 53
Knapp, Matthew 151

Lasdun, Denys 68
Laud, Archbishop William 334
Lauderdale House **148–153**
Lauderdale, John Maitland, 2nd Earl of 150, 182–188
Lawn Road 8
Leadbetter, Stiff 87
Leeds, Nancy 141
Leighton House **94–99**
Leighton, Frederic, Lord 7, 94–99
Liberty, Arthur Lasenby 292
Limerick, Lady 283, 284
Lincoln's Inn Fields 58, 60, 65
Lindsey House **100**
Lindsey, Robert Bertie, 3rd Earl of 100
Linley Sambourne House **101–106**
Little Holland House **327–329**
Lloyd, Edward 310
Longhorne, Sir William 258
Lordship Lane 299
Lubetkin, Berthold 156

[london houses]

Machell, John 172, 173
Mackmurdo, Arthur Heygate 310
McNeal, George 71
Malacrida, Peter 262, 264
Mansfield, William, 1st Earl of 138, 139
Mansion House 52
Marble Hill House **189–194**, 209, 210
Maresfield Gardens 126, 131
Marshall, P P 288
Martin, John 100
Martin, Sir Richard 148
Mary II, Queen 92, 222, 223, 225
Mary, Queen, wife of George V 25
Maryon Wilson, Sir Thomas 258
Mattock Lane 248
Maufe, Edward 175
Mead, William 151
Mellor, Hilda Pennington 115
Messel, Oliver 105
Middleton, John 315, 316
Millfield House **303**
Milward, Captain John 172, 173
Montagu House 275
Monteagle, Lord 280
Morris, Jane 286, 289, 291, 310
Morris, Jenny 288
Morris, Marshall, Faulkner & Co. 288, 310
Morris, May 288, 289, 291, 292
Morris, Roger 190
Morris, William 7, 110, 286–293, 304, 308–311, 327, 331
Morton, Archbishop John 334
Munthe, Axel 115, 116, 117
Munthe, Malcolm 114
Munthe, Peter 115, 116
Murphy, Arthur 33
Murray, William 181, 184
Mycenae House 277

Mycenae Road 277
Mylne, Robert 322

Nash, John 20, 21, 23, 24, 25
National Maritime Museum 270, 272
National Trust 123, 159, 170, 188, 238, 280
Neasden 317
Neasden Lane 317
New End Square 122
Newton, Isaac 268
Newton, Sir Adam 258
Northumberland, Algernon Percy, 10th Earl of 250
Northumberland, Henry Percy, 9th Earl of 249, 250
Northumberland, Hugh Smithson, 1st Duke of 250

Old Battersea House 7, **107–111**
Old Palace Lane 180
Old Palace, Croydon **332–334**
Orme, Denise 283
Osterley Park **235–241**
Ozenfant, Amédée 156, 158, 159

Pakenham, Kitty 17
Palladio, Andrea 212, 270
Paolozzi, Eduardo 160
Parker, Archbishop Matthew 334
Pearce, Joseph 52
Pennethorne, James 20
Pennington, John 115, 117
Pennington, Robert 114, 115, 116
Pevsner, Nikolaus 8, 52
Pitshanger Manor 58, **242–248**
Pitt, Thomas 202
Pitt, William 233
Pope, Alexander 48, 192

[london houses]

Popes Lane 218
Porteus, Bishop 87
19 Princelet Street 9
Pugin Powell, Sebastian 199

Queen Elizabeth's Hunting Lodge **304–305**
Queen's House 7, **270–272**

Rainton, Nicholas 300
Ranger's House **273–276**
Ranger's Road 305
Reade, Lady Mary 207
Red House 7, **286–293**
Red House Lane 293
Repton, Humphry 142
Reynolds, Joshua 34, 232
Richards, James 192
Richardson, Albert 199
Richardson, Samuel 32
Richmond Road 194
Robinson, William 196
Roose-Evans, James 125
Rossetti, Dante Gabriel 286, 288, 289, 291
Rothschild, Hannah 218
Rothschild, Lionel 216
Rothschild, Nathan Mayer 216
Royal Naval College 272, 273
Royal Observatory 268
Rubens, Peter Paul 241
Ruskin, John 327, 329

Sadleir, Sir Ralph 170, 172
St James's Park 66
St James's Place 70
St Mary's Catholic Teacher Training College 199
Salisbury, Frank 71

Sambourne, Linley 101–106
Saunders, George 139, 142, 143, 145, 146
Seely and Paget 260
Seely, John 260, 263
Senesino 48, 51
Severs, Dennis 39, 41
Sewell, Henry and Hannah 121
Shaw, George Bernard 289
Shaw, Richard Norman 322
The Sherlock Holmes Museum **54–57**
Sherlock, Bishop 87
Siddal, Elizabeth 288, 293
Silver Street 303
Sir John Soane's Museum **58–65**
Smirke, Robert 138
Smirke, Robert, Jr 59
Smirke, Sydney 216
Smith, J C 47
Soane, Eliza 58, 59, 60, 65, 247
Soane, Sir John 7, 23, 58–65, 231, 242–248
Somerset, Charles Seymour, Duke of 250
Somerset, Edward Seymour, Duke of 249
Somerset, Sarah, Duchess of 298
Sophia Matilda, Princess, neice of George III 275
Southside House **114–117**
Spencer House 7, **66–70**
Spencer, 1st Earl 66
Spencer-Stanhope, John Roddam 109
Spitalfields 39
Stafford Terrace 101, 106
Stafford, Archbishop John 332
Stanhope, John 273
Stanhope, Philip 275
Stanyon, Edward 208
Stephens, Henry Charles 'Inky' 314

Stirling, Wilhelmina 107, 109
9/10 Stock Orchard Street 6, 8, **164–169**
Strahan, William 32
Strawberry Hill 7, **195–202**
Street, George Edmund 286, 309
Stuart, James 'Athenian' 66, 70
Suffolk Collection 275
Suffolk, Henrietta Howard, Countess of 90, 189, 190, 193, 196, 273
Sutton House **170–175**
Sutton, Thomas 175
Suzannet Collection 30
Swift, Jonathan 48
Swinburne, Algernon Charles 288, 289
Syon House **249–255**
Sysley, Clement 280, 282

Tait, Bishop 87
Taylor, Robert 9, 178, 242
Terrick, Bishop 87
Thomas, Brian 88
Thornhill, James 92, 153, 224, 228, 229
Thornhill, John 232
Thorpe, John 90, 258
Thrale, Hester 37, 233
Till, Jeremy 6, 7, 164, 166
Tooth, Samuel 71
Townsend, James 298
Trecothick, Barlow 322
Trewby, George 125
Turner, J M W 64, 247

Uglow, Jenny 8, 228

Valence House **294–295**
Vanbrugh, John 224
Vardy, John 66, 68
Vestry House 6, **306–307**

Vestry Road 307
Vicarage Crescent 111
Victoria, Queen 20, 25, 89, 92, 94, 225
von Gersdorf, Sigismund 100
von Zinzendorf, Count 100
Voysey, Charles 74

Waldegrave Road 202
Waldegrave, Lady Frances 198, 201, 202
Walpole, Frederika 248
Walpole, Horace 7, 181, 195–202, 237
Walpole, Robert 209
Walpole, Spencer 248
Walthamstow 309, 311
Wand, Bishop 87
Ware, Isaac 273
Water House **308–311**
Waterlow Park 153
Waterlow, Sir Sydney 152
Watts, George Frederick 331
Webb, Aston 21
Webb, John 272
Webb, Philip 286–293, 309
Wellington, Arthur Wellesley, Duke of 12–17
Wesley, John 37, 71–75, 152
Westmorland, John Fane, 10th Earl of 238
Wharton, Elizabeth 114
Wharton, Philip, 4th Lord 116
Whistler, James 100
Whitehall **335–336**
Wigglesworth, Sarah 6, 7, 164–169
Wilkes, John 233
William III, King 89, 222, 223, 272
William IV, King 20, 24, 207
William Morris Gallery, *see* Water House

[london houses]

Williams, Anna 33
2 Willow Road 8, **155–161**
Wilmer, John 244
Wilmot, John Eardley 299
Windmill Hill 125
Wingfield, Thomas 317
Wolsey, Thomas 219, 220
Woodhayes Road 117
Woodlands **277**
Wren, Christopher 90, 107, 222, 225,
    227, 267, 272

Wyatt, Benjamin 12
Wyatt, George 58
Wyatt, James 12, 198

Yates, James 152

Zucchi, Antonio 145, 241
Zweig, Stefan 129

LONDON WALKING
A HANDBOOK FOR SURVIVAL

Simon Pope
Illustrations by Claudia Schenk

Packed with more information than you ever imagined you needed to
know about walking in London, this book is both a practical guide and a
pointer to new pedestrian possibilities.

Close study will give you the confidence to answer the question, 'What
is traffic?' and enable you to recognise kerbs in all their forms. Also
included is advice on walking inside buildings, how to walk to escape the
Plague, how to approach – and retreat from – cash machines, easy exer-
cises for those trying to escape their dependency on wheeled transport,
and the story of the Tufty Club. Hard fact lies alongside personal commentary and more than 70 unhelpful illustrations. Armed with the
strategies and techniques provided by this book, you will be ready to
experience the city at its haptic, hectic best.

ISBN 1 84166 056 6
£10.00

MUSEUM LONDON
A GUIDE

Andrew Wyllie
Illustrations by Emma Brownjohn

London has publically accessible collections covering almost every con-
ceivable subject. From art to sport to medicine to the city itself, and from
the houses of the extremely rich to the schools of the extremely poor, the
breadth and depth of the material available is staggering. This book
describes, in all their glorious variety of subject and curatorial approach,
some 70 London museums, providing a critical account of the whole
experience of the visit – from the exhibits to the café.

ISBN I 84166 049 3
£10.00

THEATRE LONDON
AN ARCHITECTURAL GUIDE

Edwin Heathcote
Photographs by Keith Collie

Tiny performance spaces above pubs and extravagant Edwardian auditoria shoe-horned into West End sites; the innovatory and the historicist; the little-known and the internationally famous: this book describes and illustrates the architecture of 70 London theatres.

An introduction charts the history of the genre, from the purpose-built theatres of the Elizabethan period – the city's first dramatic boom, now revisited at 'Shakespeare's Globe' – through the great age of Edwardian opulence, to the products of the current Lottery-fuelled activity. The work of the great theatre architects, Frank Matcham, C J Phipps, Walter Emden and Bertie Crewe, is well represented and the book also includes biographies of the specialist designers whose names are too often absent from the architectural record, and a section detailing ex-theatres now masquerading as cinemas, strip clubs, bingo halls and TV studios.

ISBN 1 84166 047 7
£10.00